HANDBOOK OF RESEARCH ON ENTREPRENEURSHIP POLICIES IN CENTRAL AND EASTERN EUROPE

To Robert

Handbook of Research on Entrepreneurship Policies in Central and Eastern Europe

Edited by

Friederike Welter

Jönköping International Business School, Sweden and TeliaSonera Professorship at Stockholm School of Economics in Riga, Latvia

David Smallbone

Small Business Research Centre, Kingston University, UK

Edward Elgar
Cheltenham, UK • Northampton, MA, USA

Published by
Edward Elgar Publishing Limited
The Lypiatts
15 Lansdown Road
Cheltenham
Glos GL50 2JA
UK

Edward Elgar Publishing, Inc.
William Pratt House
9 Dewey Court
Northampton
Massachusetts 01060
USA

A catalogue record for this book
is available from the British Library

Library of Congress Control Number: 2011922864

ISBN 978 1 84844 086 9

Typeset by Servis Filmsetting Ltd, Stockport, Cheshire
Printed and bound by MPG Books Group, UK

Contents

v

Figures

Tables

Contributors

Robert Blackburn, Small Business Research Centre at Kingston University, London, UK

Barbara Bradač, University of Maribor, Maribor, Slovenia

Alexander Chepurenko, Higher School of Economics, Moscow, Russia

Jerzy Cieślik, Kozminski University, Warsaw, Poland

Andrea-Rosalinde Hofer, OECD LEED, Trento, Italy

Nina Isakova, STEPS, National Academy of Science, Kiev, Ukraine

Kostadin Kolarov, University of National and World Economy, Sofia, Bulgaria

Bogdan Piasecki, University of Lodz and Academy of Management, Lodz, Poland

Miroslav Rebernik, University of Maribor, Maribor, Slovenia

Anna Rogut, University of Lodz and Academy of Management, Lodz, Poland

Zoltan Roman, Honorary Professor of the Budapest Corvinus University, Budapest, Hungary

Arnis Sauka, Stockholm School of Economics in Riga, Latvia

David Smallbone, Small Business Research Centre at Kingston University, London, UK

Kiril Todorov, University of National and World Economy, Sofia, Bulgaria

Friederike Welter, Jönköping International Business School, Jönköping Sweden and Stockholm School of Economics in Riga, Latvia

Mirela Xheneti, Small Business Research Centre at Kingston University, London, UK

1 Entrepreneurship policies in the wider Europe: a thematic perspective
Friederike Welter and David Smallbone

INTRODUCTION

This book analyses the role of government and policies in relation to the development of entrepreneurship and small businesses in Central and (South) Eastern European countries where entrepreneurship either was restricted to certain sectors and types of business as for example in Poland or Hungary, or was fully illegal until the late 1980s as in, for example, former Czechoslovakia or the Baltic States. There is an increasing interest in policy issues, as evidenced by the recent publication of a number of books on entrepreneurship policy (for example, Audretsch et al. 2007; Hart 2003; Leitão and Baptista 2009; Lundström and Stevenson 2005) and special issues of international journals (Minniti 2008; Robson et al. 2009). However, these publications emphasize entrepreneurship policy in the context of mature market economies, where the legislative and regulatory environment has evolved over decades or even centuries. In such environments, policy makers have had considerable experience in designing and implementing policy initiatives to foster entrepreneurship and societies are generally in favour of and accustomed to entrepreneurship activities. This contrasts with post-socialist economies in Central and Eastern Europe and the former Soviet Union, where, in most cases, entrepreneurship development started in the late 1980s and early 1990s with fundamental reforms, all of which presented enormous challenges to policy makers.

The recent entrepreneurship discussion has emphasized the need to view entrepreneurship within the wider political, economic and social contexts in which it takes place (for example, Baker et al. 2005; Davidsson 2003; Welter 2011). This also applies to entrepreneurship policies and support addressing those conditions that enable or constrain entrepreneurship and over which the state has a major influence. In this regard, the handbook adds to the current literature by explicitly focusing on entrepreneurship policy in emerging market economies of Central and Eastern as well as Southeast Europe and the former Soviet Union.

There are a variety of ways in which governments can influence entrepreneurship and small business development beyond direct actions and support programmes. An important issue in this regard is the under-standing of what constitutes 'policy'. Narrowly defined, 'policy' is concerned with 'policy initiatives designed to assist small firms' (Storey 1994, p. 253) and only a more broadly defined view considers the variety of ways in which government policies and actions can impact on entre-preneurship and small business development. Generally, governments can foster entrepreneurship through interventions in six policy areas (Smallbone and Welter 2001b): macroeconomic policy, which affects the willingness of (potential) entrepreneurs to set up a business and invest also with a longer time frame; the costs of legislative compliance, which can fall disproportionately heavily on newer and smaller enterprises (Bannock and Peacock 1989); tax policies, which refers to both the total tax burden and the cost of compliance that can be affected by the fre-quency with which changes are made to the tax regime and the methods used for collecting taxes; the influence of government on the development of market institutions, such as banks and other financial intermediaries, business support and training organizations; the influence of the govern-ment on the value placed on enterprise and entrepreneurship in society, which in a transition context is affected by the commitment of govern-ments towards market reforms and private business ownership; and lastly, direct intervention, to assist new and small businesses to overcome size-related disadvantages.

During the transition period, one of the main preconditions for pro-ductive entrepreneurship to develop is effective institutionalization of entrepreneurship policy (Smallbone and Welter 2010a). Key roles for the state in this regard are to remove unnecessary obstacles to enterprise creation; to establish a facilitating environment for private sector devel-opment; and contribute to the development of appropriate institutions that operate to facilitate private sector development, not to prevent or to exploit it, with, for example, punitive taxation and continual changes to the legislative and regulative frame. This chapter will examine some of these key themes for institutionalizing entrepreneurship policy in a transition context in more detail, thus building the thematic background for the country chapters of the handbook. The remainder of the chapter is structured as follows. The next section outlines institutionalization as a challenge for entrepreneurship policy. After that, the chapter dis-cusses institutional capacity building, including the regional dimension, governance issues and social dialogue, before proceeding to entrepre-neurship policies which, at least indirectly, can support institutional change, namely entrepreneurship education and targeted support. The chapter ends with a short overview of the country contributions to this handbook.

INSTITUTIONALIZATION AS A CHALLENGE FOR (ENTREPRENEURSHIP) POLICY

At the start of the reform process, post-socialist economies faced the challenge of shifting the emphasis from public towards private ownership. Creating a policy context in which new businesses could be set up and grow was a key part of this, although processes to privatize state-owned companies were also established. In this context, a broad understanding of what constitutes public policy is appropriate, because a wide range of government policies and actions can impact on entrepreneurship and small firms; not only policies that are specifically targeted in this way. In particular in a transition context, direct intervention that aims, for example, to secure small firm's access to finance may appear insignificant alongside the role of government in shaping the regulatory environment for private business; and/or influencing the value placed on enterprise and entrepreneurship in the society at large. Targeted policies will only reach a small minority of firms, at best, whereas the regulatory environment, for example, affects all businesses. Therefore, a broadly defined role for government draws attention to the important role of institutionalizing, referring to institutional development, which involves both the creation of market institutions, such as banks and other financial intermediaries, consultants and training organizations, and of public sector regulatory bodies, together with market oriented behaviour on the part of such institutions.

For a broad view on entrepreneurship policy, institutional theory, a suitable frame of reference is Douglass North's concept of formal and informal institutions as enabling or constraining influences for economic development (North 1990). North highlights the major role of governments in former planned economies in Europe for entrepreneurship development. From an institutional theory perspective, a key role for governments is related to creating and fostering an enabling environment. This involves creating a formal institutional frame which facilitates market-based transactions, but also paying attention to informal institutions and institutional inertia which has been shown to be a major influence on entrepreneurial behaviour during the transition period (Smallbone and Welter 2001a; Welter and Smallbone 2003).

The *institutional frame for entrepreneurship* can be considered at different levels of scale (Welter 1997). At the macro level, it includes the responsibility for policy making with respect to entrepreneurship and/or small to medium sized enterprise (SME) development within government, together with the mechanisms for policy implementation. At the meso level, it includes the system of banking and other financial institutions, the training and business support systems, and organizations that seek to represent special interest groups in dealing with government (such as employers' associations and Chambers of Commerce). At the micro level, this includes the local operation and behaviour of business development centres, as well as the local implementation of national policies through, for example, local offices of regulatory bodies and those of national agencies and organizations. Whether the overall institutional frame enables entrepreneurship is affected by the relationships between these different levels, as well as by the behaviour of individual organizations within them, a theme which is explored in more detail in Chapters 8 for Slovenia and 10 for Russia.

At the macro level, legal institutions are fundamental for entrepreneurship as they define property rights, set rules for market entry and exit and generally foster market-based exchange and competition. An adequate legal framework includes laws relating to property, bankruptcy, contracts, commercial activities, and taxes. However, it also involves setting up organizations and agencies with the capacity to implement the laws. Another key issue at the macro level concerns the attitude of the state and society towards entrepreneurship and private ownership, drawing attention to the impact of informal institutions on entrepreneurship development. Again, this emphasizes the importance of creating an enabling framework which is not just restricted to formal institutions, such as laws and regulations, but also pays attention to enhancing an 'entrepreneurial culture' and entrepreneurship as a career option.

The financial infrastructure represents a key element of the institutional meso level. Banks under central planning were mere accounting agencies without an active responsibility in financial transactions of households or enterprises; stock exchanges or national venture capital markets did not exist. While most countries succeeded in establishing a two-tier banking system, its adaptation to the financial needs of new and small businesses proceeded much slower. Therefore, during the early stages of the reform process, foreign donors frequently substituted for this by setting up loan programmes for new and small firms.

Institutionalization at the meso level also refers to the creation of a network which offers business services to new and established businesses. This includes self-governed membership organizations, such as Chambers of Commerce, as well as business support centres, offering information, advice, training and, in some cases, premises, many of which were supported by donor funds during the early reform stages (Bateman 2000a). State or donor involvement is usually justified on the basis of failure or deficiencies in the market for business services, combined with the need for entrepreneurs to be able to access external sources of information, advice and training from time to time, as a means of extending their limited internal resource base.

Institutional change is an integral part of the process of market reform, contributing positively to entrepreneurship where it lowers or removes barriers of entry, for example, with the introduction of private property rights at the beginning of the transformation process. However, institutional change itself can be slowed down or constrained in situations where entrepreneurs rely on previously 'trusted' actions such as evasion or non-compliance in order to deal with the uncertainties and complexities of a new and unknown business environment, since such behaviour contradicts the new regulations and laws (Peng 2003; Smallbone and Welter 2009a). For entrepreneurs, uncertainties in institutional rules, associated with institutional change, can be a mixed blessing. A deficient legal infrastructure, which includes implementation gaps and/or a lack of suitably qualified judges and economic courts, can restrict entrepreneurship development because 'institutional voids' (Polishchuk and Savvateev 2004) allow for discretionary actions and corruption on the part of administrative authorities, thus fostering non-compliant or deviant (entrepreneurial) behaviour. However, institutional voids can open up business opportunities, as shown in the case of small business service providers in Ukraine in the late 1990s (Smallbone et al. 2010).

All this indicates *institutional change*, including attitudinal changes at the level of entrepreneurs, but also governments and their implementation agencies, together with enforcement mechanisms, as key issues influencing the effective institutionalization of entrepreneurship policies. Formal institutions are enforced by coercive mechanisms, as mainly set down in government rules, whilst informal institutions are enforced by normative and mimetic mechanisms, which assist in creating legitimacy. This is of particular importance for nascent entrepreneurs and entrepreneurs in environments, where newness of the concept of entrepreneurship may be a potential liability hampering its acceptance in the wider society. It is only in situations where formal and informal institutions combine to form a coherent framework that formal regulations and the 'rule of law' will positively shape individual behaviour. In this regard, during the transition period, institutional change often contributed to conflicts between formal and informal institutions, but a key aspect of the effective institutionalization of policy is effective co-ordination between the various institutions involved, both formal and informal. This is a difficult task as illustrated by Chapter 5 for Latvia.

INSTITUTIONAL CAPACITY BUILDING

A major challenge for governments during the reform process is related to institutional capacity building. In a wide perspective, institutional capacity building extends beyond legal and administrative reforms, including behavioural change in public and private organizations and administrations, at sub-national as well as the national level. Relevant organizations are those which implement the formal institutional frame outlined above: regulatory, registration and tax authorities, private sector institutions such as banks, business support agencies and any professional providing business support, self-governing bodies such as chambers and business associations. In this regard, the next sections will explore the regional dimension of entrepreneurship policies as well as challenges of governance and social dialogue.

The Regional Dimension

Within post-socialist countries, the development of entrepreneurship varies considerably between regions and localities (Smallbone et al. 2001), as it does in most mature market economies (Reynolds et al. 1994). Local and regional governments, together with local 'bottom-up initiatives', have a role to play in creating a local entrepreneurial milieu as illustrated, for example, in the case of East Germany in Chapter 2. Therefore, institutional capacity building includes a local and regional component which is required if the contribution of entrepreneurship to local/regional development is to increase – a theme which Chapters 2, 7 and 10 illustrate for the examples of East Germany, Poland and Russia.

In socialist states, local and regional government had little responsibility for, or powers to influence, economic development (Smallbone and Welter 2010b). In some former Soviet countries, such as Belarus and, to some extent, also Russia as evidenced by Chapter 10, little has changed in this respect and central governments continue to play a (too) large role in designing policies, thereby limiting the scope for regional development programmes. This may be illustrated with reference to border regions (such as Belarus–Poland, Russia–Estonia and Bulgaria–Greece or Former Yugoslav Republic of Macedonia); where cross border cooperation involving institutions and enterprises might help to stimulate economic development, but where a lack of appropriate powers, resources and capacity at the regional level is a major hindrance (see Chapter 3). Frequently, this is aggravated by a lack of knowledge and/or discretion in interpreting regulations at the local level related to the handling of entrepreneurs, such as when handing out licenses or collecting taxes. For example, in Belarus, Moldova and Ukraine, entrepreneurs perceived the local institutional environment as more 'user-friendly' in the capital than in a peripheral case study region (Smallbone and Welter 2001b). It is at the local level where entrepreneurs typically come into direct contact with the various officials representing government, which in view of the room for discretion in interpreting laws and regulations on the part of those responsible for implementing them, increases the scope for spatial variations. This highlights the influence of 'soft' factors, such as the level of involvement of local entrepreneurs in the process, and the skills and capacities of local government in this area.

But it also shows the need for reforming local government structures, which have neither the capacity nor resources to effectively engage in regional policy. This has become a pressing issue in many Central and Eastern European countries that are now members of the European Union once the first steps in more urgent policy reforms had been carried out successfully. For example, in Poland administrative reforms in the late 1990s which resulted in the creation of 16 new *voivodeships* instead of the 49 that had existed since 1975, laid the basis of a decentralized institutional structure to facilitate local economic development, as for example reflected in the emergence of a regional innovation system in the Lodz voivodeship (Chapter 7). However, as the role of the regions in economic development policy in Poland has grown, deficiencies in the legal framework, as far as local policy is concerned, became apparent, indicating the need for further reforms.

The regional dimension of entrepreneurship policies also concerns issues such as the respective responsibilities of authorities at different levels; the coordination of national and regional support programmes, if duplication is to be avoided; the establishment of appropriate lines of demarcation of responsibility; and the need to take steps to avoid unnecessary layers of bureaucracy and duplication of effort, some of which are illustrated using the example of East Germany in Chapter 2.

Governance and Social Dialogue

Governance includes the capacities of businesses, community groups, academic institutions as well as government (Hart 2003) all of which can impact on entrepreneurship development. Since governance is concerned with the rules, procedures and practices affecting how power is exercised, it embraces both formal and informal institutions (North 1990, 2005), as well as their legitimacy and effectiveness. In countries that are now member states of the European Union (EU) the path to EU accession has highlighted issues of governance, as part of an attempt to improve the effectiveness and legitimacy of institutions at an EU level, as illustrated by the example of Hungary in Chapter 4.

The European Union highlights openness, accountability, effectiveness of institutions, coherence between policies and actions, as well as between policies and participation as key principles of good governance (Commission of the European Communities 2001). New member states of the European Union have made significant progress with respect to the openness of public institutions, participation by entrepreneurs in policy formulation, and the accountability of public institutions. Institutional capacity building in this regard includes the ability to lobby effectively, which is a function that did not exist during the socialist period.

In mature market economies, self-governing, self-regulating organizations act as professional intermediaries in the process of dialogue between government and entrepreneurs, in order to ensure that the interests of businesses are taken into account in the decision making of public authorities at different levels. But, Central and Eastern European countries have lacked a recent tradition and experience of self governing organizations, which has represented a particular challenge, as far as building institutional capacity during the Accession period is concerned. For example, Chambers of Commerce existed also during the socialist period, although they were effectively arms of the state. Their main task was not representation and lobbying, but rather they were involved in supporting state-owned large firms (Welter 1997). Once transition started, chambers lost their function, whilst many new 'bottom-up' business associations were created. However, effective consultation and engagement with new and small firms is frequently hampered by fragmentation of membership and representative organizations for entrepreneurs as well as by financial difficulties for organizations in those countries where membership of, for example, chambers is not compulsory. Differences in the level of knowledge between government and non-governmental organizations seriously limit the possibility of conducting consultations based on partnership principles. Although the weakness of these structures makes effective consultation difficult, it is important to recognize that entrepreneurs can be a difficult to reach group for consultation purposes, even in mature market economies, as Chapter 4 emphasizes.

SUPPORTING INSTITUTIONAL CHANGE

Experiences during the transition period highlighted the frequently occurring implementation gap between policy pronouncements and actions, often aggravated by a rapidly changing and unpredictable legislative and regulatory environment (Smallbone and Welter 2009b, 2010b). All of this constrained rather than enabled entrepreneurship, forcing many entrepreneurs to recur to illegal or partly legal activities which in turn had a serious impact on societal attitudes towards entrepreneurship. Clearly, the way that government recognizes and deals with entrepreneurship influences the extent to which involvement in entrepreneurship is an acceptable form of behaviour.

This draws attention to policies that promote an entrepreneurial culture and credible role models. Stevenson and Lundström (2007) classify such policies as 'entrepreneurship promotion', as they are aimed at increasing the value placed on entrepreneurship and creating more awareness for entrepreneurship in a society. In their understanding, relevant policy measures include awards programmes, media campaigns and the like. In transition environments, however, it is not just promotion policies that play a major role in supporting institutional change, but also policies aimed at educating entrepreneurs and those targeting specific groups.

Entrepreneurship Education

In recent years, promoting entrepreneurship education has increased in importance for governments across Central and Eastern Europe (Zahra and Welter 2008). Entrepreneurship education can contribute to fostering entrepreneurship, at least in the long run, but it also has a more indirect role to play in changing mindsets and in contributing to a society which positively values entrepreneurship.

In most Central European member states of the EU, entrepreneurship education is now offered through private foundations, business associations, and universities. Entrepreneurship education in these countries is usually built on existing teaching traditions, but Chapter 6 also demonstrates the need for programmes which take into account country traditions and problems arising during the transition period. These occur because often entrepreneurship education is linked to business education and management faculties and/or are equated with small business management (Zahra and Welter 2008). Moreover, where entrepreneurship education is offered by international business schools, as in Latvia or Russia, this impedes the development of local teaching expertise and materials, especially where no attempt is made to educate and train local teachers.

In countries where the pace of economic and political reforms has been slow, most entrepreneurship education still exists outside higher educational institutions, offered instead by business support centres and enterprise development agencies. This raises a question about the sustainability of these efforts as most such centres are heavily reliant on donor funding (Bateman 2000b). Some international donors have also initiated specific projects to train and educate potential entrepreneurs, focusing mostly on general management issues and neglecting 'soft' behavioural factors of teaching entrepreneurship. Isakova and Smallbone (1999) found that most private educational institutions in Eastern European countries in the 1990s focused on training managers who worked for large multinational companies. This leaves a major void in existing educational programmes which are not equipped to motivate students and graduates to pursue entrepreneurship, particularly in the early stages of transition or in those countries where reforms have stalled, since there is little reward in these circumstances for new venture creation.

However, this is exactly where entrepreneurship education aimed at higher education institutions, could make a difference in promoting a willingness to explore various opportunities for creating and growing companies.

Targeting Support

Direct interventions at the level of firms or individuals are meant to overcome or reduce systemic barriers or market failure, often with the aim to increase start-up rates of under-represented groups (Lundström and Stevenson 2005; Stevenson and Lundström 2007). While in early stages of transition, most governments embarked on direct interventions aimed at overcoming problems related to firm size and structural deficits, this changed in later stages of the transition process with targeted support aimed at increasing the participation of specific groups, gaining importance. Many governments in post socialist countries started to consider means of how to foster the entrepreneurial potential of women and young people (for example, Blokker and Dallago 2008). The participation of both women and young people is understood as contributing to economic growth and reducing unemployment, thus fostering both a competitive economy and social inclusion.

Women's entrepreneurship in a transition context is an excellent example to illustrate the complex interrelationships between institutional change and targeted support policies. On the one hand, the political and economic changes fostered entrepreneurship by both men and women. However, women faced additional challenges because of the renewal of 'patriarchal' gender orders in many post socialist countries, forcing many women back into 'traditional' gender roles and the private family sphere (Welter and Smallbone 2008). Research has shown how women entrepreneurs in such circumstances start to break out of norms which ascribe traditional gender roles (Welter and Smallbone 2010). In this regard, women's entrepreneurship has played, and continues to play, an important role in modernizing these societies and in contributing to changing public attitudes towards women, with possible benefits relating to the economic potential of female entrepreneurs. Women's entrepreneurship may foster institutional change, especially with regard to social norms and values, while institutional change is also needed for women's entrepreneurship to emerge. Therefore, targeting support policies at women entrepreneurs also requires governments to consider the wider effects of the institutional environment on their target groups and address any difficulties in this regard.

CONTRIBUTIONS TO THE *HANDBOOK*

The remainder of the Handbook is structured in three parts. Part I, consisting of seven chapters, deals with different aspects of entrepreneurship policies in the 'New Europe' which, besides East Germany, includes new member states of the European Union, joining in the first or second round during the 1990s.

Chapter 2, by Hofer and Welter is concerned with the local dimension of entrepreneurship policies in East Germany. The authors suggest that, as entrepreneurship is primarily a local event, local governments need to adopt a proactive role in order to enhance entrepreneurship development in their regions. The example of East Germany illustrates that for policy delivery to be effective, entrepreneurship policies need to be adapted to their respective local contexts. At the same time, to be effective entrepreneurship policies in East Germany require an integrated policy approach to fostering entrepreneurship development, but many local governments in East Germany continue to follow a 'piecemeal' approach, based on narrowly defined direct interventions.

In Chapter 3 Todorov, Kolarov and Smallbone analyse the development potential of cross border cooperation in border regions, emphasizing how a more effective regional policy could encourage it. The development of cross border cooperation is affected by many factors, including common or shared culture, the historical legacy, the wider political environment, as well as by economic conditions on the two sides of the border. The example of Bulgaria is used firstly, to demonstrate the development challenges facing border regions; secondly, to show the potential contribution that cross border cooperation can make to regional development in border regions; and thirdly, to highlight the types of policies needed to encourage and support this.

Chapter 4 takes up the theme of social dialogue and governance, in the context of new EU member states. Drawing on Hungary as example, Smallbone, Roman and Blackburn explore the challenges in building effective social dialogue for countries with no recent tradition of self governing organizations; a heritage of trade unions and business that were heavily politicized under the previous system; a pattern of private sector development that is dominated by small firms, which are a 'difficult to reach' group in social dialogue terms in most European countries; and a lack of resources and relevant experience. At the same time, the chapter questions the current approach to social dialogue in the EU because of the apparent mismatch between the under-representation of small firms in social dialogue alongside their widely recognized contribution to the European economy.

Sauka and Welter, in Chapter 5, consider the role of various public and private actors in shaping entrepreneurship policies in Latvia, thus contributing to or constraining institutional change in a country where until the early 1990s private entrepreneurship was illegal. Their chapter illustrates the difficulties involved in developing efficient communication and consultation mechanisms between policy makers and entrepreneurs. Although EU membership pushed institutional change in Latvia, the evidence in Chapter 5 draws attention to 'unchanged' mentalities and mindsets of politicians and entrepreneurs alike, resulting in conflicts between formal and informal institutions.

Chapters 6 and 7 discuss entrepreneurship policies in Poland. In Chapter 6, Cieślik takes up the theme of the role of (entrepreneurship) education in enhancing entrepreneurship as a career option and thus implicitly contributing to an overall positive attitude of society. The chapter discusses challenges for entrepreneurship education in Polish universities, in particular with regard to encouraging the establishment and development of dynamic, knowledge- and growth-oriented business. Touching on the difficulties inherent in any transfer of knowledge and policies, the author indicates the need to contextualize entrepreneurship education programmes into their respective socio-economic context.

Rogut and Piasecki (Chapter 7) illustrate the development of a market-oriented regional innovation system in Lodz which is aimed at helping the region to overcome its structural and economic difficulties. Although a regional innovation strategy already was adopted in 2004, this did not result in accelerating the development of a knowledge-based economy in the region. In this regard, the authors outline the recent steps undertaken by the Lodz government to overcome its regional weaknesses and enhance its regional strengths, highlighting how entrepreneurship research can help to inform local government.

Chapter 8 provides detailed insights into the institutionalization process of entrepreneurship policies in Slovenia. Rebernik and Bradač show how entrepreneurship policies and the overall institutional frame developed during the 1990s in three distinct periods, with each period being characterized by a different set of tasks, actors and policy priorities. Again, this draws attention to the role of the European Union in advancing institutional change, although a more coherent strategic approach towards entrepreneurship and SME policies was only established after 2004.

Part II of the Handbook consists of three chapters, discussing challenges of entrepreneurship policies in selected countries beyond the European Union. Chapter 9, authored by Xheneti, is an in-depth analysis of the policy transfer process in Albania. Based on the example of the endorsement of the EU SME Charter, the author demonstrates how EU discourses can shape national discourses without being embedded into a coherent national entrepreneurship strategy. Whilst policy transfer can help formerly socialist countries to develop their entrepreneurship base, it needs to be accompanied by 'policy learning', in order to take into account respective country contexts.

In Chapter 10, Chepurenko analyses entrepreneurship and SME policies in Russia, sketching developments and challenges since the mid-1990s, which again emphasizes the importance of contextualizing entrepreneurship policies. Although Russia was in need of policies to create an enabling environment for new and small firms, the Russian federal government started by establishing SME policies, mainly based on direct interventions, which tended to foster 'unproductive' entrepreneurship (Baumol 1990). The author illustrates a shift towards a more entrepreneurship-policy oriented agenda, but the persisting implementation gap reflecting 'old' socialist habits in administrations prevented a fundamental policy change.

Chapter 11 takes a closer look at women entrepreneurs in Ukraine, illustrating how institutional change can contribute to women's entrepreneurship, but also restrict it. Isakova applies both gender and entrepreneurship perspectives to analyze the complex relationships between formal and informal institutions where institutional change forced women out of the labour market. This rendered entrepreneurship an attractive opportunity whilst at the same time forcing them into housebound roles. More progress with fostering women's entrepreneurship requires appropriate policies that also take into account the impact of the overall institutional frame on women entrepreneurs.

Part III contains the concluding chapter by Smallbone and Welter, which outlines conclusions and challenges for entrepreneurship policies in a wider Europe.

REFERENCES

Audretsch, D.B., I. Grilo and A.R. Thurik (eds) (2007), *Handbook of Research on Entrepreneurship Policy*, Cheltenham, UK and Northampton, MA: Edward Elgar.

Baker, T., E. Gedajlovic and M. Lubatkin (2005), 'A framework for comparing entrepreneurship processes across nations', *Journal of International Business Studies*, **36** (5), 492–504.

Bannock, G. and A. Peacock (1989), *Governments and Small Business*, London: Paul Chapman for the David Hume Institute.

Bateman, M. (2000a), 'Business Support Centres in the transition economies – progress with the wrong model', *Small Enterprise Development*, **11** (2), 50–59.

Bateman, M. (2000b), 'Neo-liberalism, SME development and the role of business support centres in the transition economies of Central and Eastern Europe', *Small Business Economics*, **14** (4), 275–98.

Baumol, W.J. (1990), 'Entrepreneurship – productive, unproductive, and destructive', *Journal of Political Economy*, **98** (5), 893–921.

Blokker, P. and B. Dallago (2008), *Youth Entrepreneurship and Local Development in Central and Eastern Europe*, Aldershot, UK and Burlington, VT: Ashgate.

Commission of the European Communities (2001), *European Governance: a White Paper*, Brussels: EC.

Davidsson, P. (2003), 'The domain of entrepreneurship research: some suggestions', in J.A. Katz and D.A. Shepherd (eds), *Cognitive Approaches to Entrepreneurship Research*, Amsterdam: JAI, pp. 265–314.

Hart, D.M. (ed.) (2003), *The Emergence of Entrepreneurship Policy: Governance, Startups, and Growth in the US Knowledge Economy*, Cambridge: Cambridge University Press.

Isakova, N. and D. Smallbone (1999), 'The training needs of entrepreneurs in Ukraine', paper presented at the IntENT, Sofia, Bulgaria.

Leitão, J. and R. Baptista (2009), *Public Policies for Fostering Entrepreneurship: a European Perspective*, New York: Springer.

Lundström, A. and L. Stevenson (2005), *Entrepreneurship Policy: Theory and Practice*, Boston, MA: Springer.

Minniti, M. (2008), 'The role of government policy on entrepreneurial activity: productive, unproductive, or destructive?', *Entrepreneurship Theory and Practice*, **32** (5), 779–90.

North, D.C. (1990), *Institutions, Institutional Change, and Economic Performance*, Cambridge: Cambridge University Press.

North, D.C. (2005), *Understanding the Process of Economic Change*, Princeton: Princeton University Press.

Peng, M.W. (2003), 'Institutional transitions and strategic choices', *Academy of Management Review*, **28** (2), 275–86.

Polishchuk, L. and A. Savvateev (2004), 'Spontaneous (non)emergence of property rights', *Economics of Transition*, **12** (1), 103–27.

Reynolds, P.D., D.J. Storey and P. Westhead (1994), 'Cross-national comparisons of the variation in new firm formation rates', *Regional Studies*, **28** (4), 443–56.

Robson, P.J.A., F. Wijbenga and S.C. Parker (2009), 'Entrepreneurship and policy', *International Small Business Journal*, **27** (5), 531–35.

Smallbone, D. and F. Welter (2001a), 'The distinctiveness of entrepreneurship in transition economies', *Small Business Economics*, **16** (4), 249–62.

Smallbone, D. and F. Welter (2001b), 'The role of government in SME development in transition economies', *International Small Business Journal*, **19** (4), 63–77.

Smallbone, D. and F. Welter (2009a), 'Entrepreneurial behaviour in transition environments', in M.-À. Galindo, J. Guzman and D. Ribeiro (eds), *Entrepreneurship and Business in Regional Economics*, New York: Springer, pp. 211–28.

Smallbone, D. and F. Welter (2009b), *Entrepreneurship and Small Business Development in Post-socialist Economies*, London: Routledge.

Smallbone, D. and F. Welter (2010a), 'Entrepreneurship and government policy in former Soviet republics: Belarus and Estonia compared', *Environment and Planning C. Government and Policy*, **28**, 195–210.

Smallbone, D. and F. Welter (2010b), 'Entrepreneurship and the role of government in post-socialist economies: some institutional challenges', *Historical Social Research-Historische Sozialforschung*, **35** (2), 320–33.

Smallbone, D., F. Welter, N. Isakova and A. Slonimski (2001), 'The contribution of Small and Medium Enterprises to economic development in Ukraine and Belarus: some policy perspectives', *MOCT-MOST: Economic Policy in Transitional Economies*, **11** (3), 253–73.

Smallbone, D., F. Welter, A. Voytovich and I. Egorov (2010), 'Government and entrepreneurship in transition economies: the case of small firms in business services in Ukraine', *Service Industries Journal*, **30** (5), 655–70.

Stevenson, L. and A. Lundström (2007), 'Dressing the emperor: the fabric of entrepreneurship policy', in D.B. Audretsch, I. Grilo and A.R. Thurik (eds), *Handbook of Research on Entrepreneurship Policy*, Cheltenham, UK, and Northampton, MA: Edward Elgar, pp. 94–129.

Storey, D.J. (1994), *Understanding the Small Business Sector*, London: Routledge.

Welter, F. (1997), *Small and Medium Enterprises in Central and Eastern Europe: trends, barriers and solutions*, Essen: RWI.

Welter, F. (2011), 'Contextualising entrepreneurship – challenges and ways forward', *Entrepreneurship Theory and Practice*, **35** (1), 165–84.

Welter, F. and D. Smallbone (2003), 'Entrepreneurship and enterprise strategies in transition economies: an institutional perspective', in D. Kirby and A. Watson (eds), *Small Firms and Economic Development in Developed and Transition Economies: A Reader*, Aldershot: Ashgate, pp. 95–114.

Welter, F. and D. Smallbone (2008), 'Women's entrepreneurship from an institutional perspective: the case of Uzbekistan', *International Entrepreneurship and Management Journal* (4), 505–20.

Welter, F. and D. Smallbone (2010), 'The embeddedness of women's entrepreneurship in a transition context', in C.G. Brush, A. De Bruin, E. Gatewood and C. Henry (eds), *Women Entrepreneurs and the Global Environment for Growth: A Research Perspective*, Cheltenham, UK, and Northampton, MA: Edward Elgar, pp. 96–117.

Zahra, S. and F. Welter (2008), 'Entrepreneurship education for Central, Eastern and Southeastern Europe', in J. Potter (ed.), *Entrepreneurship and Higher Education*, Paris: OECD, pp. 165–89.

PART I

ENTREPRENEURSHIP POLICIES IN THE NEW EUROPE

2 The local dimension of entrepreneurship policy: the example of East Germany
Andrea-Rosalinde Hofer and Friederike Welter

INTRODUCTION

Across Organization for Economic Cooperation and Development (OECD) countries entrepreneurship policy belongs to a horizontally organized governance area with cross-ministerial responsibilities and influences and vertical connections with lower government tiers in the design, delivery and evaluation of policies and programmes. Policy effectiveness depends thus, firstly, upon the degree of institutional adaptation across ministerial boundaries, and, secondly, because of the important local dimension of entrepreneurship, upon a mix of institutional and contextual adaptation across different tiers of government to adapt objectives, targets and delivery ways to 'local' requirements. Cross-tier policy partnerships are a widely spread governance instrument to enhance the tailoring of policies to local contexts and business needs (OECD 2009). This allows for an involvement of local actors in the policy process, reflecting the fact that entrepreneurship is primarily a local event: Even if input and output are getting more and more globalized, connectivity, local availability finance and space, as well as the local institutional environment influences the decision to start and run a business. Local contexts thus have a major impact on the extent and nature of entrepreneurship development, as the literature on spatial variations illustrates (for example, Reynolds et al. 1994).

This chapter discusses some of the key features of the local dimension of the East German entrepreneurship policy framework, in which local policy actors are mainly involved in the delivery of higher-tier designed policies and programmes. The discussion around the importance of a 'local policy space' that goes beyond reaction and adaption towards a proactive role in developing new ways in enhancing innovation and growth through entrepreneurship is characteristic for, though not limited to, transition economies. The case of East Germany contributes to this discussion, even though it does not share, due to a rapid integration into the German federal republic, the experience of major institutional development processes around the establishment of local self-government and competency devolution, which are characteristic for European transition economies. The East German case study suggests that policy delivery arrangements, which maximize the degree of institutional and contextual adaptation, can increase policy effectiveness.[1]

The chapter is organized in four sections. It starts with a brief outline of the conceptual background for local entrepreneurship policies. The chapter then continues with a brief introduction to the institutional context and the local environment for entrepreneurship, and an outline of the policy framework, and its key instruments. This is followed by a discussion of key strengths and challenges illustrated by short presentations of local initiatives. The chapter concludes with recalling the importance of institutional and contextual adaptation processes for the local tailoring of policies, and advances key recommendations for entrepreneurship policy actors.

ENTREPRENEURSHIP POLICIES AT LOCAL LEVEL FROM A CONCEPTUAL PERSPECTIVE

The cross-ministerial nature of entrepreneurship policies, or what Hart (2003) refers to as the governance dimension, bears the risk of fragmentation and sub-optimal policy integration. The policy impact is often steered by ministries or their single units other than those having entrepreneurship and small to medium sized enterprise (SME) development as prime focus (OECD 2007). Moreover, the translation of different policy priorities and targets into different measures and initiatives may lead to isolated policy interventions at the local level. To address this, institutional structures were set up at different levels of governments across OECD countries. Depending on the degree of devolution, centralized, decentralized or joint structures can be distinguished. Common for a national level coordinated approach is the establishment of a cross-ministerial authority, which is tasked to design and oversee the delivery of strategies and measures. Examples are entrepreneurship and SME dedicated organizations internal to the government structure or external agencies accountable to the latter. At the sub-national level coordinating and delivering structures are established. Whereas existence and power distribution of the former are strongly interrelated with the degree of devolution, the latter are central components of the local policy delivery framework. Current delivery infrastructure and mechanisms include one- or first-stop shops, online portals, policy actor networks, mentoring schemes, and incubators.

The group of local actors involved in entrepreneurship policy is not limited to local governments and local branches of central government agencies. Private sector actors play increasingly important roles. There is growing evidence of consultative involvement of private sector actors in the priority setting and the design of policies and programmes. At the local level, support structures, such as business incubators and science and technology parks, are often jointly funded. This may lead to different expectations, motivations and interests, which can introduce goal conflicts into the system; multi-source funded business incubators are an often cited example for this. Hence, solid partnerships between public and private sector actors are needed around a comprehensive and consensus-based strategy. If these requirements are in place local policy actors are in an advantageous position to identify and rectify market and system failures. Furthermore, such strategy based partnerships are key for a smooth transition from public subsidies to private follow-up financing, which will be needed, given the envisaged time limitation of public subsidy.

In theory, the degree of local actor involvement may vary from mere mobilization or participation, the lowest level, to influence and power, which both invest local actors with decisive roles in the prioritization of policy goals, the implementation of policies and programmes, and their evaluation, as well as feeding back lessons-learned into the design phase of the policy cycle. In practice, however, the latter often sees a limited role of local actors, whereas involvement is concentrated on the delivery of policies and programmes (Audretsch et al. 2007). Cross-tier and cross-sector communication is primarily used to ensure that local actors are consulted on changes in programmes and are timely informed about changing eligibility criteria and regulations in public funding. All the same, bottom-up communication provides the ground for local tailoring of policies, and a feed-back of what worked and what did not. However, a likely pitfall of greater involvement of higher tier institutions is that local actors may perceive this as a limitation to their flexibility and creativeness in bringing forward local innovative approaches.

To make institutional adaptation processes, as described above, work out for more effective policies, the latter's contextual adaptation is needed. This requires attention to (a) the 'place' or the geographic and environmental context for entrepreneurship, and (b) the 'person' and how he or she perceives entrepreneurial opportunities. The context for entrepreneurship, or what some theorists refer to as the 'opportunity structure' (Aldrich and Wiedenmayer 1993, Thornton 1999), includes a wide range of economic, social, and cultural factors. There is an important national dimension of this, but it is the local dimension that triggers the start of a new venture or stimulates its growth. The level of recognition and appreciation for entrepreneurship, or what Etzioni (1987) refers to as the 'legitimation' or 'moral approval' of entrepreneurship within a culture is an important contextual factor. The higher it is, the wider entrepreneurship is embedded in a society and the greater the political support for it. This, according to Etzioni, will result in a higher demand for and supply of entrepreneurship. Policy intervention can be directed to the supply side, addressing the pool of actual and potential entrepreneurs or to the demand side by increasing the quantity and quality of opportunities for entrepreneurship. The supply–demand side perspective relates to Gartner's (1989) conception of business start-up as an interaction among four dimensions, which is composed of an individual dimension (personal traits), an environmental dimension (push and pull factors), a process dimension, which includes all actions that the entrepreneur undertakes to convert an idea into entrepreneurial action, and an organizational dimension (the firm).

The claim advanced in this chapter is that local tailoring, including institutional and contextual adaptation, of entrepreneurship policy is a prerequisite for its effectiveness. Local tailoring goes hand in hand with two principles of integration. Firstly, it is important that initiatives undertaken to enhance innovation and local and regional science industry linkages, general workforce development, and the stimulation and support of entrepreneurial activities amongst people with entrepreneurial potential, such as graduates, researchers and employees in certain industries, are clearly linked with each other and are part of a wider strategic local framework (Pages et al. 2003). Central to this is a local entrepreneurship strategy, which seeks to maximise the integration of different policies and measures with relevance for entrepreneurship and SME development. Such a strategy, although in most OECD countries mainly being situated on the side of policy delivery instead of policy design, can be an important instrument to increase policy effectiveness. Besides bundling efforts, and funding, it can help local institutions to be more discerning about the quality of entrepreneurship they aim to enhance, such as, for example, start-ups and young firms with growth intentions and/or potentials (OECD 2009). Secondly, the development of appropriate links between local and regional strategy building efforts should be sought, instead of considering the needs of localities in isolation from wider regional opportunities and challenges. Proximity to regional growth poles, within and outside administrative borders stipulates the need for increased integration across jurisdictions and might require a re-thinking of the scale of policy focus: if the municipal level is too small, then cross-municipal integration and joint working possibilities need to be explored.

There are, however, not many local entrepreneurship strategies that would match these two principles. In fact, likely to be found are local approaches that contain certain components strategically linked with each other, and in the best case, a high density of formal and informal networks and communication channels across different tiers of government and between the public and private side of business support (OECD 2009).

ENTREPRENEURSHIP POLICIES IN EAST GERMANY[2]

East Germany is an integral part of Germany and as such resembles key features of the German institutional context for entrepreneurship. Yet, there are some key differences in the contextual framework. Looking at both features provides some broader lessons on the opportunities and challenges for local policy approaches to entrepreneurship development.

The fall of the Berlin Wall in November 1989 commenced an integration process of six new *Länder* (states) into the federal Republic of Germany: Berlin, Brandenburg, Mecklenburg-Vorpommern, Sachsen, Sachsen-Anhalt and Thüringen. The territory of what is generally referred to as East Germany covers 107 689 square kilometres and hosts approximately 13.2 million people. Population density varies between 3800 inhabitants per square kilometre in Berlin and only 75 in Mecklenburg-Vorpommern. Only twelve cities in East Germany have more than 100 000 inhabitants compared to 70 in western Germany.

Policy Issues

At the starting point of economic transition in 1991, private entrepreneurship was nonexistent, except for around 80 000 private craftsmanship firms. The industrial sector was organized in approximately 3400 large state-owned industrial companies, with on average 500 to 1000 employees (Schrumpf 1990). The reallocation of resources across the industry sector's activities and the latter's restructuring resulted in an increase in the production capacities, which was, however, not reflected in the level of research and development (R&D) activity, as these units largely remained in the headquarters in West Germany or abroad. The density of firms with more than 50 employees is 24 firms per 10 000 inhabitants, significantly lower than in the west (30), and the average number of personnel is 164 employees per company, two-thirds of the western measure (BMVBS 2008). The differences in density and size are reflected in a lower rate of industrial productivity, less local demand for SME suppliers, and fewer private business support service providers, such as legal and management consultancies, financing and business investment services.

East Germany is host to both lagging and shrinking regions as well as places becoming the source of new local economic growth. Factors stipulating high growth rates include the degree of connectivity of a place, the presence of high-growth companies, and the effectiveness of the local innovation system (Ragnitz 2009). Regional productivity rates, for example, are high in places where subsidiary companies of large global corporations have settled. Teltow-Fläming (Daimler-Chrysler, BMW), the city of Dresden (Infineon, AMD, VW) and Eisenach (General Motors) provide evidence for this. The East German labour market is characterized by a persistent East–West migration of the young labour force and high unemployment rates, with youth unemployment being a major challenge. Wages as well as the average labour productivity are lower than in the west. Demographic changes, largely due to the continuous out-migration of the young (women) and talented (Kröhnert and Klingholz 2007), are likely to hamper entrepreneurial activity and economic development, if not properly addressed by policy. Many rural areas, but also smaller cities that are distant from economic growth poles, will thus need to define their own genuine strategic approach.

In this regard, promoting entrepreneurship and SME development has been taken up by many local governments as a local policy strategy to foster job creation and economic development (Hofer and Potter 2009b). Support in this comes from federal and state government policies and programmes to enhance the entrepreneurial activity rate by getting individuals to start businesses and by attracting existing firms to locate or extend their activities in East Germany. Providing the right framework for starting one's own business, for business succession or matchmaking business needs for skilled with high-skilled labour are key components of the entrepreneurship agenda of local governments and partnering organizations and individuals from private sector and civil society.

Policy Framework and Policy Delivery

The policy process for entrepreneurship and SME policies is embedded in a multi-level governance system in which federal ministries and the state governments are decision-making tiers and local governments are the key implementers. Table 2.1 gives an overview of the different actors involved. Business support initiatives at local levels therefore seldom reflect genuine 'new' approaches of local government, but they are embedded in federal and state programmes and policy approaches (Welter 2009). At the federal level different ministries are involved in entrepreneurship and SME policies. Key responsibilities are with the Federal Ministry of Economics and Technology, and the Ministry of Education and Research. For East Germany, the Federal Ministry of Housing, Construction and Urban Development has been given the role of coordinating and integrating

Table 2.1 *Key actors involved in SME and entrepreneurship policies*

Federal level	State/Land level	District level*	Municipal level**
Ministry of Economics Gen Inv Fin Skills	Ministry of Economics Gen Inv Fin Skills	District administration department for economic development, publicly owned development corporation (*Regionalmanagement*) Gen Inv Fin Skills	Municipal department for economic development Gen Inv Fin Skills
Ministry of Education and Research Skills	Ministry of Education and Research Skills		
Ministry of Labour Skills	Ministry of Labour Skills		
Ministry of Housing, Transport and Urban Affairs co-ordinating East Germany focused policies	Ministries responsible for/involved in respective policy areas		
KfW Bankengruppe Fin	State-owned public banks (*Landesbanken*), private–public sector jointly owned guarantee banks, etc. Fin	Regional and local branches of state-owned public banks, local representatives of guarantee banks, etc. Fin	
Unions of business associations Gen Fin Skills	Business associations Gen Fin Skills	Regional/local branches of business associations, local business associations Gen Fin Skills	
Bundesagentur für Arbeit (federal public employment service) Gen Inv Fin Skills		District level public employment service Inv Skills	Local offices Inv Skills

Table 2.1   (continued)

Federal level	State/Land level	District level*	Municipal level**
Confederation of Chambers of Industry and Commerce Gen Inv Fin Skills	Regional branches of Chambers covering in general more than one administrative district		Gen Inv Fin Skills
Confederation of Chambers of Skilled Crafts Gen Inv Fin Skills	Regional branches of Chambers covering in general more than one administrative district (*Kreishandwerkerschaften*) for certain professions		Regional branches of Chambers covering in general more than one administrative district, plus local guilds Gen Inv Fin Skills
Federal association of German innovation and technology centres and business incubators Gen Inv Fin			Science parks, technology centres, business incubation facilities (often co-ownership municipality and university and partly state/federal funded) Gen Inv Fin

Notes:

*   District level is equal to LAU-1 level, or a regional government level, according to the Nomenclature of Territorial Units for Statistics (NUTS) used in the European Union.

**   The municipal level in Germany is equal to LAU-2, the lowest NUTS level.

Gen: business start-up and SME support; Inv: Inward investment promotion; Fin: Business financing; Skills: skills development (entrepreneurship education in schools, business needs dovetailed training, SME training initiatives, etc.).

Source: Adapted from Wehrle (2009).

different policy areas. Involving the private sector in tailoring policies to business needs is considered to be crucial for effective policy making and was taken up into strategic alliances. Examples of counselling and policy evaluation boards are *Gründerbeirat*, which is an institutionalized public–private board that discusses current challenges for business start-up and SME development in Brandenburg, and *Denkwerkstatt 2020*,[3] a major undertaking by the state government that involves locally well-known personalities in making Mecklenburg-Vorpommern an attractive place to live and work in, both as an employee and an entrepreneur.

Policies nowadays are often delivered through competitions that encourage local and inter-regional partnership building, also between public and private actors. *Lernende Regionen*[4] and *Unternehmen Region*[5] are examples of competitions that provide financing for innovation and technology inter-firm networks and the establishment of business support partnerships and regional skills initiatives. The current distribution of winners shows a north–south and an urban–rural divide, with projects clustering around larger cities in the southern parts of East Germany, despite the emphasis of policy to establish regional growth centres also across jurisdictions (Welter 2009). The delivery structure is similar across the six East German states. In all states a development and investment agency has been established and tasked with the attraction of foreign investment to the state's territory and the provision of innovation and entrepreneurship support. Some states have established additional agencies at the local level, often directly managed by local governments as an integral part of the local entrepreneurship support infrastructure. These agencies have a broad range of tasks that include business advisory services, assistance in finding appropriate premises and in accessing public grant and loan schemes, and often also the management inter-firm networks.

Public development banks deliver a broad range of public financing schemes (Grichnik 2009). These banks have no commercial banking activities but design and oversee public financing programmes from the respective state and the European Union. They act as one-stop shops for entrepreneurs and local governments and are involved in key local policy partnerships. In addition, some states have encouraged the establishment of public guarantee banks as a form of self-help to overcome information asymmetries and gaps in financing business start-up and SME development. Typical shareholders are the Chamber of Industry and Commerce, the Chamber of Skilled Crafts, business associations and guilds, insurance companies, and private, mainly savings banks. Guarantee banks are financially backed up by the federal and respective state governments.

The Chamber of Industry and Commerce, and the Chamber of Skilled Crafts with their national umbrella organisations and local branches, are the most important non-governmental organisations lobbying for business needs across all levels of government. They also deliver policies and programmes at the local level, including training and assistance in business management, marketing and export promotion. Central for the latter is an overseas network of German Chambers of Industry and Commerce. Export credit guarantees and financial support for the participation in international fairs abroad are well-taken up measures to facilitate the internationalization of East German SMEs. The role of the Chambers in providing business support has increased over the last few years. According to a national survey in 2004 almost 40 per cent of businesses referred to the Chambers for support and advice, whereas it was only 22 per cent in 2002 (Wallau 2007). Also universities, business incubators and technology centres became more frequent points of referral for businesses (Wallau 2007).

Local governments are getting more actively involved in entrepreneurship and SME support than they have been in the past (Welter 2007). Business support is considered a voluntary task for which no extra state transfers are available. Hence, often smaller towns and rural districts do not provide services on their own, but collaborate with neighbouring jurisdictions. Where they provide business support services, they either establish a dedicated unit in-house or outsource to private sector. Often, business advisory services for existing companies are considered more important than enhancing new business start-ups. The focus is on building and strengthening regional and supra-regional intra-firm networks and clusters, and to increase the share of tradable products and services. There is a trend towards a greater emphasis on the soft infrastructure for entrepreneurship and SME development and locational factors in general, and successful project based cooperation with the European Structural Funds increased the possibilities of local governments to become active. Despite a broad range of local activities, comprehensive and clearly communicated local strategies for entrepreneurship and SME development are, however, rare. In 2001, less than half of all towns with more than 10 000 inhabitants had a written strategy for local economic development that goes beyond industrial real estate development and retail trade which are seen as the 'traditional' business policy areas for local governments (Blume 2001).

Key Policy Instruments

Pre-start up support is provided solely by the regional/state governments, whereas the federal government took over post-start-up support. Business start-up advisory services are provided for new and young companies up to the age of 60 months (BMVBS 2008). The support period is longer than the OECD average of 42 months. In order to increase the transparency of services and their effectiveness, a working group composed of the federal and regional governments agreed a coordinated approach. *Gründercoaching Deutschland*[6] is an example of a Germany-wide approach, financed by the federal budget and European Social Fund money, which provides services through regional contact points. The focus is on businesses in trade, handicrafts, manufacturing, transport, tourism and non-tradable services. In addition to general information and advice, the programme offers interested firms access to subsidized counselling services.

Grants and subsidized loan schemes, and investment allowances for companies to locate to, or extend their activities in, East Germany are key policy instruments that local governments can use to attract firms into their jurisdictions or increase the local entrepreneurial activity rate (Ragnitz 2009). The attraction of companies to settle in localities economically lagging behind is practiced as part of local job creation strategies. For companies, accessing these 'location grants' is becoming increasingly competitive. In order to be eligible, applying companies need to demonstrate innovativeness, high levels of R&D activity and their potential and commitment to create new jobs. In addition, schemes for individual applicants target different groups, including university students, graduates, young talented workers as well as the unemployed.

Private equity is still less frequent in East Germany than in the west and business start-ups and young firms are thus more dependent upon private and public financing (Grichnik 2009). A wide range of public financing instruments has been developed and is used by a large number of companies. The delivery is organized through local commercial banks following the so-called 'Hausbank' approach, according to which commercial banks deliver public financing programmes. This approach has a number of advantages, but can also create obstacles, if the applicant, according to the decision of the superior banking level, does not fulfil the loan criteria. Table 2.2 gives an overview of current policies with an East Germany focus or exclusivity.

CHALLENGES AND STRENGTHS OF THE EAST GERMAN LOCAL ENTREPRENEURSHIP POLICY DIMENSION

Key challenges for entrepreneurship and SME development in East Germany lie in the actual structure of the business stock, which is characterized by a low density of large and globally connected industry, whose

Table 2.2   Selected federal entrepreneurship financing programmes

Initiative	Description	Objectives
High-tech start-up financing (High-tech Gründerfonds)	Financing of research-results based business start-ups and young companies (<1 year) with up to EUR 500 000 equity capital. Own contribution is 10% in East Germany and 20% in the rest of Germany.	● Overcome gaps in high-tech business start-up financing.
EPR start-up financing (EPR-Startfonds)	Co-financing of equity capital in young technology companies. Terms of investment are equal to those of private investors. Maximum amount of investment is EUR 3 million.	● Overcome gaps in financing young technology companies.
Investment allowance	Financial support for primary investments in SMEs in manufacturing, services, and tourism.	● Strengthen competitiveness and growth potentials of existing companies.
Joint task to enhance the regional economic structure (Gemeinschaftsaufgabe 'Verbesserung der regionalen Wirtschaftsstruktur')	Financial support for investments by manufacturing SMEs, investments in local business infrastructure, regional clusters and inter-firm networks, and the establishment of regional development agencies (Regionalmanagement).	● Job creation and maintenance in lagging regions. ● Attracting of inward investment and off-shore settlement of large firms.

Source: BMVBS (2008).

activities are concentrated on production rather than on R&D. This clearly impedes local supply chain development and thus restricts SME growth opportunities. In addition, there are challenges that impact the effectiveness of entrepreneurship and SME policies. Pitfalls resulting from a multi-level governance system, the less prominent position of entrepreneurship in society, and existing gaps in private financing are discussed below. A key strength of the East German entrepreneurship policy environment is the abundant supply of support programmes that cover the different stages of the business life cycle (OECD 2009). In the following, initiatives to enhance skills development and investment in skilled labour, current policy practice to enhance the R&D activity of SMEs, and local policy partnerships and collaboration with the private sector are presented.

Governance Pitfalls and Local Policy Partnerships

As mentioned earlier, the local tailoring of policies requires close cooperation, coordination and integration across different levels of government. Current arrangements at regional government level in East Germany appear to constrain stronger integration and coordination at the local level, as often different priority setting is translated into strategies that are then implemented by different agencies at local and/or state level. An illustrative example can be found in the increasingly important field of enhancing entrepreneurship in higher education institutions. Here, the education and science policy portfolio overlaps with that of economic development promotion. Universities will need to find their way in communicating with both partner ministries, who, however, often pursue different agendas.

In general, limited competencies of local governments for entrepreneurship and SME policy design lead to a top-down approach with varying degrees of local discretion and input. A systematic analysis of local needs and policy options with regard to entrepreneurship and SME development is often underdeveloped and evaluation practices are limited to the enumeration of the outputs of specific projects and programmes rather than a more qualitative evaluation that aims at feeding back lessons-learned into the policy process (Hofer and Potter 2009a).

Yet, local governments work hard to reduce administrative burdens and to make localities attractive for businesses. A key task has been to introduce clearly visible and easily accessible entrance points to the local business support system. Maintaining an overview and selecting the best suitable option can, however, be time intensive and not without difficulty for the entrepreneur. Lambrecht and Pirnay (2005), having assessed public and private business advisory support in the Walloon region of Belgium, suggest the establishment of a single integrated office, accountable to government, to be tasked with the certification of private consultants, the promotion of their services, the financial management and the *ex-post* evaluation.

The introduction of a broker to disseminate information, ensure quality checks and avoid adverse selection is followed also by eastern German regions. In Brandenburg, for example, this has been addressed by the establishment of a state-wide network of 26 *Lotsendienste*,[7] first-stop shops for entrepreneurs attached to existing agencies. Technology and incubation centres, the Chambers, regional development agencies, institutes of higher education, and agencies focusing on social groups under-represented in business start-up and business ownership, like women and migrants, are participating in this initiative and contribute with dedicated personnel to a one-to-one advice and counselling approach. The package is tailored for different target groups, like pupils, youth, women, migrants and university graduates, includes first orientation about challenges and opportunities related to the start of a business, pre-start coaching, assessment centres and training needs identification as well as coaching in the post-start-up phase. *Lotsendienste* is an initiative co-funded by the Ministry of Labour and the European Social Fund. It is part of a wider government initiative to increase business creation and entrepreneurial activities that brings together the Ministries of Economy, Labour, Science and Research, and Education and Youth in partnership with Chambers. This state-wide initiative, together with its local outreach, the *Lotsendienste*, can be considered an effective approach to address the earlier mentioned risk of fragmentation in entrepreneurship policy delivery, especially when it concerns business start-ups in regions characterized by demographic changes and high levels of unemployment.

There is a great offer in premises-based support structures and many local governments run their own business parks, technology centres and various forms of business incubation structures (Welter 2009). Where there is no local presence of a university or research institutions, local governments are often hesitant to commit to the huge investments needed for the establishment and maintenance of incubator space and technology centres. This, however, stands against the growing need of businesses to increase their competitiveness on national and international markets and the resulting likelihood of a dislocation or bankruptcy in case adequate support, networking and clustering opportunities and skilled labour are not locally available. It is interesting to look at how local governments dealt with this conflict of interests and development needs. For example, the Innovation and Technology Centre *PITZ*[8] in Parchim (Mecklenburg-Vorpommern), was established by the municipality despite the absence of a university or a research institution. Nevertheless *PITZ* gained wider regional importance, mainly because of the co-location of *NUKLEUS*;[9] a federally subsidized inter-firm networking and business advice initiative. This partnership initiated a successful clustering process around nanotechnology, offering expert advice to firms and connecting regional, national and international research organizations with businesses in the region. The ever growing number of network partners considers the access to strategic information an incentive to meet. *PITZ* strengthened the local science industry base and led to the creation of a local value chain.

Another example is an inter-regional partnership that the City of Altenburg in Thüringen initiated in 2007 with the University of Applied Sciences in Jena, 70 kilometres away from Altenburg, to deal with the problems of no local university, underdeveloped science–industry linkages and limited access to highly skilled young workers by starting a partnership.[10] Young people from Altenburg that are studying in Jena are offered the possibility of a placement in a technology-based business in Altenburg. This brings them in contact with local firms and the overall business environment. As SMEs in Altenburg usually have no dedicated research and development departments, students can add real value to the business by providing research assistance. The student exchange activity allows SMEs to have access to current technology that they would otherwise be unable to afford. This keeps their skills up-to-date and alleviates the disadvantage of size. As these examples illustrate, business support partnerships are an excellent way of levelling out the playing field at local level.

Struggling with SME Growth

The generation of intrapreneurial attitudes among company managers and staff is an important ingredient in the process of raising a firm's innovation potential and readiness. The East German regions have on average a higher share of people with completed tertiary education in the labour force (OECD 2009, latest data). This suggests an expansion of current business start-up support initiatives, as widening the target group and including high-skilled employees with great potential for entrepreneurial activities, in light of the still limited interest in business succession compared to start-up activities. With its geographic advantage of a central European location, and the substantial investment that has been made in infrastructure, East Germany is well-positioned to become a competitive centre for traded goods and services. Local companies, particularly those with a focus on traditional products and services, however, often lack adequate skills and information to best access export markets. The general shift in federal and state policies towards innovation support and away from investment allowances has had a positive impact on the level of SME innovation activity (Hofer and Potter 2009b). There is a great supply of training and counselling for business start-ups, young firms and established companies. Yet, wider aspects of business modernization and economic activity diversification appear to be limited to a small number of firms, mainly those operating in high-tech and growth sectors, where competition for market shares is a stimulating factor, whereas for the majority of local SMEs, growth has not yet become a key objective. This raises the question of what is needed to stimulate growth tendencies and to improve the capacities of firms to recognize and take up new business and market opportunities, or, with regard to the contextual framework of East Germany, what is needed to turn the necessity entrepreneurs of today into the opportunity entrepreneurs of tomorrow?

Results from the Regional Entrepreneurship Monitor (REM) illustrate a link between entrepreneurial attitudes, the propensity to enter entrepreneurship and overall regional economic development: More individuals in economically prospering regions, which have a higher share of entrepreneurship already, perceive opportunities for setting up a venture compared to those in depressed regions or regions with a deficient business support infrastructure (Bergmann 2005). Overall, the recent socio-economic legacy in East Germany has not been favourable to the emergence of an entrepreneurial culture: people seem to be less entrepreneurial and starting a business is often considered the last exit from unemployment. Whilst there are hotspots of entrepreneurialism in certain sectors and population groups, the current culture favours undertaking standard tasks and nurtures the expectation of career development within well-established companies rather than encouraging the types of capacities that support the development of new and growing businesses, such as creativity, adaptability, self-direction and measured risk taking, and an expectation of career moves between firms and potential periods of self-employment and business management (Hofer and Potter 2009a).

Actions to increase entrepreneurial motivations and to develop skills for business growth are thus important, not just for increasing the pool of people interested in and capable of starting and running a business, but also for shifting the nature of business activity towards opportunity entrepreneurship and towards incremental innovations in products, markets and production techniques that will make local businesses more competitive. The importance of an entrepreneurial culture that encourages start-ups and enhances SME growth has already translated into government action and a slew of public–private networking and partnership development (Grimm 2009, Welter 2009). It is important to bear in mind that this kind of policy initiative needs time as well as integration into a locally genuine approach to stimulate and strengthen entrepreneurship and SME development.

Getting the Entrepreneurial Skills Base Right

Companies that wish to grow need skilled labour to develop new products and services. Professional reorientation, widespread in East Germany, needs to be adapted to the requirements of local labour markets in order to help supply local business with appropriately skilled workers. In some regions out-migration and the changing career wishes of young people make it difficult for companies to locally recruit appropriate personnel. The existence of individualized training schemes and a close cooperation between training providers, as already practiced in many places, can be considered good practice. Smaller firms often face difficulties in getting the personnel they want and in accessing public grant schemes that subsidize employment as well as training participation. Good relationships with the public employment service can help in this regard. In Mittweida (Saxony), for example, the local business support environment is characterized by its strength in networking companies with support organizations. Often referred to as *Bestandspflege*, or maintenance care, local governments and the public employment service are working closely together in assessing the needs of local companies for skilled labour and training of the existing labour force. In Uckermark, a district in Brandenburg, the *Luchs* network is a formalized local business support partnership. *Luchs* is one of five regions in Brandenburg that receive funding from the above mentioned federal competition *Lernende Regionen*. *Luchs* contributes to local firm development through the provision of skilled labour. It has around 50 partners, including training providers, business associations, the Chambers and individual firms, the employment service, trade unions, local governments, and cultural organizations.

Besides finding the right personnel, staff costs might put off expansion and growth plans, especially if other costs take over. To address this, the programme *Innovationsassistenten* has been introduced in most of the East German states. In Brandenburg for example, the programme, which receives European Structural Fund money, is run by the *Brandenburg Investitionsbank*, the state development bank. The aim is to raise innovation and competitiveness of local SMEs, and to increase the adoption of environmentally sustainable production methods by taking on university students and graduates as skilled employees. Firms can employ up to two, and companies younger than five years up to four innovation assistants. Their employment is subsidized for a period of up to two years.[11] Whilst these policies present solutions to the skills problem at firm and local level, they also need to be assessed in the wider context of out-migration in East Germany which might counterfeit local policy efforts in this regard.

Enhancing Local Science–Industry Linkages

Taking into account the differences in size, location and sectoral structure there is no significant gap in the research and development (R&D) activity of

SMEs in both parts of Germany. However, East German SMEs are less efficient innovators.[12] According to Aschhoff et al. (2008) reasons for this are:

- low R&D capacity of firms;
- low dynamic of technology oriented start-ups;
- insufficient integration into national and overseas markets;
- low direct private investment and high dependency upon public R&D support;
- insufficient technology transfer;
- low dynamic in skills upgrading; and out-migration.

Enhancing the R&D activity of existing SMEs and the technology orientation of new firms are key areas for policy intervention. Public policy intervention is mainly directed at stimulating the interest of existing companies to increase their R&D activity through inter-firm networks and through greater contacts with research and higher education institutions (Aschhoff et al. 2008). In 2008, the federal ministries ran 83 programmes for the whole of Germany. Table 2.3 gives an overview of current federal programmes with an East Germany focus or exclusivity. In addition, East German regional governments run between three (Mecklenburg-Vorpommern) and nine (Sachsen) programmes that provide grants, loans and silent or open forms of shareholding for innovative and technology oriented SMEs.

In all East German states, programmes are in place to stimulate the establishment of local innovation systems. Regions with a high density of innovation infrastructure are Wismar and Rostock at the Baltic Sea coast, Berlin and its hinterland, Magdeburg and Halle, Dresden, Chemnitz, and Freiberg. Positive results have been achieved from locating advice and counselling services in business start-up and growth in local technology and innovation centres, as this can be offered best at a decentralized level (OECD 2009). With dedicated technology and innovation centres, business support infrastructure has been used to initiate and develop SME clusters. Typical innovation-focused business advice includes the provision of general information and referral to technological advice, and assistance in the planning and implementation of joint R&D projects that bring together firms, industry organizations, higher education institutions and research organizations. Inter-district and inter-municipal cooperation in financing and managing technology, and innovation support infrastructure, is practiced in economic regions and in places with high levels of inter-firm networking and clustering. Institutional partnerships with universities and research institutions help to overcome administrative difficulties in inter-jurisdictional cooperation.

Table 2.3 *Policies and programmes to enhance local innovation capacities and competences*

Policy/programme	Description	Objectives
INNOWATT	Financial support for R&D activities of SMEs and research institutions in East Germany in high-market potential and high-risk areas.	Stimulate and strengthen the innovation potential of SMEs and research institutions, and make them carriers of growth potentials and engines for local economic development.
Industrial research capacity of lagging regions	Financial support for industrial research of non-profit research partnerships.	Enhance the capacities of non-profit industrial research partnerships.
Innovation management capacities of SMEs	Financial support for manufacturing SMEs and craftsmanship utilizing external innovation management and consultancy services.	Increase the innovation potential of SMEs.
PRO INNO II	Financial support for national and international R&D cooperation of SMEs and research institutions.	Increase the innovation potential of SMEs and a greater incorporation of research results in SMEs; Cooperation capacity of SMEs; job creation and maintenance; increase of turnover and export rates of SMEs.
NEMO	Financial support for technology oriented external management and consultancy services to build and expand inter-firm networks.	Increase the engagement in inter-firm networks and R&D and innovation benefits for SMEs; job creation and maintenance; increase of turnover and export rates of SMEs.
Regional innovation initiative ('Unternehmen Region')	Financial support for innovation initiatives by administrative and economic regions.	Regional partnership building by actors from business, science and education to stimulate and strengthen local innovation capacities.

Source: BMVBS (2008).

For all firm sizes, the presence of a university can stimulate growth intentions and be a source of innovation. Often universities and research institutes are, however, not the usual interlocutors of small firms. Even high-technology and growth companies direct, in the first place, an interest in technology transfer and a request for support to the Chambers which have specialized structures to serve high-technology firms. Central to their business advice activity is assisting individual member firms to survive and grow, and facilitating the establishment of inter-firm networks. The latter bears the potential for greater local cooperation and strategic partnership building. Yet, often higher education institutions and Chambers remain on two, often distant, sides of the local innovation support system; and a so-called 'high communicator' is needed to further develop the local innovation system (Welter and Kolb 2006).

Higher education and research institutions can act as key promoters of local science industry linkages, by doing the first step towards the 'business side' (Harding 2009). In Halle, for example, the Martin-Luther University of Halle-Wittenberg plays an important role in bridging this gap and instigated a closer cooperation in technology transfer that facilitates the exploitation of knowledge and technology through a wider group of firms, and brings additional financial resources and human capital into the University that can be mobilized for joint R&D activities. *UNIVATIONS,*[13] a publicly financed network, links the four universities in the region and connects them with other networks in Germany, including a recently started international outreach. The spirit of cooperation amongst the partnering universities is exemplified by the fact that each university refers student entrepreneurs to the most appropriate resources for their needs, even when those resources are at one of the other institutions. This allows participating universities to develop both individual and collaborative strengths and helps to establish and spread local linkages between spin-off firms and local companies. Each university is thus also in a position to foster local inter-firm exchanges. With this second type of networking, *UNIVATIONS* seeks to link universities with local firms and start-ups. Extending the target group, from the initial core group of university students, graduates and academic staff, to local business clusters, financing institutions and venture capitalists, as recently launched with the *Scidea*[14] project, can be seen as a promising approach to make full use of the network's potential to contribute to a wider economic development in Halle. The aim of *Scidea* is to become the main interface between key local industries and the local science base in facilitating technology transfer from laboratory to industry and from company to company. The approach is meant to assist in the channelling of public support and private funding into business ideas with high growth potential and small firms with growth intentions, and further, to foster networking between these firms. Time will prove whether the University of Halle has a comparative advantage over any other actor in the local innovation support system in running such an interface.

CONCLUSIONS AND IMPLICATIONS

The East German case study revealed a number of interesting conclusions on the relevance of institutional and contextual adaptation processes in the local tailoring of policies. Institutional adaptation cannot be steered by local actors; it needs to be considered as a 'hand-in-hand' exercise, supported by central government authorities. Such an arrangement is, however, not always easy to achieve, in particular in transition economies where institutional changes are still intermingled with political power struggles. Yet, as the East Germany case shows, the effective existence of a local strategy, combining different paths of actions, can prepare the ground for wider institutional changes in how and on what evidence basis SME and entrepreneurship policies are designed, implemented and evaluated. Contextual adaptation, in particular, moving entrepreneurship and SME development and growth, into the centre of policy attention, plays an important role.

The following key lessons from the East Germany case are presented as recommendations for national, regional and local entrepreneurship policy actors.

Institutional Adaptation

Local actors constitute important pillars for the East German entrepreneurship policy framework. Although their involvement is more or less limited to the delivery of policies and programmes, it is the way the latter is organized, which has an impact on the effectiveness of entrepreneurship policy. The following key recommendations can be advanced:

- *Fostering institutional innovation.* Institutional arrangements characterized by high levels of integration and coordination have a positive influence on entrepreneurship and SME development. Institutional innovation will need to include all levels of government, but short term positive results can be achieved by starting from the delivery side. Increasing the level of coordination and integration through a local strategy for entrepreneurship and SME development can be, despite the costs of consensus building (that is, getting different actors on board and overcoming goal conflicts), a concrete means to steer and increase the impact of policy.

- *Tailoring policy to local and regional contexts.* The target setting process in entrepreneurship policy-making ideally reflects to a certain degree the characteristics of local contexts. Communication channels between different levels of government, involving beneficiaries and their representative bodies, can be very useful instruments. The more localized they are, the more valuable the information gathered from them. Optimized communication can positively impact output rates and the outcomes of certain measures; timely communication on changing eligibility criteria and regulations in public grant and loan schemes is an example.

- *Incentivizing the design of an overarching local strategy for entrepreneurship and SME development.* The existence of a local strategy for entrepreneurship and SME development can greatly contribute to bundle current efforts, and helps to identify bottlenecks or overlap and distortion caused by goal conflicts or a duplication of activities. Across OECD countries there are to date only a few comprehensive local entrepreneurship strategies, but many different policy documents that make reference to, or prescriptions for, entrepreneurship and small firm development (OECD 2009). National governments can incentivize the drafting of clear and mutually agreed strategy by making it a prerequisite for evaluation exercises or a requirement for tapping into government transfer payments and special development budgets. Furthermore, involving key local and national level actors in systematic evaluation efforts helps to identify goal conflicts and potential synergies between different strategies. This provides a valuable source of information for upper tier governments to tailor policies and measures to the local context, and for their local partners to adjust delivery.

- *Optimizing the local support environment.* The local support environment ideally responds to current needs and allows timely identification of new areas of intervention reflecting the changing needs of local businesses in general, and potential growth companies in particular. A suite of support activities is needed as well as foresight intelligence. Public and private sector actors will need to closely work together in partnership to provide tailored and timely hands-on support. A well functioning partnership can prepare a regularly updated inventory of local companies, their growth intentions and orientations. It is important that public and private actors in business support grasp growth prospects of different segments of companies and respond to growth needs. This is about recognizing new ideas, business concepts and company features and identifying and segmenting the companies displaying them. Such a system needs clear and transparent criteria for the categorization of business support measures and their delivery. The latter requires the introduction of regular quality and fit-for-purpose checks to evaluate the current offer in order to identify and adjust access and take-up barriers, bottlenecks and offers that no longer meet business needs.

Contextual Adaption

The level of recognition and appreciation for entrepreneurship is an important contextual factor. Local governments and local business support organizations are key actors in developing a strategic approach to enhance entrepreneurial attitudes and fostering their translation into business start-ups and growth enterprises. Key recommendations for achieving such an approach include:

- *Improving the image of places.* Changing entrepreneurial attitudes also means changing the image of a place. If people do not believe that a place is attractive to live in, and that it allows for being entrepreneurial and innovative, then they will not set up businesses, or will set up or operate their businesses in more attractive places. It is important to generate trust in local assets and strengths and in the future of places.
- *Promoting entrepreneurial attitudes and increased awareness of entrepreneurial opportunities.* It is important that entrepreneurship is not seen as a cure for unemployment but rather as a means to dynamic economic development. Practical real life stories and happenings provide people with better understanding of what it is like to be an entrepreneur. Regions and localities need to be innovative in initiating special promotion activities to raise entrepreneurial attitudes amongst all segments of society. In the long run, promoting entrepreneurship education throughout the education system, also through extra-curricular activities, up to university level stimulates entrepreneurial aspirations, attitudes and behaviour.
- *Clarity about the sources for new entrepreneurship and motivations.* It is important for local entrepreneurship policy actors as well as for actors in the wider policy framework, to have clarity about the sources for new entrepreneurship and their support needs. Often, business support organizations have limited knowledge of potential entrepreneurial groups and their needs and barriers, as they are too involved in taking care of those already in the start-up 'pipeline' and existing businesses. Yet, it is important to recognize the motivations for entrepreneurship of those currently entrepreneurially underrepresented. Although, often found to be not amongst the

top drivers, altruistic motivations, such as helping others and doing something in favour of the environment, should find entrance into entrepreneurship support initiatives.

- *Entrepreneurial attitudes are not confined to the individual, but need to include the support framework.* A business- and entrepreneurship-friendly atmosphere is an important ingredient for encouraging firm birth and fostering growth. The involvement of all relevant stakeholders and actors in a society-wide process will help to bring forward the idea of an entrepreneurial society, where enterprises can be established and grow, and administrative barriers are removed.

Outlook

Since reunification, East Germany has made enormous progress in developing entrepreneurship and local entrepreneurship policies. These, as demonstrated in this chapter, can help foster transition at local level, while at the same time a local dimension is a key requirement for successful entrepreneurship and SME development. However, the evidence throughout the chapter also illustrates the difficulties in tailoring local policies and setting up adequate delivery mechanisms, both of which are a prerequisite for policy effectiveness at local level. In particular, the local context for entrepreneurship in East Germany challenges traditional approaches to entrepreneurship development at local level, instead asking for an integrated approach whose elements have been outlined in the previous sections. In this regard, it remains to be seen as to whether all local governments in East German will be able to switch from a more piecemeal approach to an overall local strategy.

NOTES

1. For an overview of key market and system failures and potential local actions see Potter (2005).
2. The information in this chapter on East Germany is based on an OECD review of the local dimension of entrepreneurship policy that the OECD Local Employment and Economic Development Programme conducted over the period 2005–07. The authors have been part of this exercise, see Hofer and Potter (2009b), Welter (2009). The full report is downloadable at http://www.oecd.org/cfe/leed/entrepreneurship/compendium.
3. See http://www.denkwerkstatt-mv.de/ for more information.
4. See http://www.lernende-regionen.info/dlr/index.php for more information.
5. See http://www.unternehmen-region.de/ for more information.
6. See http://www.kfw-mittelstandsbank.de/ for more information.
7. See http://www.lasa-brandenburg.de/Lotsendienste.664.0.html for further information.
8. See http://www.pitz-parchim.de/ for further information.
9. See http://www.unternehmen-region.de/en/269.php for further information.

10. See http://www.altenburgerland.de/sixcms/detail.php?id=46589&_lang=de&_css_tem plate=altenburgerland_css for further information.
11. During the first year 50 per cent of the gross wage is subsidized up to a maximum of EUR 20 000, decreasing to 40 per cent, up to a maximum of EUR 10 000 in the second year. See http://www.esf.brandenburg.de/sixcms/detail.php/land_bb_boa_01.c.20536. de for further information.
12. The current share of turnover increase resulting from new products is 21 per cent for East German manufacturing enterprises, compared to 29 per cent in the west. In knowledge-intensive services the respective shares are 15 per cent and 21 per cent. Similar patterns can be found for the impact of market novelties on turnover and unit cost reduction achieved by process innovation (Aschhoff et al. 2008).
13. See http://www.univations.de/ for further information.
14. See http://www.scidea.de/ for further information.

REFERENCES

Aldrich, H.E. and G. Wiedenmayer (1993), 'From traits to rates: an ecological perspective on organizational foundings', in J. Katz and R. Brockhaus (eds), *Advances in Entrepreneurship, Firm Emergence, and Growth*, Vol. 1, Greenwich, CT: JAI Press, pp. 145–95.
Aschhoff. B, T. Doherr, C. Köhler, B. Peters, C. Rammer, T. Schubert and F. Schwiebacher (2008), *Innovation in Germany. Results of the German Innovation Survey 2007*, Mannheim: ZWE.
Audretsch, D.B., I. Grilo and R. Thurik (2007), 'Explaining entrepreneurship and the role of policy: a framework', in D.B. Audretsch, I. Grilo and R. Thurik (eds), *Handbook of Research on Entrepreneurship Policy*, Cheltenham, UK and Northampton, MA, USA: Edward Elgar, pp. 1–17.
Bergmann, H. (2005), 'Entrepreneurial attitudes: Wodurch werden sie determiniert und welche Rolle spielt die Region?', *Zeitschrift für Wirtschaftsgeographie* (3–4), 185–99.
Blume, L. (2001), *Erfolgsfaktoren kommunaler Wirtschaftspolitik in Ostdeutschland*, Berlin: DIW.
BMVBS, Bundesministerium für Verkehr, Bau und Stadtentwicklung (2008), *Jahresbericht der Bundesregierung zum Stand der deutschen Einheit 2008*, Berlin: BMVBS.
Etzioni, A. (1987), 'Entrepreneurship, adaptation and legitimation', *Journal of Economic Behavior and Organization*, **8**, 175–89.
Gartner, W.B. (1989), '"Who is an entrepreneur?" is the wrong question', *Entrepreneurship Theory and Practice*, **13**, 47–68.
Grichnik, D. (2009), 'Policy issues in financing entrepreneurship', in A.R. Hofer and J. Potter (eds), *Strengthening Entrepreneurship and Economic Development in East Germany: Lessons from Local Approaches*, available at http://www.oecd.org/cfe/leed/entrepreneurship/compendium, pp. 109–32.
Grimm, H. (2009), 'Fostering entrepreneurship in East Germany: multi-level governance in a transitional economy', in A.R. Hofer and J. Potter (eds), *Strengthening Entrepreneurship and Economic Development in East Germany: Lessons from Local Approaches*, available at http://www.oecd.org/cfe/leed/entrepreneurship/compendium, pp. 29–54.
Harding, R. (2009), 'Fostering university–industry links', in A.R. Hofer and J. Potter (eds), *Strengthening Entrepreneurship and Economic Development in East Germany: Lessons from Local Approaches*, available at http://www.oecd.org/cfe/leed/entrepreneurship/compendium, pp. 139–54.
Hart, D.M. (2003), 'Entrepreneurship policy. What it is and where it came from', in D.M. Hart (ed.), *The Emergence of Entrepreneurship Policy. Governance, Start-ups and Growth in the U.S. Knowledge Economy*, Cambridge, UK: Cambridge Press, pp. 3–19.
Hofer, A.R. and J. Potter (2009a), 'Conclusions and overarching policy recommendations', in A.R. Hofer and J. Potter (eds), *Strengthening Entrepreneurship and Economic*

Development in East Germany: Lessons from Local Approaches, available at http://www. oecd.org/cfe/leed/entrepreneurship/compendium, pp. 225–28.

Hofer, A.R. and J. Potter (eds) (2009b), *Strengthening Entrepreneurship and Economic Development in East Germany: Lessons from Local Approaches*, available at http://www. oecd.org/cfe/leed/entrepreneurship/compendium.

Kröhnert, S. and R. Klingholz (2007), *Not am Mann: Vom Helden der Arbeit zur neuen Unterschicht? Lebenslagen junger Erwachsener in wirtschaftlichen Abstiegsregionen der neuen Bundesländer*, Berlin-Institute for Population and Development, Berlin.

Lambrecht, J. and F. Pirnay (2005), 'An evaluation of public support measures for private external consultancies to SMEs in the Walloon Region of Belgium', *Entrepreneurship & Regional Development*, **17** (2), 89–108.

OECD (2007), *OECD Framework for the Evaluation of SME and Entrepreneurship Policies and Programmes*, Paris: OECD.

OECD (2009), *Local Entrepreneurship Strategies*, Paris: OECD (in press).

Pages, E., D. Freedman and P. Van Bargen (2003), 'Entrepreneurship as a state and local economic development strategy', in D.M. Hart (ed.), *The Emergence of Entrepreneurship Policy. Governance, Start-ups and Growth in the U.S. Knowledge Economy*, Cambridge, UK: Cambridge Press, pp. 240–58.

Potter, J. (2005), 'Local innovation systems and SME innovation policy', in Organisation for Economic Co-operation and Development (ed.), *OECD SME and Entrepreneurship Outlook*, Paris: OECD, pp. 127–42.

Ragnitz, J. (2009), 'Prospects for regional development and entrepreneurship in East Germany', in A.R. Hofer and J. Potter (eds), *Strengthening Entrepreneurship and Economic Development in East Germany: Lessons from Local Approaches*, available at http://www. oecd.org/cfe/leed/entrepreneurship/compendium, pp. 13–27.

Reynolds, P.D., D.J. Storey and P. Westhead (1994), 'Cross-national comparisons of the variation in new firm formation rates', *Regional Studies*, **28** (4), 443–56.

Schrumpf, H. (1990), 'Selbständige in der DDR', *RWI-Mitteilungen*, **41** (1–2), 105–16.

Thornton, P.H. (1999), 'The sociology of entrepreneurship', *Annual Review of Sociology*, 25, 19–46.

Wallau, F. (2007), 'Gründungsgeschehen und Unternehmensnachfolgen in Deutschland', presentation at the Theorie-Praxis-Genossenschaftsforum 'Potenziale der genossen-schaftlichen Rechts- und Wirtschaftsform für neue Unternehmen', 3 July, Cologne, Germany.

Wehrle, M. (2009), 'Strengthening entrepreneurship and economic development in East Germany: youth, economy and innovation. Study case: Berlin', unpublished.

Welter, F. (2009), 'Policy delivery: challenges and opportunities for entrepreneurship and SME development', in A.R. Hofer and J. Potter (eds), *Strengthening Entrepreneurship and Economic Development in East Germany: Lessons from Local Approaches*, available at http://www.oecd.org/cfe/leed/entrepreneurship/compendium, pp. 195–216.

Welter, F. and S. Kolb (2006), *How to Make Regions RTD Success Stories? Good Practice Models and Regional RTD*, Beiträge zur KMU-Forschung, 2, Siegen: PRO KMU.

Webpages (accessed 29 April 2009)

http://www.altenburgerland.de/sixcms/detail.php?id=46589&_lang=de&_css_template=alten burgerland_css.

http://www.denkwerkstatt-mv.de/.

http://www.esf.brandenburg.de/sixcms/detail.php/land_bb_boa_01.c.20536.de.

http://www.kfw-mittelstandsbank.de/.

http://www.lasa-brandenburg.de/Lotsendienste.664.0.html.

http://www.lernende-regionen.info/dlr/index.php.

http://www.pitz-parchim.de/.

http://www.scidea.de/.

http://www.univations.de/.

http://www.unternehmen-region.de/en/269.php.

3 Promoting cross-border entrepreneurship in Bulgaria: a case for policy treatment?
Kiril Todorov, Kostadin Kolarov and David Smallbone

INTRODUCTION

This chapter is concerned with cross-border cooperation between enterprises in border regions in one of the EU's new member states. Since these regions are peripheral to the core of national economic activity, with few assets for economic development, cooperation between enterprises across the border represents one of the ways of reducing locational disadvantages associated with peripherality. In this context, creating a policy environment to enable and facilitate productive forms of cross-border entrepreneurship may be viewed as a necessary part of the regional development strategies for these border regions. Whilst European Union (EU) membership offers access to funding to support such a strategy, a lack of regional policy, competing policy priorities and a weak institutional framework combine to make achieving this a challenging prospect.

Bulgaria's regions are very varied both geographically and historically. For the purposes of national regional development policy, six large regions are defined, namely South-Western, South-Central, South-Eastern, North-Western, North-Central and North-Eastern, which also represent statistical units at the NUTS II level. Recently the capital city, Sofia, has been separated as a statistical region due to its significant economic and urban development and the large disparity with the other regions. However, with the exception of Sofia, demographic and economic inter-regional disparities are relatively small compared with intra-regional disparities. A tenfold difference exists between the levels of net income at the municipal level and a clustering of municipalities with low economic development may be observed in all planning regions (Ministry of Regional Development and Public Works 2006).

For more than five decades, regional development in Bulgaria has been affected by policies that excluded any form of cross-border cooperation due to specific political relations with the neighbouring countries. In recent Bulgarian history border regions are associated with the defence policy of the country, especially during the Cold War years, and this has had consequences for their current level of development. It is only in the post-socialist period that some of the border regions have been perceived as places with potential for development, linked to the abolition of a number of restrictions associated with the accession of Bulgaria to the EU. Unfortunately, this has brought positive benefits in some regions whilst significant negative economic and demographic processes have occurred in others.

Contemporary policy for regional development in Bulgaria partly reflects common EU policy, which Bulgarian governments needed to pay attention to in the course of the negotiation process leading to accession. However, some achievements of regional development policies can be identified even in the socialist years when a number of administrative measures were introduced with regard to the population and the economy (mainly regional subsidiaries of state-owned enterprises). Governments at that time tried to regulate the migration processes in the country, to ensure equality in the distribution of income and investment and to develop economic and social infrastructure. On the positive side, although regional differences have always existed, core-periphery differences were less historically than more recently, when regional GDP data from 1995 to 2007 from the National Statistical Institute revealed a process of increasing regional differences (http://www.nsi.bg). On the negative side, border regions typically suffer from poor infrastructure, as well as from restrictions on the movement of people. In the years of transition, however, any positive benefits were lost because of the retraction of the state from its role as the main engine in regional development. The liberalization of the economy accelerated processes such as migration, concentration of investment in more developed regions, and decline of regions with lower infrastructural provision. This intensified regional differences, with border regions particularly negatively affected (Totev 2004). For example, in the period 2000 to 2007 the share of investment in Sofia grew from 50 to 56 per cent of total investment in the country; and a similar trend is apparent in the industrial regions such as Plovdiv and Stara Zagora. By contrast, in the provinces, including the border regions featuring in this chapter (Blagoevgrad and Kyustendil) investment dwindled from 1.2 per cent to 0.8 per cent and 0.2 per cent to 0.06 per cent respectively.

The current national strategy for regional development (2005–15) (Ministry of Regional Development and Public Works 2005a) emphasizes the importance of entrepreneurship and cross-border development as potentially significant instruments for regional development. Measures which could positively influence entrepreneurship development in border regions are those related to overcoming the disadvantages of a peripheral location, including investment in physical and economic infrastructure, the development of local agencies for regional development to support entrepreneurs in making contacts, building networks, and finding market and technological opportunities both domestically and in neighbouring countries.

The development of entrepreneurship and cross-border cooperation are also subjects of other national strategies, such as the employment strategy (2004–10), innovation strategy, strategy for encouragement of investment (2004–10), the national strategy for encouragement and development of small to medium-sized enterprises (SMEs) (2002–06), each of which concentrates in specific elements of the environment for entrepreneurial activity. Increased entrepreneurial activity at a regional level is affected by: change in economic structure of the regions, such as from traditional to new industries; the development of entrepreneurial attitudes and a new entrepreneurial culture; the creation and strengthening of regional and local support organizations; and the provision of infrastructure for exist-ing and new businesses. Along with the challenges to entrepreneurship as a whole originating from the border context, in the case study regions featured in the chapter changing circumstances included a softening of the border regulations between EU members (with Greece and Romania) and a hardening of the external borders of the EU (with Turkey, Macedonia and Serbia). The rest of this chapter analyses the experience of cross-border cooperation and entrepreneurship in two contrasting Bulgarian regions.

PROFILES OF THE REGIONS STUDIED

The material presented in the chapter is based on two regional case studies of entrepreneurship development and cross-border cooperation, which were part of a wider European project that included 12 cross-border regions in six countries.[1] For Bulgaria, the selected regions are two municipalities in the South-Western planning region – Petrich and Kyustendil. The choice of these municipalities is justified by their specific geographic location. Both are located at the border and both are crossed by international transport corridors of increasing regional and European importance. An additional argument for the choice of Petrich municipality is that one of the most important border checkpoints to Greece (Kulata), and one of the three checkpoints to the Republic of Macedonia are within its territory. For these reasons the chosen municipalities were judged to have significant potential for realizing cross-border cooperation.

Petrich

The municipality of Petrich borders the former Yugoslavian Republic of Macedonia to the west and Greece to the south. The population of Petrich

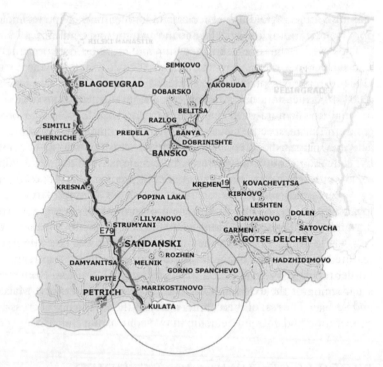

Figure 3.1   Petrich region

municipality is 58 744 (as of June 2007), with 30 013 in the town of Petrich itself (Ministry of Regional Development and Public Works 2008). The main trunk road E-79 (connecting Sofia and Thessaloniki) passes through the Petrich municipality as does the Zlatarevo–Strumica–Petrich–Sofia motorway. Both are extremely important to the region in terms of its economic development and the history of cross-border cooperation. The E-79 is the main connection from Sofia to Greece and forms part of the pan-European Transport Corridor IV, linking Central European countries with the Aegean Sea through the port of Thessaloniki. The road connecting Petrich and Strumica in Macedonia can be used for international traffic towards the Southern Balkans. The Petrich locality along the Strumeshnitsa Valley is also one of the most fertile in Bulgaria, producing citrus fruits, grapes and early vegetables. The municipality of Petrich is 13km west of the border checkpoint of Kulata (on the border with Greece) and 20km east of the border checkpoint of Zlatarevo (on the border with Macedonia).

According to National Statistical Institute data, unemployment at the end of the first quarter of 2006 was 9.7 per cent, although there was a decreasing trend. In terms of professional and educational characteristics, 26 per cent of the registered unemployed had specialized secondary education and 34 per cent were unemployed specialists (17 and 7 per cent in 2004).

In Petrich municipality, there are 2164 registered companies that are active, with a higher proportion of medium-sized enterprises than in neighbouring municipalities. The main economic activities are clothing production, shoes and furniture. Around 70 per cent of industrial enterprises are joint-venture companies with foreign investors, which mainly work with customer's materials. The only wholly state owned enterprise is Petrich Forestry enterprise (Parvomai). The manufacturing industry is the key for the municipality because of its dynamic development in recent years. The total number of companies in manufacturing industry is 490, generating 36 per cent of the total net income and 67 per cent of total employment.

Kyustendil

Kyustendil municipality is also located in the South-western planning region of Bulgaria. The municipality has a common border with the Republic of Macedonia and also the Republic of Serbia. The distance to Macedonia is 22km and to the border with Serbia 30km. Kyustendil is traversed by Road No. 6 which is the main road artery connecting the capital city of Sofia to Skopje (in the former Yugoslavian Republic of Macedonia) through Koumanovo. The trans-European corridor No. 8 (Vlyora–Tirana–Skopje–Sofia–Bourgas–Asia) also passes through Kyustendil Municipality.

The semi-mountainous and trough-like terrain of the municipality, combined with its climate is conducive to fruit growing. There are also hot mineral springs (known as thermals) which have proven curative qualities for spa treatments and natural resources, including coniferous and deciduous forests and materials for the construction industry. The region's cultural and historical heritage dates from the Roman period, the Middle Ages and the National Revival period (eighteenth to nineteenth century), which offers favourable conditions for the development of cultural, rural and winter tourism.

The population of Kyustendil municipality is 69034 inhabitants (December 2003): 71 per cent urban and 29 per cent rural spread across some 71 villages. The unemployment rate for the municipality was 13.4 per cent (2004), which was similar to the average rate for the country for the same period (13.7 per cent). In terms of economic structure, data for the 2001–03 period show an increase in the relative share of the contribution

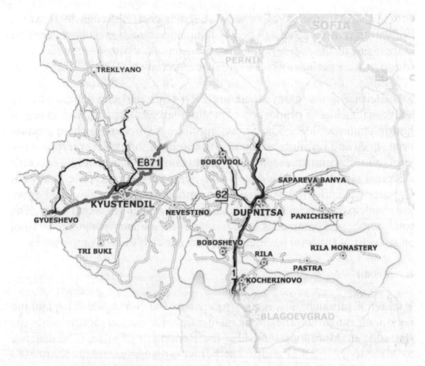

Figure 3.2   Kyustendil region

of services; a strong decrease in the share of the agricultural sector; and a decreasing contribution of the manufacturing industry. The agricultural and industrial sectors together only contribute about half of the contribution of the services sector to Gross Value Added (GVA). The transition from central planning to a market economy and the loss of traditional markets in the former Soviet Union negatively affected industry in the Kyustendil municipality. The current industrial structure in the municipality is made up of companies operating in kitchen equipment, textiles, clothing, shoes, transformers, capacitors, foodstuffs, toys and spirits.

ENTREPRENEURSHIP DEVELOPMENT AND CROSS-BORDER COOPERATION IN PETRICH AND KYUSTENDIL

The empirical data for the present analysis were gathered from a combination of primary and secondary sources. The main primary source of data comprised a total of 39 semi-structured interviews with entrepreneurs, managers, small business owners, representatives of business support organizations, local authorities and non-governmental organizations (NGOs) undertaken in the period March to July 2007. One of the major aims of the case study regions was to identify and assess the state of entrepreneurship development in the border regions as well as the existing and potential practices with regard to cross-border cooperation. A special emphasis was put on the implications for policies towards the development of entrepreneurship and its cross-border dimensions. The case studies also sought to reveal the enabling and constraining forces of cross-border entrepreneurship in the light of policy demands and requirements.

The Context

Cross-border cooperation in the case of Bulgaria is a relatively new phenomenon in view of the long period of isolation of the country not only from its immediate neighbours, but also in the wider international context. This isolation was dictated by the desire of the country to protect its borders but also to totally isolate the population from external influences, mainly for ideological reasons. With few exceptions, the possibilities for Bulgarian citizens to travel abroad, including short-term visits to neighbouring countries, were strictly limited. This situation, combined with an almost complete liquidation of private enterprise in the years of socialism and the establishment of state monopolies in foreign trade activities, created preconditions for an almost total absence of cross-border cooperation at the individual, local and enterprise levels, which lasted for more than four decades.

At the same time the high rates of industrialization of the country in the 1960s and 1970s and the successful specialization of the national economy within Comecon placed Bulgaria among the leading countries for foreign trade activities, outstripping many East European countries at the end of 1980s. For example, the export share in gross domestic product (GDP) for Bulgaria at this time was 34 per cent, while the same indices for Czechoslovakia were 19 per cent, 15 per cent for Hungary, 7 per cent for USSR and Poland. This can be explained in terms of the strong centralization of foreign trade relations, which in practice detached Bulgarian enterprises from their foreign suppliers and clients, although the latter subsequently had negative impacts on both operational and strategic cross-border capabilities of economic entities in border regions.

However, the changes that occurred after 1989 created a radically different environment for cross-border cooperation for citizens and newly established companies who, despite the visa restrictions which some neighbouring countries introduced at the beginning of the 1990s, enjoyed significantly better opportunities for engaging in economic cooperation with neighbours in bordering countries. At the same time, the inheritance from previous decades in terms of uneven economic development, together with the demographic and social profiles and the locational disadvantages of peripheral regions problems, had a strong influence on the nature and character of the emerging cross-border cooperation.

The economic decline that followed the collapse of socialism resulted in some very unwelcome effects. The most important, from the standpoint of cross-border cooperation, was the diminishing industrial base caused by the decline of state-owned enterprises (Todorov 2004). In addition, the depopulation of some regions due to economic out-migration is a further constraint on the economic potential of these regions. The emerging private sector was not able to compensate for the losses from the restructuring processes. The new enterprise structures lacked critical mass (in terms of the number and size of small firms) to form a significant network for cooperation (including cross-border) and/or any industrial clusters.

After EU enlargement the situation regarding both institutional and enterprise-based cooperation with Greece did not change significantly, but there are some indications of future improvements. The opening of the Greek–Bulgarian border and its change of status from 'hard' to 'soft' is expected to foster social and cultural exchange and also facilitate cross-border trade and business relations. Meanwhile the 'hard' border between Bulgaria and Macedonia and the visa regime (which was revoked in December 2009), has negatively influenced cross-border cooperation at the institutional, enterprise and household levels in this case.

In the short term, EU enlargement has caused significant difficulties as a result of the visa regime introduced for the citizens of neighbouring countries, namely Macedonia and Serbia. Notwithstanding the fact that enlargement is favourable for entrepreneurship and the development of cross-border cooperation between Bulgaria and Greece, it exerts a negative influence over cooperation between Bulgarian and Macedonian and Serbian entrepreneurs.

Enterprise and Institutional Cross-Border Cooperation: Some Empirical Evidence

For historical reasons, the volume of inter-regional cross-border cooperation in the two case study regions has been low, and essentially only started to develop in the mid 1990s. This was because until 1990 Bulgarians travelling abroad were strictly controlled, leaving no room for any non-centrally controlled cross-border activity. Until the end of the socialist regime, all foreign trade activities were concentrated in less than 200 special organizations – all of them central.

Following the collapse of communism, Petrich entered a new period of economic development. Situated near two borders, the town became a foothold for cross-border trade as well as for smuggling activity between Bulgaria, Macedonia and Greece. It was especially important for Macedonian traders during the time of the economic embargo imposed by Greece as a result of the latter's name and flag. During this time, Macedonian traders could not enter the territory of Greece and in order to maintain their economic relations with Turkey they were forced to cross Bulgaria. Cross-border cooperation at enterprise level is based mainly on the establishment of personal contacts with Greek entrepreneurs, as stated by each interviewed entrepreneur or manager. Triggers for this type of cross-border cooperation included the removal of border controls imposed during the socialist period; differences in labour cost; the relatively high rate of unemployment in Bulgaria at the beginning of the transition period; the readiness of the local population to work in unfavourable conditions; the weak institutional control over retaining labour; and tax and other business regulations as emphasized by key informants interviewed. There is evidence that some of the larger Greek clothing companies have moved their production bases into the Petrich region in the last few years, replacing small Bulgarian subcontractors. However, it is not evident whether EU enlargement has affected this tendency or not. Dimitar Kandzhikov, one of the entrepreneurs interviewed by the authors, emphasized that until now, there has not been any evidence suggesting how EU enlargement will affect existing cross-border cooperation in the future.

The Kyustendil region, similar to Petrich, has a relatively short history of cross-border cooperation in recent times. It began with the opening of borders after the end of the communist regimes on both sides of the border. During the transition period this region was under pressure for a number of reasons. Cross-border cooperation between Bulgaria and Macedonia originally began as a result of the initiative of individual communities on the two sides of the border and has gradually expanded to involve both central and local administrations. Several attempts at cross-border projects have been registered at the local level. Among the most sustainable is the establishment of the first local cross-border structures between Kyustendil–Kriva Palanka, which involves a training centre in Kriva Palanka, commonly organized cultural events and business initiatives. However, these structures are limited to cooperation between development agencies and local authorities play only a supportive role in them. Cross-border cooperation in Kyustendil is still in its initial stages, both at the local administration and business levels, with very few examples of businesses that have cooperated on a regular basis for a significant period. Most of the enterprises maintain relations with enterprises in more distant areas in the country than in neighbouring regions.

In both case study regions, the municipal administrations are the main actors involved in cross-border cooperation as they have a common interest in developing good relationships with the administration in the neighbouring countries. In second place are Greek investors in Petrich who have more advantages than their Bulgarian counterparts. In Petrich, regional entrepreneurship activity is higher than the average in the rest of the country, with a particularly high rate of new start-up firms, which has included the emergence of young entrepreneurs (Ministry of Economy and Energy 2007, 2008; Municipality of Petrich 2000, 2005). The main characteristics of the region's businesses include a preponderance of very small enterprises producing low value added goods, oriented towards services and trade, with competitive advantages focused on price. The private sector firms in Petrich municipality are mainly involved in services, light industry, trade, and agriculture that allow quick realization of production and profits. The new workplaces created in the last year for which data are available (2006) are mainly in the textile sector, accounting services, and construction sector.

Cross-border price differentials have stimulated the development of services and trade, which means that a key factor influencing entrepreneurship development in the region is its proximity to Greece. However, EU enlargement is likely to negatively affect local SMEs through a decrease of cross-border price differences. At the same time, there are expectations, as stated by interviewed entrepreneurs, that EU enlargement will stimulate regional tourism development, and tourism is probably the only sector which has potential to attract considerable amounts of foreign direct investment.

Although the current state of the agricultural sector in Petrich municipality is poor, agriculture has strong development potential. Agricultural products include tomatoes, peppers, salads, spinach, tobacco, peaches, apples, figs, peanuts and strawberries, with some attempts by local agricultural entrepreneurs to cultivate olives and some exotic fruits (Municipality of Petrich 2005). Textile firms are disproportionately represented in the region's business stock. Most are some form of joint venture between Bulgarian and Greek partners. There is a high rate of investment in textile enterprises from Greek firms in Petrich. These firms are often based in villages where the salaries are lower because of the monopsonistic position of one or more firms functioning in the village over the local labour market.

Some of the Petrich respondents stated that the lack of a labour force is currently a problem for the textile sector. In the Petrich region there are many clothing enterprises working with materials supplied by the clients. This type of production is characterized by very low value added and the use of cheap labour. The reasons for labour shortages are structural because the young generation prefer employment in service sectors where working conditions are better in contrast to hard manual work in clothing production. Another weakness is the poor local and regional support for entrepreneurship development (especially for small businesses).

By contrast, in the Kyustendil region, local entrepreneurship is weak. Respondents explain this in terms of the diminishing local market and the low purchasing power of local population. In Kyustendil municipality, micro-enterprises accounted for 92 per cent of the total number of enterprises in 2003. The second largest share was enterprises employing up to 50 persons with 6 per cent (137 businesses). The share of large-scale enterprises in 2003 amounted to only 0.4 per cent (just 8 enterprises).

More detailed investigation paints an even more negative picture. The training and education programmes for entrepreneurs are sporadic, as they depend on different initiatives providing grants for projects, which have a limited period of activity. From 2007, a project encouraging entrepreneurship in young people will start at one of the secondary schools in Kyustendil. An active entrepreneurial culture is lacking in Kyustendil for a number of reasons (Todorov et al. 2007). These include the long period of the planned economy which neglected peripheral (border) regions; the domination of political over economic considerations, which was associated with a strongly protected border leading to the isolation of these regions; and the fear of potential conflicts during the Cold War, which led to a complete lack of development policies and investments in border regions. Between Sofia and Skopje (in the region of Kyustendil) a railway connection is still to be completed, because of a lack of political will. The same is true in the case of roads to the border with Serbia. As a consequence, many young people have migrated to the large industrial centres inland, leading to school closures in many villages. Many small facilities of large-scaled state-owned enterprises were also closed, with negative economic impacts. Finally, Kyustendil has been adversely affected by structural change at a national level, contributing to a state dependency culture and a preference to work in state-owned enterprises, leading to neglect of traditional occupations. The significantly reduced and ageing population is neither willing to take risks, nor identify opportunities for profitable business for a combination of objective and subjective reasons.

The overall assessment is that the scale and the scope of cross-border partnerships in the Kyustendil region are limited and the cross-border cooperation that does exist is typically ad hoc, developed on the basis of informal agreements. The small number of companies that have long-term cooperation with firms from the other side of the border mainly exploits informal and personal relationships. In most cases, where enterprises are involved in cross-border cooperation, it is limited to export and import activities, rarely involving the engagement of complex relation with the neighbouring country's partners, such as sharing resources and other forms of cooperation. The reasons include unsolved legislative issues to protect the rights of the foreign enterprises and the symbolic institutional cooperation between the concerned countries. The consequence is the adoption of risk-avoiding practices by businesses as evidenced by the low degree of resources allocated to cross-border cooperation activities.

Institutional cross-border cooperation is also weakly developed and is mainly concentrated in the cultural field, as evident when reviewing the implemented projects in the frame of EU neighbourhood programmes (Neighbourhood Programme 2004). At the same time, there is much broader scope for cooperation in relation to sustainable development, including environment protection; illegal import/export and traffic of women, children and drugs; and discrepancies between cross-border regions with different level of economic development. Institutional infra-structure for cross-border cooperation in the region is lacking or ineffective. All these issues have been raised in various strategic papers developed at the national level (for example, Ministry of Finance 2006; Ministry of Regional Development and Public Works 2005b, 2007) and also in some documents of the European Union (European Commission 2006, 2007). The main constraints on the development of cross-border cooperation at the institutional level include: inadequate background or training for the administrative personnel (in municipalities, local structures of the civil society, including NGOs); a lack of knowledge how to make cross-border cooperation sustainable; the limited number of staff available that speak foreign languages; and a lack of knowledge of the mechanisms of functioning of cross-border cooperation and possibilities for funding.

Challenges for Cross-Border Cooperation in the Case Study Regions

Greek entrepreneurs are active in seeking out cooperation with Bulgarian partners, although their interest is exclusively in rather unsophisticated economic activities involving the export of textile products and the import of clothing materials (subcontracting relations). The interest of Greek entrepreneurs is in exploiting lower labour cost in Bulgaria, with little apparent interest in higher levels of cross-border cooperation. The propensity of Bulgarian entrepreneurs to proactively seek to develop cross-border cooperation is low, due to the absence of a deeply rooted business mentality inherited from the old economic system, combined with a lack of financing. Although Bulgarian entrepreneurs seem less inclined towards cross-border cooperation than their Greek counterparts, their propensity to engage is definitely higher than among Macedonian entrepreneurs, who are affected by the less developed state of their border region. This is because of the importance of the relative levels of development on the two sides of the border. Factors that influence enterprise-based cross-border cooperation in a positive way include the consistently high quality of goods produced by Greek firms, which means Bulgarian firms have access to innovative products that are not produced in the country; free access after EU enlargement to an enlarged market.

A common opinion among respondents interviewed in the case study regions was that the various stakeholders often do not work together for the common goal of a region's development priorities. The various actors at the institutional, business and individual levels appear fragmented and lacking in trust in many cases, rather than operating effectively as a network. Constraints identified on the development of cross-border cooperation at the micro level include a lack of highly skilled professional staff; poor marketing skills; short-term profit orientation by some business owners; ineffective cooperation between business and local public structures influenced by bureaucratic and corruption practices; insufficient opportunities for financial support of cross-border cooperation development. In addition, a lack of knowledge in the cross-border partner's language impedes cross-border cooperation in many cases.

The changes in relations with neighbouring countries at the beginning of 1990s, involving bilateral agreements and regulations created opportunities for establishing and further developing cross-border cooperation. However, after the promising start of many cross-border activities, a series of internal and external events hindered the development of cross-border cooperation in the region. Among these events was the deep economic crisis during the transition, the Yugoembargo, the economic migration from the region to more developed regions and the inconsistent policies on both sides of the border (Bulgaria–Macedonia, Bulgaria–Serbia). As a result, the current nature and extent of cross-border cooperation is limited. Accessibility in terms of the road infrastructure is another important factor that can hinder and/or facilitate the development of cross-border cooperation between enterprises with Macedonia and Greece. From this point of view, Greece is more attractive as a destination than Macedonia where the road infrastructure is poorer and cross-border movement impeded by the visa regime. Notwithstanding geographic proximity, Macedonian partners typically lack sufficient financial resources and information to develop cross-border cooperation with Bulgarian firms.

Factors favouring the development of relations with Macedonia are a common identity and the absence of language barriers. While political factors do not have a strong impact, the historical legacy burdens the cooperation and generates some tensions between Bulgarian and Macedonian partners. Cultural barriers also exist in cooperation with Greek partners, who are typically unwilling to speak the Bulgarian language, despite the fact that a large part of the Greek population in the border area can speak it. One interviewed Greek entrepreneur had registered a firm in Bulgaria but declared that he could speak neither in Bulgarian nor in English, only Greek.

The common identity with Macedonia and close identity with Serbia plays an ambiguous role in cross-border cooperation. It is one thing to have common roots but another to behave in the same way in the present. The perceptions about 'ours' and 'theirs' are very strong and are often exploited subjectively, according to the current interests and situations. The similarities, even the fact that they prevail, are often shadowed by the small but arguably artificial, differences created in the most recent decades, mainly for political reasons. These 'artificial' differences are a source of disputes which negatively influence cooperation in some cases.

The lack of trust between potential partners is a barrier for the development of cross-border cooperation, dominating relations between some entrepreneurs. Key institutions support regular contacts but no traditions exist with respect to information exchange. In other words, the main stakeholders in cross-border cooperation at both the institutional and business levels (municipalities, NGOs, enterprises) cooperate with each other but this cooperation is not as effective as it could be. Experience is a key factor that helps to build trust. The absence of a language barrier, especially in Macedonia, facilitates communication, yet it does not in itself create trust. Local people are ready to participate in cross-border cooperation and are open to other cultures and countries but the level of economic development, institutional factors and EU enlargement all influence the processes of building trust between potential partners, both within the region and to develop cooperation across the border.

THE POLICY ENVIRONMENT AND EMERGING POLICY ISSUES

The policy environment at the national level in Bulgaria includes regulations, strategic documents and national plans. On the basis of their scope and content they could be positively assessed as a basis for encouraging both entrepreneurship and cross-border cooperation. The criticism, however, is twofold; first, the particular needs of entrepreneurs and regions remain unexplored to a great extent, and second, regarding the need to allocate resources to implement proposed policy initiatives. In the first place, it is sufficient to point to the almost total unfamiliarity with the main strategic documents on the side of both enterprises and citizens. In the second case, and in a similar vein, there is an absence of effective local institutions to contribute to and implement national strategies.

One of the key issues constraining effective policy development and implementation to encourage cross-border cooperation is a lack of resources and institutional capacity at the level of the provincial and local authorities. Another is a lack of effective regional policy in Bulgaria, which could provide resources to promote institutional and enterprise based cooperation as an economic development tool. EU policy is broadly supportive, providing specific opportunities for financing from Structural Funds through the regional operational programmes, and there is a lack of significant barriers caused by foreign policy between neighbouring countries. However, the challenge is to provide the required technical assistance as well as financial resources to strengthen the role of local and provincial authorities in economic development, set within the context of an effective regional policy at the national level. Resources are a key constraint, but so too is the inadequate administrative capacity of local authorities, reflected in their inability to recruit appropriately prepared specialists and provide them with an environment that motivates them.

The question of strengthening local policies to encourage the development of entrepreneurship at both the national and regional levels is also constrained by a lack of institutional capacity. As a result, existing policies tend to be limited to declaring good intentions but without measures, supported by budget allocations to achieve them. An additional consideration is that the development of cross-border cooperation depends on bilateral rather than just unilateral efforts, involving positive interaction between provinces and municipalities in neighbouring countries. In this regard, the empirical research in the case study regions has revealed significant discord in local authorities, as well as other local organizations (business and non-business), firstly between local policy makers and central government; and secondly, between the local authorities from the two sides of the border. There is no established mechanism at the policy level for key issues including the provision of seed finance and business support for start-ups and new businesses, such as mentoring programmes and/or business incubators.

The results of the research in the two case study regions point to a number of specific policy issues that need to be addressed if

Table 3.1   Summary of the main empirical findings in the Bulgarian case study regions

	Petrich	Kyustendil
Entrepreneurship development	Above the country average	Below the country average
Enterprises involved in import – export activities	Many	Few
Joint ventures in the region	Many (dominantly with Greek entrepreneurs)	Few
Direct investments in the region	Many small investments by Greek entrepreneurs	Few, not by the neighbouring country
Use of special support	No special support provided; couple of newly established chambers claim as providers of such support	Advised by the local Chamber of Commerce and Industry
Impact of national entrepreneurship policy on CBC	No visible impact	No visible impact
Impact of local entrepreneurship policy on CBC	No particular policy	No particular policy
Impact of EU membership on CBC	Positive, reducing many barriers	Neutral to negative, setting new barriers
Enabling factors for CBC	Good location, fertile land, improving demographics indices, historical heritage, mineral water springs, light industries capacity, cost advantages	Good location, nature, fertile land, historical heritage, mineral water springs, light industries capacity, cost advantages
Constraining factors for CBC	No significant threats. Minor negative impact from the competition of close towns such as Sandanski	Worsening demographic picture, economic difficulties in the neighbouring countries (FYROM and Serbia); closeness of the capital city (orientation to the centre); shrinking local market

Table 3.1   (continued)

	Petrich	Kyustendil
Policy issues (common for both regions)	Lack of proactive behaviour of the local administration – 'hands off' approach; Irrelevant advertising of the local opportunities; Lack of specific support to SMEs; Underutilization of local resources – restrictive regulations for exploitation of natural resources and ineffective agrarian policy; No room for implementation of local regulations in regards to taxation and social insurance policy; Poor business support infrastructure; Selective support to politically close circles of entrepreneurs	
Specific regional policy issues	Miscommunication between the local authorities and the emerging business chambers. Insufficient informational provision for business regulations in the neighbouring countries	Lack of proper budget for business support infrastructure. Insufficient training in entrepreneurship. No specific promotion of the region as touristic destination

entrepreneurship is to be promoted in these border regions and the potential benefits of cross-border cooperation exploited. These include:

- The development of local infrastructure to facilitate cross-border cooperation and especially the provision of business support services. This issue could be addressed centrally through the establishment of an effective national network of business support agencies, although a strong local input is essential to maintain a local focus.
- The provision of targeted support to enterprises involved in, or having potential for, cross-border cooperation. Specific support measures may include tax concessions linked to participation in approved joint projects and participation in business delegations.
- The creation of new and strengthened roles for local business associations, (including the participation of enterprises). Such associations would benefit from some financial support and technical assistance to strengthen their capacity for the development and

implementation of cross-border projects, as well as to strengthen their lobbying function with local and national authorities.

- Training local entrepreneurs to manage cross-border business and joint ventures, including joint projects in third countries. The transfer and adaptation of foreign best practices in cross-border cooperation, for example, cluster formation in appropriate industries.
- The promotion of cross-border entrepreneurial networks and subcontracting chains in traditional and emerging branches.

To be effectively addressed, these policy issues require the coordinated efforts of national and local authorities, NGOs, as well as interested businesses and their associations. Strengthened national regional policy could be the key to unlock more of the potential contribution of cross-border cooperation to regional economic development. At the same time, there are two key questions that need to be considered in formulating a national regional policy for Bulgaria: firstly, how to balance the need for infrastructural investment in border regions with the return on such investments, which are typically higher in the more urbanized and congested centrally located regions; and secondly, how to balance the special targeted measures needed for border regions with the principle of equity in the conditions of the business environment.

CONCLUDING REMARKS

Bulgarian regions have limited freedom to make decisions in the current political framework in the country. They were characterized by regional informants as implementers of policies designed at the national level, although the process of decentralization of policy making is reported to have started. Not surprisingly, a lack of delegated responsibility for economic development is associated with a lack of capacity to fulfil this function. Interviews with key informants in the Bulgarian regions show that local authorities typically lack staff with the appropriate skills to develop cooperative initiatives and, most importantly, to set clear and adequate objectives. This also affects their willingness to coordinate their activities with those of other local actors that operate in the region (Smallbone and Xheneti 2008).

The need for capacity building exists at all levels of government. In many ways the question of 'what a policy should be?' is easier to answer than 'how to make a policy?'. Possible answers to the first question may be found by looking at relevant experience in other European countries, but the preparation of policy-makers is in many ways more challenging. This is because it is more than a technical exercise, affected not just by knowledge and know-how but also by the policy culture and a willingness to accept responsibility. Effective institutional change is one of the most challenging aspects of the transformation from central planning to a market system and a key element of this is the redefinition of the role of the state in relation to business activity (Smallbone and Welter 2011). Effective policy making and implementation is central to this process at different levels of government.

NOTE

1. The project which was funded under the EU's 6th Framework Programme was titled 'Challenges and Prospects of Cross-Border Co-operation in the Context of EU Enlargement (CBCED)'. It involved partners in 7 EU countries, undertaking detailed empirical investigation in 12 border regions.

REFERENCES

European Commission (2006), *European Territorial Cooperation Programme Greece-Bulgaria 2007–2013*, CCI 2007CB163PO059, 2006. Brussels: EC.

European Commission (2007), *Bulgaria – Republic of Macedonia IPA Cross-Border Programme*, available at http://www.sep.gov.mk/content/Dokumenti/EN/англиска%20 верзија%20-%20BG.pdf (accessed August 2010).

Ministry of Economy and Energy (2007), *Annual Report on the Condition and Development of SMEs in Bulgaria 2006*, Special Edition, Sofia: Ministry of Economy and Energy, Bulgaria.

Ministry of Economy and Energy (2008), *Annual Report on the Conditions and Development of SMEs in Bulgaria 2007*, Special Edition, Sofia: Ministry of Economy and Energy, Bulgaria.

Ministry of Finance (2006), *National Strategic Reference Framework 2007–2013*, Sofia: Ministry of Finance, available at http://www.europe.bg/upload/docs/ENNSRF_LAST. pdf (accessed August 2010).

Ministry of Regional Development and Public Works (2005a), *National Regional Development Strategy of the Republic of Bulgaria for the Period 2005–2015*, Sofia: Ministry of Regional Development and Public Works.

Ministry of Regional Development and Public Works (2005b), *Regional Development Programme of South-West Planning Region 2007–2013*, Sofia: Ministry of Regional Development and Public Works.

Ministry of Regional Development and Public Works (2006), *Operational Programme Regional Development 2007–2013*, Sofia: Ministry of Regional Development and Public Works.

Ministry of Regional Development and Public Works (2007), *Regional Development Operational Programme 2007–2013*, Directorate General 'Programming of Regional Development', Sofia: Ministry of Regional Development and Public Works.

Ministry of Regional Development and Public Works (2008), *The Regions in Bulgaria, Portraits*, Sofia: Ministry of Regional Development and Public Works.

Municipality of Petrich (2000), *Strategy for Development of Municipality of Petrich 2000–2006*, Petrich: Municipality of Petrich.

Municipality of Petrich (2005), *Municipal Plan for Development of Petrich 2007–2013*, Petrich: Municipality of Petrich, available at http://www.petrich.bg/pag/upload/uploaded/petrich%20md%20plan.pdf.

National Strategic Ministry of Regional Development and Public Works (2008), *The Regions in Bulgaria, Portraits*, Sofia: Ministry of Regional Development and Public Works.

Neighbourhood Programme (2004), *'The Republic of Bulgaria – The Former Yugoslav Republic of Macedonia' – Joint Programming Document 2004–2006*, Sofia.

Smallbone D. and F. Welter (2011), 'Entrepreneurship and institutional change in transition economies: the commonwealth of independent states, Central and East European countries and China compared', *Entrepreneurship and Regional Development*, forthcoming.

Smallbone, D. and M. Xheneti (2008), *Policy Issues Related to Entrepreneurship Development and Cross Border Cooperation in Case Study Regions*, Deliverable 16: CBCED Project, Kingston: SBRC, http://www.crossbordercoop.net.

Todorov, K. (ed.) (2004), *Foundations of Small Business*, 2nd edn, Sofia: Next Ltd.

Todorov, K., K. Kolarov and D. Smallbone (2007), 'Cross border cooperation in the triangle Bulgaria – Greece – Macedonia: some preliminary findings and policy issues', paper presented at the ICCEES Regional Congress, Berlin, 2–4 August.

Totev, S. (2004), 'Regional economic disparities in Bulgaria and the rest EU candidates member countries', *Economic Thought Journal*, **2**, 3–17.

4 SMEs and social dialogue in the new Europe: the case of Hungary
David Smallbone, Zoltan Roman and Robert Blackburn

INTRODUCTION

This chapter is concerned with the role of small to medium-sized enterprises (SMEs) in social dialogue in the New Europe, with particular reference to the case of Hungary. It focuses on the nature and extent of the involvement of SME owners/managers and their employees in the social dialogue and the challenges this brings. According to the International Labour Organization (ILO), social dialogue includes 'all types of negotiation, consultation or exchange of information between or among governments, employers and workers on issues of common interest, related to economic and social policy' (http://www.ilo.org/public/english/dialogue/themes/sd.htm). An alternative but similar definition is that it is a 'process by which the representatives of employers, workers and government exchange information and views, consult, negotiate and reach agreements on issues of concern to them' (Kenworthy and Kittel 2003, p. iii). Hence, the main goal is to promote consensus building and democratic involvement among the main stakeholders in the field of employment relations, although it can also have a role in providing a forum for consultation and dialogue on issues of common interest. Social dialogue can exist as a tripartite process with the government involved as an official partner or on a bipartite basis between labour and management or their representative organizations. Moreover, social dialogue can take place at the cross-national, national, regional, sectoral or enterprise level.

The definitions included above are broad and reflect what is generally recognized as social dialogue within individual countries. However, at the European Union (EU) level, social dialogue refers more specifically to a process underpinned by the European Treaties to bring institutions representing employers and employees at the national level (the social partners), together at the European level, giving them the right to be consulted on matters coming under the banner of 'social affairs'. The institutional framework for EU social dialogue derives from Articles 137–39 of the European Union. Article 137 covers the social policy areas where social partners have to be consulted by the Commission, including, for example, working conditions and health and safety at work. Article 138 specifically provides for a two-stage consultation procedure. The first stage is where the Commission is required to consult the social partners on the direction of a potential initiative. The second is further consultation on the details of the proposal. Article 139 provides the implementation methods for contractual agreements that result from social dialogue between social partners.[1]

In practice, evidence shows that social dialogue at the EU level takes place on both a bipartite and tripartite basis. The bipartite dialogue takes place between the organizations representing employers (that is, BUSINESSEUROPE, CEEP, UEAPME) and employees (ETUC[2]) at an EU level, each of which consists of national membership organizations. The 'Social Dialogue Committee' is the main forum within the EU where bipartite social dialogue takes place, through three 'technical' subcommittees taking care of macroeconomic, labour market, and education and training issues. In addition, 31 sectoral social dialogue committees have also been established.

Within the EU, social dialogue is viewed as a central peg in the European social model. It has a key role in achieving the strategic goals of the Lisbon agenda: namely full employment and reinforced social cohesion (Commission of the European Communities 2002). Within an enlarged Europe, social dialogue has also been promoted as a partnership approach to facilitating the integration of new member states, which only 25 years ago were operating under the rules of central planning. The process of EU Social Dialogue has undergone dramatic developments since the initiation of bipartite dialogue in 1985, linked to the Single Market Project (European Commission 2006a, 2006b). At the same time, it has now entered a new phase as a result of enlargement of the EU, to include member states that have no recent tradition of such processes, while at the same time the EU is facing a need to adjust to increased globalization and the challenges this presents to social partners. In this context, the European Commission has been promoting a renewal of Social Dialogue as part of good governance, in order to allow both employers and employees to contribute to a common understanding of the challenges faced and develop appropriate responses together. Fundamentally, this is based on a commitment to maintaining the existing 'European social model' and an assumption that effective social dialogue will contribute to greater competitiveness and increased employment.

In new member states of the EU in Central and Eastern Europe, the post-communist period has brought with it enormous economic and social changes, which have implications for social dialogue. Now that these countries are members of an enlarged Europe, establishing the basis of social dialogue involving both sides of business is a necessary part of the EU social model, as well as an integral part of establishing an appropriate system of governance to enable ongoing private sector development. It is seen as a necessary part of these new member countries playing their full role within the EU. However, this presents a major challenge for countries with no recent tradition of self governing representative organizations; a heritage of trade unions and business organizations that were heavily politicized under the previous system; a pattern of private sector development that is dominated by small firms, which are a 'difficult to reach' group in social dialogue terms in most European countries; and social partners which lack both resources and relevant experience.

Some of the new challenges facing EU social partners are associated with varying economic disparities within the EU, which have implications for labour markets and working conditions. In this regard, analysis of social dialogue in established member states suggests that achieving economic stability can be a key factor influencing the successful operation of social dialogue. Changes in the French and German systems, for example, demonstrate how economic downturn can put pressure on the social dialogue system, raising doubts about the direction of causality, in terms of the relationship between economic performance and social dialogue.

The rest of the chapter is divided into four sections. The next section discusses the challenges associated with engaging SME owners, managers and their employees in social dialogue processes. Section three focuses on the particular challenges associated with establishing effective social dialogue processes in new member states of the EU. These challenges are then illustrated in section four with reference to Hungary. The conclusion pulls together the evidence presented and draws out some implications for the development of a system that is more likely to tackle existing challenges.

THE SME DIMENSION OF SOCIAL DIALOGUE

The European Union has an estimated 20 million enterprises of which 99 per cent are SMEs employing 67 per cent of the total number of employees in the European economy (European Commission 2010a).[3] A key question to ask, therefore, is whether this economic contribution is reflected in their involvement with EU social dialogue partners. In this context, the evidence suggests that SMEs are under-represented in the existing model of social dialogue. Although the national organizations that are members of BUSINESSEUROPE contain some SMEs among their members, they are mainly comprised of larger enterprises (Greenwood 2002, p. 121). UEAPME is the main representative organization of SMEs in Europe at the EU level, drawing on 85 member organizations from 34 countries and representing an estimated 12 million enterprises and 55 million employees across Europe (http://www.ueapme. com). Whilst the acceptance of UEAPME as an EU social partner since 1998 (as part of the BUSINESSEUROPE delegation) offers SMEs a voice, the strength of EU wide organizations representing SMEs is dependent on the national platforms from which they draw. For example, the strength of the Austrian SME representation in the EU is based on the high level of activity of UEAPME in the EU, which is itself based on strong SME representation in Austria. Where member states are less well endowed with strong representative organizations, platforms for small firm engagement are weak or underdeveloped. This leads to conditions for representation at the EU level that are less than satisfactory, because the national base of UEAPME's membership organizations is often not representative of the full range of SMEs within member states. An exercise undertaken by the Commission (European Commission 2005) found unevenness in engagement with small firms, appearing to support the view that 'the fragmented and variable nature of organisations representing SME interests at the national level is reflected in EU organisation' (Greenwood 2002, p. 139).

One of the fundamental problems faced by policy makers seeking to engage small business owners in formal processes of social dialogue is the reluctance of the latter to join and participate in representative organizations. Moreover, within the SME sector, small firms with less than 50 employees can be particularly difficult to reach for consultation and social dialogue purposes, for various reasons. One reason is that irrespective of the national base, most owner-managers tend to avoid engagement with government or quasi-government agencies and SME membership bodies over and above for compulsory reasons (Curran and Blackburn 1994). This is an important part of the challenge of bringing SMEs into social dialogue. This reluctance has been explained by Hart (2003) in terms of three main factors: first, a lack of time, energy and enthusiasm on the part of entrepreneurs for activities that are not directly connected with their businesses; second, a lack of information about the possible benefits of participating; and third, doubts about whether any policies resulting from their contribution can be implemented quickly enough to make a difference to their particular venture. As a consequence, it is inevitable that only a small minority of entrepreneurs typically become involved directly in policy and/or social dialogue processes, through representative organizations. Mobilizing entrepreneurs and small business owners to become involved is not easy, even if policy makers have a will to do so. In addition, if the potential benefits to small business owners are perceived to be distant (if they exist at all) and the approach used is perceived to be based on an outdated model of collective bargaining, engaging a representative group of SMEs in social dialogue appears doubly difficult.

It is important to recognize that social dialogue involves employees as well as employers. From the perspective of an employee in a small business, a key problem with respect to the current EU social dialogue model is that membership rates of trade unions are non-existent, or typically much lower in small firms than in large enterprises. Although it may be argued that social dialogue can, in principle, benefit employers and employees in firms of all sizes, a lack of engagement with trade unions in small firms may be associated with ambivalence on the part of employees and antipathy on the part of small firm employers towards unions. If so, then this may affect the perceptions and attitudes of both groups concerning the value of existing social dialogue processes. It may be argued that the potential benefits for employers and employees of engaging in social dialogue include opportunities to influence agreements, and possibly EU directives affecting the business/working environment in which they operate, regardless of firm size. Indeed, supporters of the current model argue that with respect to EU employment and social affairs, for example, social dialogue can offer a more pragmatic and less rigid solution to certain regulatory issues than EU derived legislation. Nevertheless, a key problem is how to convince SME owners of this, particularly in situations where their orientation towards autonomy and independence is associated with an unwillingness to associate, and where the national social dialogue context may not encourage them to do so.

Whilst small business owners and their employees may have an opportunity to be involved in social dialogue processes through involvement with national social partners, they cannot be forced to do so any more than an individual voter can be forced to vote in an election. However, such an argument fails to recognize that participation rates are one indicator of how well a system is valued. In this context, it might be suggested that the existing model(s) of social dialogue in Europe is/are based on an approach, which fits better with the experience of collective bargaining practices in large rather than small firms, where levels of trade union membership are low and employment relations practices (for example, wage setting; firm level employee representation) are typically informal. This appears to be one of the fundamental reasons why participation rates of small firm employers and employees in social dialogue processes are low, which should be a major concern of Europe's policy makers.

CHALLENGES FACING NEW MEMBER STATES

The enlargement of the EU to include countries which less than twenty years ago were operating under central planning, presents specific challenges to the successful operation of European social dialogue. Since these countries have joined the EU, establishing effective social dialogue has been promoted by the European Commission and existing EU social partners as a necessary part of the EU social model. This presents a major challenge for countries with little or no recent experience of self governing organizations; a heritage of trade unions and business organizations that were effectively arms of government; and social partner organizations that lack both resources and relevant experience.

Vatta (2001) has described the involvement of social interest groups in public policy-making in Central and Eastern European Countries (CEECs) as 'irregular, if not totally ineffective'. Others have referred to the weakness of bilateral dialogue in most of the new EU members (European Small Business Alliance 2005), with bipartite dialogue being the exception (for example in Latvia) rather than the rule. At the same time, Due and Mailand (2003) have painted a somewhat less bleak picture as part of a comprehensive summary of social dialogue in six accession states.

National social dialogue in new member states is generally tripartite (that is, involving government, employers and organized labour), reflecting a lack of culture and experience of autonomous industrial relations, because of the all-embracing control of the state during the socialist period. In addition, social partners were given political legitimacy by national governments in the early years of transition to share responsibility for difficult reforms, almost irrespective of their membership, which is arguably not the best foundation. The participation of social partners in tripartite fora was taken as a de facto criterion for their representativeness, although there is clearly a difference between political recognition and representativeness based on membership. Since social dialogue institutions in Central and Eastern European countries (CEECs) do not usually have statutory authority, their legitimacy is sometimes called into question.

For the new democracies of CEECs, the establishment of effective social dialogue involving SMEs presents a particular challenge, for a number of reasons:

(i) *Restructuring processes in the economy* that involved a shift away from an emphasis on large state owned companies towards an emerging privately owned SME sector have been associated with a reduction in the importance of trade unions and a more fragmented context for employers to form associations. Restructuring has also involved a shift from a narrow focus on heavy manufacturing, which was central to the socialist economic model, to a greater emphasis on a range of service activities, in which small firms are dominant. In combination, these changes represent a major challenge to the establishment of social dialogue institutions and processes that engage with smaller enterprises, because of the greater fragmentation that is implicit in them.

(ii) *The involvement of organized groups, other than political parties, is not always understood in countries where there is no recent tradition of self governing organizations.* As a result, social partnership has sometimes been confused with the corporatism, or neo-corporatism, practised by totalitarian regimes, rather than as a complement to classic parliamentary democracy (Rychly and Pritzer 2003).

(iii) *In terms of employee representation, the inheritance from the Soviet period included a tradition of trade unions that were strongly linked to the Communist Party.* Although trade unions have typically disconnected themselves from association with the Communist Party, in the majority of countries the reformed communist trade unions have the largest political influence. At the same time, the structure of trade unions varies significantly from state to state. For example, in Latvia and the Czech Republic one single trade union has near monopoly representation of employee interests. In Poland and Estonia, two major trade unions compete for members and for influence on the political system. By contrast, Lithuania and Hungary are characterized by pluralistic trade union structures, with evidence of considerable tension between organizations. However, one consistent aspect of the transformation process across CEECs is that trade union membership has declined rapidly since the end of communism, when approximately 90 per cent of employees were members. Levels now vary from 10 to 40 per cent of employees, with representation and trade union membership much weaker in the emerging private sector, particularly in the case of SMEs.

(iv) *In contrast to most established EU states, where employers' organizations developed initially as a response to trade union power, in the emerging market economies of Central and Eastern Europe, employers' organizations grew out of a desire for more effective lobbying with government on behalf of an emerging private sector.* In the absence of regulation by the state, this has resulted in a multiplicity of SME employers organizations, based on locality, in some cases, and sector in others. Fragmentation has dispersed the representation of the interests of SMEs, thereby weakening their position. No tradition of independent employers' organizations existed before the collapse of the communist regimes, which means that since 1989, it has been necessary to start to build these from scratch. In most CEECs, it is difficult to distinguish between employer organizations and associations of entrepreneurs, most of which have developed as interest or lobby groups, focusing their attention on aspects of economic policy. In terms of membership, it is estimated that employer organizations in the CEECs represent on average only 2 to 5 per cent of the total number of enterprises (UEAPME ENTER Project 2003).

Another result of the historical legacy is that it is often difficult in CEECs to distinguish between employers' organizations and Chambers of Commerce, many of which were built on the basis of former chambers of commerce and industry. These 'old' chambers had a special role under the previous system that in effect made them an arm of the state, dominated by large state owned companies. Under transition in the 1990s, this offered some benefit in terms of political recognition and the ability to use institutional resources in some cases, although the resultant organizations were very different institutions from the employers' organizations existing in established EU countries. As a consequence, it has proven difficult for some social partners on the employee side in new member countries to find employer organization counterparts, particularly at a sectoral level.

(v) *In new member states, organizations involved as social dialogue partners, have often lacked sufficient resources and capacity to contribute effectively to social dialogue processes.* For example, although in most new member states, the negotiations leading up to EU accession involved consultation with entrepreneurs and employers' organizations, doubts have been expressed about the effectiveness of this consultation. In the case of Poland, for example, social partners have been described as deficient, first, because they had insufficient familiarity with procedural aspects of preparations for negotiations; and second, because of insufficient knowledge about integration processes themselves and negotiations connected with them (http://www.ukie.gov.pl). In practice, differences in the level of knowledge between government and non-governmental organizations seriously limit the possibility of conducting consultations based on the partnership principle. Specific practical issues that social partner organizations in new member states have needed help with include how to obtain a mandate from their members; how they report to members; and how they present compromises to members (Wild 2008).

As a consequence, social partners and non-governmental organizations in EU new member states have often been insufficiently prepared to undertake discussions on the most important issues concerning them, although this is an issue being addressed by EU capacity building programmes. Many employers' organizations face considerable difficulties in attracting sufficient membership fees and thus the resources required to run their organizations effectively. On the trade union side, the dramatic and continuing fall in membership, associated with rising unemployment, privatization and sectoral shifts, has weakened them both financially and politically.

(vi) *Social dialogue is typically not well developed at the sub-national level.* A common issue in this regard is a shortage of resources and know-how required to establish social dialogue at a local level. A lack of sectoral and firm level dialogue has been identified as one of the weakest aspects of social dialogue in new member states, contrasting with 'numerous tripartite consultation mechanisms' (Ghellab and Vaughan-Whitehead 2003). Sectoral level collective agreements are rare and where they do exist, they are normally confined to wages, rarely covering employment issues, working conditions, health and safety or training. In addition, they usually have weak regulatory force. At company level, most social dialogue centres on discussions over pay and working conditions.

Although the development of social dialogue mechanisms and processes in new member states presents many challenges, it is important to recognize the developments that have taken place in recent years. The process of preparing to join the EU has contributed to awareness of social dialogue issues and to the development of social dialogue mechanisms and processes, in order to implement the 'acquis communitaire'. Existing EU social partners have played a role in this, initially in disseminating information, stressing the potential role of social dialogue as a credible alternative to EU legislation, because of its more pragmatic and less rigid solutions.

There have been various attempts to help new member states develop their social dialogue capacity. One of the most significant was a joint project of the four social partner organisations (BUSINESSEUROPE 2006, Joint Project of the European Social Partner Organizations 2005).[4] The European Sectoral Social Dialogue has also emphasized a need to engage with new Member States and the Sectoral Social Dialogue Committees have actively targeted them with a series of initiatives to help in capacity building (European Commission 2006b). Despite these initiatives, however, it would appear that social dialogue in the new member states is still in its infancy, although more advanced in some countries (for example Poland) than others (for example Hungary).

SOCIAL DIALOGUE IN NEW EU MEMBER STATES: THE CASE OF HUNGARY

Whilst the new EU member states from Central and Eastern Europe share many characteristics associated with their common heritage, they also represent a varied group of countries. From a social dialogue perspective, it is important to recognize the differences in the starting points for the transformation process, as well as differences in cultural heritage. As a result, whereas in a number of CEECs, such as Hungary and Poland, some private business activity was able to exist during the communist period, in other countries, such as the Baltic States, all private business activities were illegal. The heterogeneity of background and experience is reflected in differences between countries in the characteristics and behaviour of social partner institutions and in differences in the levels of membership of both trade unions and employers' organizations.

In Hungary, there were attempts at economic reform before the collapse of the Berlin Wall in 1989 and the changes it triggered, most notably in 1968. Whilst this did little to change the basic characteristics of the centrally planned system, the 1970s and 1980s saw the toleration of various forms of the entrepreneurial 'second economy' and private microbusinesses that provided some basis for understanding and implementing the requirements of the systemic changes that occurred in 1989/90. As in other CEECs, the early 1990s saw an explosion of entrepreneurial activity (Piasecki and Rogut 1993) in Hungary, resulting in an increase in the number of registered enterprises from 360 000 in 1989 to 746 000 in 1992 and 1 002 000 by 1994. Based on the latest data available (2009), the enterprise structure of the non-financial business economy in Hungary is converging with the EU average, with SMEs contributing a higher share of employment (71.1 per cent compared with 67.4 per cent in EU-27) and a lower share of GDP (51.9 per cent compared with 57.9 per cent in EU-27).[5]

An institutional framework for tripartite social dialogue was set up in the late 1980s, making it the first to be established in the CEECs. This involved the creation of the first National Council for the Reconciliation of Interests (NCRI) in 1988, which consisted of representatives of employers, employees and government, although formed on the basis of agreement than legal statute (which did not come until 2009). The NCRI was reconstituted after the political changes in 1990. During the turbulence of the early 1990s, when more than one million jobs were lost (in a country of just 10 million inhabitants), official sources suggest the NCRI played an important role in helping to moderate and resolve social conflicts (http://www.szmm.gov.hu). At the same time, questions concerning the representativeness and weakness of social partner organizations affected their legitimacy and effectiveness.

The NCRI was connected to the Ministry of Labour, or the Ministry of Social Affairs and Labour, as it is now. The government's permanent representative in the NCRI has been the State Secretary of this Ministry, although other ministries were invited to participate, depending on the agenda. From May 2010, the new government restructured the ministries, so there is now no longer a separate Ministry of Labour or Social Affairs and Labour, although so far the role and composition of the NCRI has not changed.

The NCRI is said to 'provide national social partners and the government with a formal structure for their continuous dialogue. It ensures the institutional framework for discussing economic and labour related issues, with a view to reaching agreements reflecting the interests of the government and social partners alike' and 'its competence covers all issues related to the world of labour, including any major economic policy issue that has an implication on the distribution of state revenues' (http://www.szmm. gov.hu/main.php). Within this framework, social partners are consulted by government on draft economic, social, employment and other labour-related laws, as well as the underlying policies and priorities.

In a recent (April 2010) publication of the (former) prime minister's office the role of the NCRI has been defined 'to reveal, coordinate, and form agreement with respect to the interests and endeavours of employees, employers and government; to anticipate and settle potential national conflicts; as well as to exchange information, assess suggestions and alternatives. With this interest it discusses all topics related to labour, the economy and employment, including themes influencing changes in income, taxation, social contributions, state budget and drafts of legal measures'.[6]

The NCRI has nine specialized committees, a National ILO Council (NILO), four Sectoral and two Professional Councils. Its major forum is the plenary session, prepared by one or more of these committees, namely: the Wage and Collective Agreements Committee, Equal Opportunities Committee, Economic Affairs Committee, Labour Market Committee, Labour Law Committee, Labour Safety Committee, National Development Plan Committee, Vocational Training Committee, Social Committee.

In the NCRI nine employer and six employee organizations represent the two major partners, although these organizations show considerable differences in their past experience, traditions, coverage and influence. With respect to the employer organizations, a temporary period in the mid-1990s, when Chamber of Commerce membership was obligatory, weakened the employer's representation in the longer term by sharply reducing membership in voluntary organizations. Low membership results in a weak financial situation and limited access to expertise. It has also contributed to increased fragmentation with overlap in the activities of the Chambers and professional associations. This fragmentation is aggravated by a low level of cooperation, influenced by the heritage from the former centralized system, in which the state administration did not recognize the principle of social partnership. Although in all these organizations, the vast majority of members are micro-, small or medium-sized enterprises, the voice of the large enterprises dominates. Four organizations with only SME members have created a framework for cooperation, attempting to fulfil the role of an umbrella organization called the 'Interest Representation Association of Small and Medium-Sized Enterprises' (KÉSZ).[7]

On the employee side, the role of trade unions in Hungary weakened in the early 1990s, during the period when more than one million jobs were lost. Their weakened position was reinforced by a divergence between emerging trade unions, difficulties faced in trade unions finding their place in a new political situation, and the legacy of a monolithic trade union structure that had existed in the past. As in other transition countries, structural changes in the economy were reflected in the rapid growth of small private enterprises which are not unionized, adding to the weakening of organized labour. Since a high proportion of both employees and employers are not covered by collective agreements, the legitimacy of social dialogue in Hungary has proved difficult to establish. As a consequence, social dialogue in the late 1990s reached a particularly low ebb, degrading to consultations or forums for receiving information and hearing opinions, rather than a process for achieving consensus and reaching agreements.

However, becoming an EU member and the preparations for membership undoubtedly boosted the system of social dialogue in the country. Attempts at harmonization with the EU system has included a growing emphasis on the Sectoral Dialogue Committees (SDCs), which Hungary has received support from the EU to develop. The Hungarian representative organizations have become members of the EU social partner organizations, that is the European Trade Union Confederation (ETUC), the Confederation European Business BUSINESSEUROPE, the European Centre of Enterprises with Public Participation and of Enterprises of General Economic Interest (CEEP) and the European Association of Craft Small and Medium-Sized Enterprises (UEAPME), which participates in EU social dialogue as a member of the BUSINESSEUROPE delegation.

EU membership also has increased the stated commitment of government to pursuing meaningful social dialogue with social partners, with respect to both consultations and to concluding agreements. Fostered by EU initiatives, this has included steps to strengthen social dialogue at the sectoral level, so that now 23 Sectoral Committees discuss specific sectoral questions. A recent publication from the (former) prime minister's office[8] presents 22 further committees and councils with members from the social partners, attached to various ministries. These offer fora for consultation, discussion and social dialogue, although at the time of writing their status has yet to be confirmed by the new government. Although these organizations include SMEs among their members, the voice of SMEs is generally weak.

In addition, there are two further forum for social dialogue. The first is the Economic and Social Council (ESC), which was established in 2004 with a role similar to that of the Economic and Social Council (ECOSOC) in the EU. Chaired by the Prime Minister, it has 43 members, including representatives of employers, employees, civil and science organizations. This is a wider circle than the NCRI since it includes, among others, two Chambers of Commerce, the Council of Co-operatives, the Council of the Exchange, the Joint Venture Association, the Hungarian Association of International Enterprises, major civil organizations, the Hungarian Academy of Sciences and the Hungarian Economic Association. In addition to the Prime Minister, it also includes seven other ministers and the President of the Central Statistical Office. According to its mandate the ESC primarily deals with national strategic questions, such as the National Development Plan, the National Sustainable Development Strategy and recently the Hungarian Lisbon Action Programme for 2008–10, which attracted many critical comments.

The second forum is the Enterprise Development Council (EDC), established in the Ministry of Economy in December 1995, with a role to formulate SME policy. It is chaired by a representative of the Minister in charge of SME policy (currently at the National Development and Economic Ministry). At present, the voting members of the ECD include 12 state organizations and 10 organizations representing SMEs; and a few other organizations are invited to participate with 'consultation rights'. In former cycles, some academics were also members, although this has now been abandoned. The EDC has three to four sessions per year discussing programmes for, and reports on, SMEs in the country, as well as draft regulations. However, recurrent complaints of the social partners are that they receive the drafts of new regulations too late to study and evaluate them effectively.

The Hungarian experience illustrates the wider difficulties of establishing effective social dialogue mechanisms in former socialist countries, as well as the specific challenges faced in engaging with SME employers and employees. Although 'all the social partners (in Hungary) acknowledge that significant proportions of employees and employers are not formally members of an organization' (Joint Project of the European Social Partner Organizations 2005, pp. 26–7), it is fair to point out that this issue is not confined to Hungary, since the experience in most countries is that many SME owners are not 'joiners'. Another issue identified is that 'Social dialogue has up to now been very political, depending on the reigning Government's attitude towards the partners . . . often the partners agree on many important issues, but cannot move forward for political reasons' (Joint Project of the European Social Partner Organizations 2005, pp. 26–7). Whilst an institutional framework for consultation has been established by government, encouraged by the demands of and opportunities presented by EU membership. It remains to be seen whether this framework is sufficiently robust to provide an effective basis for the full participation of Hungarian employers and employees in EU social dialogue processes.

Moreover, it can be argued that even at a national level, some of the consultation mechanisms established appears weak and rather partial. For example, whilst the EDC may provide a forum for an exchange of ideas and views between government and SMEs, an official spokesman for the Ministry chairing the EDC has pointed to the lack of involvement of other relevant government ministries in the work of the Council.[9] A more fundamental weakness is that many important regulations call for quick coordination, and since the Enterprise Development Council is only a professional coordinating forum and not a mandatory part of the coordinating process for new regulations, not all draft regulations are submitted to the Council.

CONCLUSIONS

This chapter has dealt with two interrelated themes: first, issues concerned with establishing social dialogue mechanisms and processes in new members of the EU, that until 1989/90 were operating under the rules of central planning; and second, the challenges of engaging with SME managers and employees in social dialogue processes.

In relation to the first theme, the economic and social transformation of Central and Eastern Europe is a remarkable phenomenon by any standards, not least because it involves a redefinition of the role of the state, with implications for political processes. The challenges faced in establishing social dialogue mechanisms and processes is an illustration of this, since many of the challenges reflect structural factors that are part of the legacy inherited from former regimes. In this respect, joining the EU has been an important driver of change in these countries. Yet, based on the experience in Hungary, this has been more about government establishing consultation mechanisms than creating fora for reaching joint agreements. It may be argued that in countries where the principle of social partnership is relatively new, any attempt to initiate a process of exchange of views between employers, employees and government may be viewed as a positive step. However, there is a danger that participants will become disillusioned if these fora become little more than 'talking shops'. Since social dialogue institutions in CEECs do not usually have statutory authority, their legitimacy is sometimes open to question.

The question of the involvement of SME managers and employees in social dialogue processes is a Europe-wide issue, particularly in new member countries, because the private sector that has emerged since transformation began is essentially a SME phenomenon. Nevertheless, there are established EU member states, such as the UK, where engaging SMEs in social dialogue is also underdeveloped. The limited involvement of small firm managers and workers in social dialogue processes must be a concern to policy makers when considered alongside the widely acknowledged contribution of small firms to the European economy. Clearly, there is a need to either significantly improve small business engagement in the existing models or alternatively look for other approaches. Whilst it may be argued that it is in the interests of SME owners to participate in a social dialogue, which can influence employment and social policies that ultimately affect them, in practice there are various barriers to increasing this involvement. These barriers include the fragmentation of the SME voice; the limited management time which SME owner-managers can spare to take part in representative organizations and forums; plus the fact that owner managers are often focused on day-to-day issues of managing their business, which is a world away from that of representation in the social dialogue.

Finally, a distinction needs to be made between creating fora for dialogue and consultation between employers, employees and government, in the process of public policy making and monitoring and the more narrowly defined concept of social dialogue that operates at the EU level. In the latter case, it is particularly important that small as well as large firms are fully involved in social dialogue processes, if EU Social Dialogue is to have credibility throughout the EU. Whilst EU social partners have some engagement with small firms, very few small firms' owner-managers or employees are drawn into the process. The role of UEAPME is important in the SME dialogue process although the representativeness of some of UEAPME's national membership organizations can be questioned.

One of the underlying problems is that the model of EU social dialogue is based on a process of collective bargaining, which is unfamiliar, and arguably inappropriate, in a SME context. As a consequence, whilst there are measures that could be taken by national and EU social partners to encourage more small business involvement, the fundamental problem may be seen as inherently flawed at the institutional-structural levels. The result is that SMEs appear marginalized with a weak voice in EU social dialogue processes.[10]

Achieving significant improvement in SME representation and input into EU employment and social policies may be difficult to achieve in the context of the existing social dialogue model. A combination of the fragmentation of SME representation, very low trade union density in SMEs, a lack of corporate recognition of SME priorities, combined with behavioural characteristics of SMEs themselves, make it difficult to engage them in existing arrangements. Indeed, if small firm employers and employees are to fully engage in the process of EU policy making, it will need a culture shift in their engagement patterns, but also in the approach of policy makers. This may lead to a questioning of the underlying assumptions of dominant notions of social dialogue and practical pillars upon which it currently stands. More radical approaches could involve the European Commission and national governments stepping outside the current social partner system, to undertake more broadly based consultations of small firm managers and workers on European social dialogue issues, feeding in to the decision making process.

NOTES

1. For a more detailed description of the legal basis of EU social dialogue see Smallbone et al. (2005).
2. BUSINESSEUROPE was previously known as UNICE. The name was changed in 2007. CEEP is the European Centre of Employers and Enterprises, UEAPME is the European Association of Craft, Small and Medium-sized Enterprises, and ETUC is the European Trade Union Confederation.
3. In fact, there are only an estimated 43 000 large scale enterprises in the EU; that is firms employing 250 or more (European Commission 2010a: Table 4).
4. The pilot project involved the design and organization of two day workshops in each of the pilot countries in 2003–4, during which representatives of national partner organizations were invited to identify their needs with respect to building their capacity to represent the view of their members in the European social dialogue. On the basis of the needs identified, action plans were developed by social partners, both individually and jointly to address these.
5. European Commission (2010b).
6. Eszter and Tóth (2010).
7. Kállay, Kissné Kovács, Kohegyu and Maszlag (2009).
8. Eszter and Tóth (2010).

9. Statement by a representative of the Ministry of Economy and Transport at the EU Charter Conference in 2005.
10. See for example the view of the European Small Business Alliance (2005) which has called for the creation of a new forum for small businesses and entrepreneurs.

REFERENCES

BUSINESSEUROPE (2006), *Final Report: Joint Report of the Social Partner Organisations: CEEC social partner participation in the European Social Dialogue*, UEAPME, available at http://www.ueapme.com/spip.php?rubrique28 (accessed September 2010).
Commission of the European Communities (2002), *The European Social Dialogue, a Force for Innovation and Change*, Communication from the Commission, Brussels, 26 June, COM (2002) 341 final.
Curran, J. and R. Blackburn (1994), *Small Firms and Local Economic Networks: The Death of the Local Economy?*, London: Paul Chapman, Sage.
Due, J. and M. Mailand (2003), 'Social Dialogue in Central and Eastern Europe – present state and future development', paper for IIRA congress 2003, Berlin.
Eszter, M. and L.M. Tóth (eds) (2010), *Institutions and Forums of the Social Dialogue*, prepared under the editorship of the Office of the Prime Minister, Bureau of Co-ordination for Social Dialogue (published in Hungarian).
European Commission (2005), *Consultation with Stakeholders in the Shaping of National and Regional Policies Affecting Small Business*, Final Report of the Expert Group's Final Version October, DG Enterprise and Industry, Unit E1, Brussels, available at http://europa.eu.int/comm/enterprise/entrepreneurship/index.htm (accessed September 2005).
European Commission (2006a), *20 Years of European Social Dialogue, Social Dialogue Summit, 29 September, 2005*, Directorate-General for Employment and Social Affairs and Equal Opportunities, available at http://ec.europa.eu/employment_social/social_dialogue/docs/sds_actes_en.pdf (accessed September 2007).
European Commission (2006b), *Recent Developments in the European Sectoral Social Dialogue*, Directorate-General for Employment and Social Affairs and Equal Opportunities, Unit D1, available at http://ec.europa.eu/employment_social/social_dialogue/docs/sectoral_sd_2006_en.pdf (accessed September 2007).
European Commission (2010a), *European SMEs under Pressure, Annual Report on EU Small and Medium-sized Enterprises, 2009*, EIM and DG Enterprise, Brussels, available at http://ec.europa.eu/enterprise/policies/sme/facts-figures-analysis/performance-review/pdf/dgentr_annual_report2010_100511.pdf (accessed September 2010).
European Commission (2010b), *SBA Factsheet: Hungary*, DG Enterprise and Industry, DG Enterprise, Brussels, available at http://ec.europa.eu/enterprise/policies/sme/facts-figures-analysis/performance-review/pdf/final/sba_fact_sheet_hungary_en.pdf (accessed September 2010).
European Small Business Alliance (2005), *Press Release: Independent Small Businesses and Self-employed want to be heard in European Social Dialogue*, available at http://www.esba-europe.org/9F5FB/News/Press_Releases/Pre-2006_-_Press_Rel/14_April_05_Social_Dialogue.aspx (accessed August 2005).
Ghellab, Y. and D. Vaughan-Whitehead (2003), 'Sectoral social dialogue: a link to be strengthened', in Y. Ghellab and D. Vaughan-Whitehead (eds), S*ectoral Social Dialogue in Future EU Member States: The Weakest Link*, Geneva: ILO, available at http://www.ilo.org/public/english/region/eurpro/budapest/download/sectoral_sd.pdf (accessed August 2005).
Greenwood, J. (2002), *Inside the EU Business Associations*, Basingstoke: Palgrave.
Hart, D.M. (2003), 'Knowledge, power and entrepreneurs: a first pass at the politics of entrepreneurship policy', in D.M. Hart (ed.), *The Emergence of Entrepreneurship Policy: Governance, Start-Ups and Growth in the US Knowledge Economy*, Cambridge, pp. 227–39.

Joint Project of the European Social Partner Organizations (2005), *Study on Restructuring in New Member States. Hungary – Country Dossier (2005)*, available at http://resource-centre.etuc.org/ReportFile-20080229105245_Restructuring-Hungary-country-dossier-EN%5B1%5D.pdf (accessed September 2010).

Kállay, L., E. Kissné Kovács, K. Kohegyu and L. Maszlag (2009), *The State of Small and Medium Sized Business in Hungary 2008*, Budapest: Ministry for National Development and Economics.

Kenworthy, L. and B. Kittel (2003), 'Indicators of Social Dialogue: concepts and Measurement', ILO Working Paper No 5. ILO, Geneva, available at http://www.ilo.org/wcmsp5/groups/public/---dgreports/---integration/documents/publication/wcms_079091.pdf (accessed August 2005).

Piasecki, B. and A. Rogut (1993), 'Self-regulation of SME sector development at a more advanced stage of transformation', paper presented to the 20th Annual Conference of E.A.R.I.E., Tel Aviv, September.

Rychly, L. and R. Pritzer (2003), 'Social dialogue at national level in the EU accession countries', Working Paper, International Labour Office Geneva, February, available at http://www.ilo.org/public/english/region/eurpro/geneva/download/events/malta2003/soc_nat_dial.pdf (accessed August 2005).

Smallbone, D., R. Blackburn and M. Hart (2005), *Effective Social Dialogue in an Enlarged Europe*, report commissioned by DTI, Small Business Research Centre, Kingston University, available at http://webarchive.nationalarchives.gov.uk/+/http://www.berr.gov.uk/files/file26223.pdf.

UEAPME ENTER Project (2003), *Social Dialogue in the CEECs*, background factsheet No 4, 13/10/03, available at http://www.ueapme.com/enter/dwnlds/IsSocD_3A.doc.

Vatta, A. (2001), 'The enlargement of the European Union and social dialogue in Central and Eastern Europe', *Perspectives on European Politics and Society*, **2** (1), 127–46.

Wild, A. (2008), *Final Report of Joint Project of the European Social Partner Organisations: CEEC Social Partner's Participation in the European Social Dialogue, What are the social partners needs?*, available at http://resourcecentre.etuc.org/ReportFile-20090624155147_IP1---Bulgaria-Seminar-Report-Final-EN.pdf (accessed September 2010).

Webpages

http://www.szmm.gov.hu.
http://www.ueapme.com.
http://www.ukie.gov.pl.

5 Mentalities and mindsets: the difficulties of entrepreneurship policies in the Latvian context
Arnis Sauka and Friederike Welter

INTRODUCTION

Along with the economic and political processes prior to the collapse of the Soviet Union, entrepreneurship development in Latvia as well as other countries of Central and Eastern Europe started 20 years ago. This process of change from a centrally planned to market-oriented system is often referred to as 'transition' in entrepreneurship literature (Smallbone and Welter 2001). The fundamental transformation of the role of the state, along with the development of a suitable political structure and institutional change, in particular with regard to a *framework* shaping economic, financial and legal institutions underpinning the market economy, had to be achieved first in each and every country of Central and Eastern Europe (EBRD 1995). North (1990) refers to this framework, generally enforced by governments and relatively easily adaptable to the changing economic circumstances, as formal institutions. Due to the total collapse of the former system, the introduction of new formal institutions was not an easy task to carry out. In this context, 'framework uncertainty'[1] shaping the environment in the countries of transition is often mentioned amongst the major constraints in entrepreneurship literature (Van de Mortel 2002). As emphasized by North (1990), along with the development of formal institutions, informal institutions, for example invisible 'rules of the game', made up of norms, values, acceptable behaviour and codes of conduct in a society, also have to change while a country progresses towards a market economy. Such informal rules often evolve either to substitute or to complement formal rules and they have a fundamental influence on economic development (Raiser 1999). For example, if piracy is rewarded by the institutional framework, unproductive entrepreneurship will almost certainly emerge, whereas if legal entrepreneurship is rewarded by the institutional framework, organizations will tend to engage in 'fair' activities (North 1990).

It is thus important to understand how norms and values of a society interact with formal institutions when it comes to analysing the process of change within the transition context. In this light, however, it is perhaps of even more importance to consider the role of actors in shaping entrepreneurship policies, including civil servants, business support agencies and policy makers themselves, by analysing their attempts in changing the institutional framework. During the transition process, it is crucial for those actors to reassess their own norms and values while simultaneously introducing a new legal framework or contributing to the framework's development (for example, Aidis 2006; Van de Mortel 2002).

Few studies have attempted to address this issue empirically, apart from studies exploring informal institutions by entrepreneurs in a transition context (Aidis 2006; Aidis and Sauka 2005), irrespective of the fact that a good conceptual background has been developed which allows the exploration of factors influencing development and implementation of entrepreneurship policies within transition context (North 1990; Smallbone and Welter 2001, 2006; Van de Mortel 2002). This chapter aims to fill this gap by drawing on the example of a new European Union member state, Latvia. In order to provide the reader with an in-depth analysis of the difficulties of entrepreneurship policy design and implementation, 23 interviews with public and private actors who are involved in the process of entrepreneurship policy making were conducted during June and August 2006. These include the representatives of Ministry of Economics of Latvia, Ministry of Interior of Latvia, Ministry of Foreign Affairs of Latvia, business support organizations such as the Latvian Chamber of Commerce and Industry and the Latvian Development and Investment Agency as well as all major associations representing the main business sectors of the country. Interviews were conducted by selecting experts so that they represent the viewpoint of their organization and have access to all necessary information, thus in most organizations respondents hold a top position. Apart from focusing on the impact of norms, values, behaviour and codes of conduct in the development of a framework for entrepreneurship activity within a transition setting, factors such as capacity, communication and overall impact of the environment on the development and implication of entrepreneurship policies are addressed in the chapter.

The rest of the chapter is structured as follows. The next section provides a brief introduction to the development of entrepreneurship-related policies in Latvia during the various stages of its transition to a market economy. The chapter then continues to identify the major challenges of current entrepreneurship policies in Latvia, followed by an exploration of the communication between entrepreneurs and actors shaping entrepreneurship policies in Latvia. Positive trends brought on by EU accession are then explored, and the chapter concludes with policy suggestions and implications.

DEVELOPMENT OF ENTREPRENEURSHIP, LAWS AND SUPPORT MECHANISMS IN LATVIA

Emphasizing the role of the external environment, empirical evidence highlights that although not unique, entrepreneurship in a transition setting has specific features as compared with more advanced market economies (Smallbone and Welter 2006). Furthermore, previous research also suggests that it is not appropriate to refer to transition countries as a 'unified group' since important difference exists between countries as a result of different starting points, traditions and the success of ongoing reforms (Smallbone and Welter 2001). In this light, while emphasizing that no clear cut-offs exist and various transition stages can overlap, a number of attempts have been carried out in order to distinguish between different stages of development from a centrally planned towards a well developed market economy.[2] Regardless of how the transition stages are determined, however, it is often emphasized that the transition process is not linear by nature, meaning that a country can regress to a less developed stage (Smallbone and Welter 2001).

Taking this into consideration, up to the EU accession in 2004, entrepreneurship development in Latvia, along with the development of entrepreneurship laws and support mechanisms, can be divided into three major stages (Kuzmina 1999). The first stage of transition to a market economy started with reforms instigated by the former Soviet leader Michail Gorbachev which resulted in the legislation of cooperatives in the late 1980s as the beginning of private sector development in the country. The first stage of transition is usually very short, given that the country has a willingness to reform (Van de Mortel 2002). This notion holds true for Latvia, because the early 1990s, when the Law on Entrepreneurship was introduced almost at the same time as the country declared independence from the Soviet Union, is already considered as the beginning of the second transition stage in the country (Kuzmina 1999).

Overall, the second stage of transition is mainly characterized by the introduction of the legal framework, including banking laws, protection of private property, competition law, and bankruptcy law (Van de Mortel 2002). In Latvia, along with the Law on Entrepreneurship, a number of related laws regulating the entrepreneurial climate were introduced during this period.[3] Furthermore, several organizations were established to support entrepreneurship development, including the Latvian Chamber of Commerce and Industry,[4] the Investment and Development Agency of Latvia[5] and the Latvian Technology Centre.[6] According to Van de Mortel (2002), the second stage of transition ends when the introduction of a formal framework is roughly complete, although Smallbone and Welter

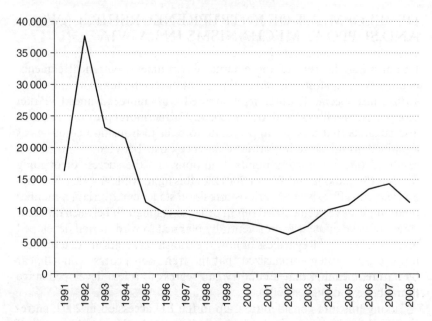

Source: http://www.lursoft.lv.

Figure 5.1   Number of registered companies in Latvia (1991–2008)

(2009) emphasize the behaviour of institutions as important, which is not guaranteed by solely implementing the formal institutional framework. Moreover, informal institutions have to change during the second stage as well. In this light, research has emphasized that without harmony between formal and informal institutions, people will not accept the new legal and institutional framework, which may result in the regression of the transition process to the previous stage (Aidis 2006; Van de Mortel 2002).

As a result of the development of legal and market reforms in Latvia, including the liberalization of purchase prices and privatization, as well as other reforms implemented during the first stages of transition, enterprises mushroomed (see Figure 5.1). Needless to say, the high numbers of start-up rates during 1991–93 were certainly not the result of economic development in the country. On the contrary, these were hard times for Latvia. For instance, the gross domestic product (GDP) fell by more than 50 per cent from 1990 to 1993, but inflation was as high as 958 per cent in 1992. Mushrooming of the companies is usually explained by the fact that most forms of the entrepreneurship were restricted during the Soviet Union regime and individuals took advantage of the transition to market economy to start their firms (for example Aidis, 2006). Here it should be also mentioned that lack of experience and know how, however, further caused a steady decline in entrepreneurship activity just a few years later in 1994–95 (Sauka and Welter, 2010).

According to Kuzmina (1999), the third stage, often referred to as the contemporary stage of entrepreneurship development, started in Latvia around 1994, and can be characterized by the emergence of many new laws[7] and programmes, numerous changes implemented in the existing legal framework and the establishment of business promotion organizations, complementing those developed in the previous stage of transition. The main difference in the majority of these legal initiatives as well as in the nature of the newly established business promotion organizations during the advanced transition stage in Latvia, however, was that these were focused on the development of specific aspects of the framework for entrepreneurship development. Support for innovative and knowledge-intensive companies or increasing the availability of external finance for nascent entrepreneurs can be mentioned as examples in this regard.

As admitted by representatives from various associations, policy makers have worked hard in order to establish a framework for entrepreneurship development in the country since the reforms started. In this light, the majority of the interviewees highlighted *the role of the accession process to the European Union* in fostering an entrepreneurial climate, which can be seen as the distinctive stage in the entrepreneurship development of Latvia. According to the interviewees, the process towards EU accession and accession itself has had a *positive influence on entrepreneurship legislation in Latvia* and has ensured higher quality standards. The improvement of customs work, for example, is very often emphasized in this regard. Still, there are also other points of view. For example, a number of associations, including one representing major business sectors in Latvia, argue that *due to their mentality* policy makers in Latvia were only 'too willing to accept all EU regulations', referring to civil servants wishing to look good to the EU, by, for example, introducing EU directives with recommendation power, such as directive-regulating requirements for personal protective equipment, into the legislation of Latvia. 'Hand in hand with poor quality translations of the EU directives, this has actually created many unnecessary problems for entrepreneurs in Latvia', argues the representative of a business association, again bringing up the question of competencies, political will and trust between entrepreneurs and policy makers. What is the reason for this? According to the representative of one of the leading business support organizations in Latvia, especially right before and also after accession to the EU, it was frequently the case that the creation of a new bureaucratic or administrative burden was justified by policy makers as requirements from the EU. 'In many cases it was actually less of an EU requirement than the inability to understand what a particular EU directive actually implies', he continues. 'It is not only a question of understanding the recommendation status of the directives, but also of being aware of the extent to which we need this "safety". For example, if the EU recommends minimum requirements regarding the smoking of fish, we see that in Scandinavia people still follow their traditions by exceeding these recommendations many times. The question arises as to why Latvia should then adjust to all of these recommendations.'

Apart from improvements in the legal framework, as confirmed by policy makers, accession to the EU in many ways increased the possibilities of *cooperating with companies on an international scale* and opened new, attractive markets. Entrepreneurs in Latvia also faced challenges brought on by increasing competition resulting from companies from other EU markets entering Latvia. According to the representatives of policy makers, business support organizations and business associations in Latvia, it is still too early to come to any conclusions as to whether these processes fostered or actually damaged the entrepreneurial climate in Latvia. All agree, however, that not only the initiatives and strong positions of the Latvian government but also the ability and creativity of local entrepreneurs play a major role in this regard, as emphasized by one of the representatives of policy makers; 'Entrepreneurs not only have to take advantage of but also avoid threats brought by the EU.'

Apart from the laws and regulations mentioned above, an increasing number of policy planning and strategic documents have been introduced recently with the aim of improving the entrepreneurship environment in the country. Arguably, not without the influence of these efforts, Latvia, with a population of 2.3 million inhabitants, had approximately 86000 legally registered, active enterprises in 2009 (http://www.lursoft. lv). Furthermore, as illustrated by Figure 5.1, with the exception of a downturn from 2008 onwards, influenced by the worldwide financial crisis, nascent entrepreneurship shows an overall positive tendency in the country by continuously increasing since 2002. A similar tendency can be observed also with regard to other indicators in Latvia since 1994. For instance, by the end of 2005, Latvia's gross domestic product (GDP) per capita reached 11962 USD with almost constant growth in real GDP since 1995 and an increase in the private sector share of GDP from 55 per cent in 1994 to 70 per cent in 2005 (EBRD 2005). Regardless of these positive figures, however, even during the steady economic growth in 2007 Latvia still lagged behind most EU countries both in terms of GDP per capita and the number of registered businesses per 1000 inhabitants (both approximately 40 per cent of the EU average, http://www.lursoft.lv).

In this light it could thus be appropriate to ask how efficient the measures undertaken by the actors shaping the entrepreneurship climate in Latvia have been. The question arises as to how various factors, including mentalities and mindsets of policy makers, civil servants, and business organizations, the overall technical capacity of the state as well as mechanisms for the communication between government, business promotion organizations and entrepreneurs influence the contents and the application of these policy measures. These issues are explored in the following sections.

EXPLORING MAJOR CHALLENGES FOR THE DEVELOPMENT AND IMPLEMENTATION OF ENTREPRENEURSHIP POLICIES

Creating an Enabling Business Environment

When it comes to addressing the challenges of entrepreneurship policy making practices in Latvia, the very first and foremost problem emerging from the interviews refers to formal institutions, for example to the legal framework established to regulate and promote entrepreneurship in the country. More specifically, as highlighted by all interviewees, although being constantly reviewed, there are still simply too many laws, regulations and programmes even after accession to the EU to regulate the entrepreneurship climate in the country. The overall situation is well illustrated by the representative of the major business support organization in Latvia who stated that: 'Entrepreneurs are tired of all these documents, aimed at promoting their businesses. Who can follow all of them, not to mention understand how they may be interrelated, which is often the case . . . I can tell you that even business organizations do not have enough strength to deal with this issue', he concludes. Several explanations were provided by interviewees when asked what, in their opinion, could be the main reasons for such, in their view, major shortcomings in the legal framework. One group, not surprisingly mostly consisting of representatives of business associations as well as business support organizations, pointed to the *inefficient work of policy makers*. For example, as argued by several interviewees, all of whom preferred to stay anonymous, policy makers in Latvia tend to create entrepreneurship support programmes even though it is clear that most of them will never become established. One of the reasons for this is the lack of financing to implement these programmes, but 'even if there is money available or at least the potential to attract funding, it is quite often the case that processes stop because of a lack of political will. Thus many good plans remain only on paper', states the representative of one of the leading business support organizations in Latvia.

Interestingly enough, a few representatives from public organizations such as interviewees from the Ministry of Economics of Latvia admitted that it is quite often the case that 'political games' overshadow the interests of promoting entrepreneurship in Latvia. Thus, it should come as no surprise that one interviewee from the Ministry of Economics stated: 'Even today many entrepreneurs do not believe that somebody, including the government, can help them and so they actually rely only on their own efforts.' On the other hand, the question has to be raised whether it really can be the case that all efforts on the part of policy makers, resulting in various laws, regulations and programmes to promote entrepreneurship during various transition stages, have no value to entrepreneurs? Previous research pointed out that although support programmes cannot be treated as a single group as differences regarding the aims and thus also expected benefits should be distinguished, the value entrepreneurs receive through entrepreneurship support programmes or new laws and legislation in general consists of both primary and secondary benefits (Chrisman and McMullan 2002; Wood 1999). The primary benefits are 'direct revenue gains', including increase in profits or turnover, for example. Secondary benefits, on the other hand, include taxes paid by entrepreneurs or employment generated as a result of the promotion programmes or laws and legislation (Chrisman and McMullan 2002). Research has argued that entrepreneurs will usually value those policy measures which bring direct value and will not care too much about secondary benefits (Chrisman and McMullan 2002), regardless of the fact that primary and secondary benefits are actually closely correlated (Davidsson 2004). In this context, since the number of entrepreneurs has more or less constantly increased during the process of transition, one could argue that the policy makers' efforts to foster an entrepreneurial climate in Latvia by introducing laws, regulations and various programmes have brought important value to entrepreneurs in terms of both primary and secondary benefits. The data from our interviews, however, suggests that entrepreneurs during the period when interviews were conducted were not happy with these support measures. Why is that the case?

Although the answer seems to be quite complex, a number of arguments expressed by entrepreneurship support organizations and leading business associations highlight that entrepreneurs do not link their success with the actions undertaken by policy makers. As emphasized, for example, by one of the representatives from leading industry associations, 'the government of Latvia has become very good at writing plans. Unfortunately, for some reason, most of those plans are declarative by nature and do not bring much value for the entrepreneurs. Because of this, entrepreneurs often see policy makers as "composers", describing positive and negative tendencies in entrepreneurship, making plans for the unforeseeable future at the same time without much involvement in solving problems which are actually faced by entrepreneurs.'

Apart from the policy makers' intentions to develop appropriate entrepreneurship policies in Latvia, many of the interviewees expressed doubts also towards the policy makers' competencies. As argued by one of the interviewees representing a business support organization: 'I am not sure whether there is consensus in the government about what has to be done in order to promote entrepreneurship in Latvia, and I am talking about cooperation between various ministries involved in the process.' 'Yes, there has been progress in recent years in this regard', admits another interviewee, mentioning working groups which have recently been organized in different ministries of Latvia, working closely with experts in a specific field when particular problems are addressed. 'Still', he continues, 'I am not sure whether policy makers in general understand what is happening in entrepreneurship so there is no illusion that they could come up with something meaningful as a result.'

Adjusting Mindsets and Attitudes

Apart from the above mentioned challenges with formal institutions, the role of informal institutions as well as conflicts between formal and informal institutions (North 1990) was also emphasized by the interviewees. To be more specific, many interviewees, mostly from business associations, referred to *'shortcomings' in the norms and values* of policy makers, pointing out that even in cases where the appropriate legal framework is in place, problems often arise because of the implementation of these laws or regulations.

In this light, policy makers themselves admit the problem arguing that 'unfortunately it is still not uncommon that regardless of the time and resources invested in development of regulations and business promotion mechanisms, there are sometimes challenges faced at the administration and implementation level'. The tax collection mechanism in Latvia, for example, is a good example for challenges faced by entrepreneurs in other areas. That is, referring to the problem from the policy makers' standpoint, the whole tax collection and business monitoring mechanism in Latvia is oriented towards punishment rather than the education of entrepreneurs. 'This, of course, is a very negative aspect,' says one of the interviewees, pointing out that 'the problem here is that it is very easy to control and thus, punish, the "fair" entrepreneurs in Latvia. After all they report all their income and provide all required statements. With illegal business it is much more difficult,' he continues, adding that 'monitoring organizations actually are not even aware of the activities illegal entrepreneurs conduct and often lack the resources to trace them.' As a consequence, the willingness to 'fight against evil' by punishing legal deviations, but thus creating new (legal) barriers, fees and other burdens, makes life more difficult for honest entrepreneurs, without much influence on the illegal entrepreneurs who are usually 'creative enough' in finding new ways around these burdens. But knowing the extent of the grey and illegal business in Latvia, we can only imagine what disadvantages all this might bring and most probably is bringing to the country. 'So perhaps it is time to change the mindset for the benefit of everyone, starting with trusting entrepreneurs and thus also fostering entrepreneurs' trust towards policy makers?' asks another interviewee.

Furthermore, highlighting the role of entrepreneurs themselves in shaping the business environment, most interviewees also emphasized that it is actually meaningful to implement various business support programmes and offer funds for business activities, even if only a limited number of people take advantage of this opportunity. As argued by a representative of the SME Council, for example, on the one hand it is, of course, important for the policy makers to know whether they want flourishing entrepreneurship in the country. On the other hand, the general public also have to be aware of their interest in becoming entrepreneurs. For instance, a representative from the financial sector claimed that: 'It is really meaningless to expect government or banks to discover new talents and promote high-growth, value added entrepreneurship. Come with your ideas, develop competitive enterprises and fight for the opportunities yourselves!' he concludes. 'Entrepreneurs often lack education and are not always willing to learn and develop business management, economic and juridical skills', he continues. In this light, from the business support organizations' viewpoint, not only does the lack of experience and motivation on the part of entrepreneurs play a role. Even more important, becoming an entrepreneur is still far from prestigious in Latvia. 'Unfortunately people have a tendency to study, get an education and then do "something for a living" by working for someone else,' says one of the interviewees, adding that 'this phenomena can be explained by a mentality which is partly based on the fact that people in Latvia still hold old fashioned beliefs, a heritage from Soviet times, namely that somebody will solve their problems for them', thus pointing to the need to also adapt prevailing norms and values to the requirements of a market economy (for example Aidis 2006).

'Regarding the awareness of entrepreneurs, we have had several rather sad cases', continues the representative of the SME Council. 'For example, in one Latvian town we met with a nice couple that produces high quality wooden toys for kids. Being unemployed, instead of making a business out of this activity, they are still doing this on the "hobby level" for the reason that they are afraid to start a business', she explains. Arguably, this example points to the conclusion that, apart from developing complicated programmes, a focus on fostering an entrepreneurial spirit, especially in the countryside, is of great importance. In this light, many interviewees emphasize the role of the education system, agreeing on the necessity of developing entrepreneurial thinking already in kindergartens and continuing this process throughout higher education.

To sum up, using the words of the policy makers themselves, in this case the representative of the Ministry of Economics of Latvia: 'Lots of resources are involved, different plans, policy documents and also money is spent – this should be more than enough for any entrepreneur to be happy.' Interestingly enough, the same person admits that the 'main problem, however, seems to be with the exchange of information between the government and entrepreneurs when it comes to the engagement and consultation and this is something that needs to be solved as soon as possible'. He also asks rhetorically: 'After all, what is the sense in spending tax payers' money to develop different programmes and get access to financing possibilities, when those at which all these actions are aimed do not have enough information about all these activities?'

The next section will assess the challenges of policy making practices in Latvia, focusing on interactions between entrepreneurs and policy makers in terms of information exchange and consultations.

EXPLORING INTERACTIONS BETWEEN ENTREPRENEURS AND POLICY MAKERS

As highlighted by a representative from the Latvian Academy of Science: 'Problems in communication start when one of the sides does not follow either legal or ethical rules. Unfortunately, in Latvia often policy makers are to be blamed in this regard.' Since exchange of the information is a twofold process, the question, however, arises as to whether the entire responsibility falls onto the policy makers. After all, by introducing a variety of programmes and policy documents for the development of the entrepreneurial climate in Latvia, we can argue with certainty that policy makers have prepared a message to entrepreneurs. But is this message understood, and, has it been sent to the right target audience? Or could it also be that the target audience is not always willing to listen to the message?

Referring back to the discussion in the previous section which high-lighted the entrepreneurs' disbeliefs towards policy makers' intentions and competencies, the *issue of trust* comes up not only when the benefits of regulations and programmes aimed to promote entrepreneurship develop-ment are assessed, but also in the context of exploring the consultation and engagement patterns between two sides. Various forms of trust exist, including personal, collective and institutional trust. Moreover, all these types of trust are determined by the interaction between formal and infor-mal institutions within a given context (Welter et al. 2004). Institutional trust is of major importance when it comes to the formation of formal institutions (Raiser 1999; Welter et al. 2004). However, formal institutions need to be accepted by society and should not conflict with general norms and values. If this is not the case, weak levels of institutional trust not only enhance illegal and shadow activities (Welter and Smallbone 2006), but may also reduce the level of entrepreneurial activity and companies' growth in general (North 1990). In such cases, personal trust often substi-tutes for institutional trust, which may have a negative impact on changes required in informal institutions. This is certainly of major importance for governments attempting to install consultation mechanisms with entre-preneurs. So what are the major problems and challenges both sides face in this regard?

As emphasized by a number of business associations, one of the major engagement problems seems to be that even in cases when official infor-mation reaches the entrepreneurs, very often it is already 'deformed'. According to policy makers, this in turn could be the fault of both inex-perienced clerks and business associations. 'Nowadays, when there is so much information available everywhere, all information should be tar-geted to the right people at the right time and, even more importantly, in the right format, which very often is a big problem', says a representative of the Ministry of Economics of Latvia. 'Maybe we should have more spe-cialists dealing with consultation and engagement here in the government to control the situation?', he adds.

When asked about the role of business support organizations and associations in fostering interactions between policy makers and entrepre-neurs, many associations admit that they could work harder to ensure this. The Association of Construction Contractors, for example, emphasizes the lack of a unified system in business support as one of the problems. Namely, there are more than 60 different associations representing various industries and sectors, but 'some of these associations consist only of two or three members, some are established with a purpose to lobby their busi-ness interests in a way that can actually harm the sector. Even though the SME and Craft Council was established with the purpose of representing all associations on the institutional and government level, this system is not always efficient, especially with regard to communication,' concludes a representative of the association.

Furthermore, as emphasized by the Latvian Chamber of Commerce and Industry as well as a representative of the Ministry of Economics of Latvia, associations very often do not represent more than 20 to 30 per cent of companies from one industry and only 20 to 30 per cent of those companies play an active role in their associations. Indeed, most of the interviewees representing business organizations admitted that they would like to see much more activity from their members. As highlighted by the Latvian Chamber of Commerce and Industry, almost all companies sooner or later complain about their unsolved problems and are waiting for someone who will solve them. 'When asked to summarise their main problems and send us the summary within ten days so that we can further plan our activities to improve the situation, we rarely receive anything,' he continues, concluding that 'this is why in business promotion you cannot really rely on direct feedback from companies facing actual problems. It is more the art of guessing on the basis of intuition and practice you have acquired yourself.' In the light of the latter comment, it might thus be advisable for business support organizations to follow a more proactive approach in building evidence based policies and support.

The lack of activity from entrepreneurs and shortcomings in the performance of associations and business promotion organizations are far from being the only problems with regard to interactions between policy makers and entrepreneurs. As emphasized by the Latvian Chamber of Commerce and Industry, the Information Technology and Telecommunication Association as well as the Association of Textile and Clothing, consultation with entrepreneurs is difficult because of inadequate actions from the government side. For example, it is rather common that business associations receive a request for comments on legislative documents only one or two days before the deadline. 'It is thus not possible to get professional feedback from member organizations, of course', highlights a representative of one of those associations, arguing that both lack of experience and professionalism from the side of government, and maybe also their general attitude, can be a major problem in this regard. The representative of the Ministry of Economics of Latvia admits this 'answer-in-one-day-request' problem and suggests that associations should be more active themselves in representing the interests of their members, for example in checking the web for new legislative documents which are currently in discussion. 'Ministries are very often overloaded with work and do not have enough resources – this is one of the main reasons why such a situation arises,' he explains. Obviously, there is a lack of mutual understanding between entrepreneur and government, which seems to be a much bigger problem than expected before conducting these interviews.

More specifically, both sides admit that very often they do not understand (and maybe also do not know) what is going on in the other 'camp'. This is a problem that seems to characterize all communication between policy makers and entrepreneurs and certainly does not foster an increase in trust on both sides. One of the reasons for this, as argued by a representative of the Latvian Investment and Development Agency, is that most policy makers have never worked in the private sector and vice versa. In the context of this discussion, as emphasized earlier in the chapter, entrepreneurs often claim that they do not have any trust in the qualification of persons involved in business promotion. No wonder we have quotes coming from entrepreneurs such as 'Those students working for the government cannot actually understand the problems of entrepreneurs, much less how to solve them.'

It should also be mentioned that the consultation and engagement issue is even more dramatic in the regions of Latvia because of a deficient communication infrastructure. As emphasized, for example, by the Trade Association, 'A lot of companies outside Riga do not have email and Internet connection in general and thus are often difficult to reach.' This is an even bigger problem, as both government and associations admit that most communication nowadays is through Internet and email. Communication problems with and in regions are emphasized also by the Investment and Development Agency of Latvia, arguing that 'Often it seems like a lot of information does not reach entrepreneurs. Possibly, the problem is within the associations – very often there are people who do not have enough communication with companies in industry, especially in the regions.'

In the light of this discussion, representatives of the government agree that there are indeed too many obstacles and burdens for both nascent entrepreneurship and business development in Latvia, although they claim that a lot of effort is made to overcome these: 'The lack of seed capital and the availability of information are only a couple of important aspects which need to be improved in this regard . . . Still . . .' this interviewee continues, 'not everything is so bad as sometimes expressed by entrepreneurs – a lot of things have been done in Latvia in the past 20 years and nobody can say this is not true.' In particular, as argued by most of the interviewees, and emphasized previously in the chapter, EU accession process has played a significant role, shaping the environment for entrepreneurship development and policy making practices in Latvia.

CONCLUSIONS

In the light of the above discussion it should be highlighted that although most of the problems described below still hold true, at the time this chapter was written (2009), new challenges for entrepreneurship policy making occurred in Latvia. The major reason for that is the sharp economic downturn in the country influenced by the financial crisis in Europe and the US. Still, when comparing Latvia with neighbouring countries, such as Lithuania or Estonia, (which are comparably better off but had very similar starting points and development paths over the past 15 years) questions relating to the efficiency of political actors shaping the economic and political situation in the country arise. This demonstrates the non-linear nature of transition process by highlighting the important role of the state in shaping the business environment.

In a rather short period of time Latvia has achieved remarkable progress in economic development and the development of entrepreneurship in particular. Still, when listening to statements such as 'entrepreneurs often do not take the programmes and policy documents seriously, saying that they do not believe in the government's interest in promoting their business', we have to conclude that a lot of effort is still needed in order to promote an entrepreneurial climate in Latvia. Improvements in the legal framework might still be necessary, but the results also illustrate a serious need for a change in mindsets, attitudes and the culture of the Latvian people, both entrepreneurs and policy makers. In this regard, one policy suggestion comes from the Association of Traders, which argues that 'Apart from continuous improvements through legislation, including taxes, mentalities have to be changed according to the requirements of the relatively new markets conditions. In Latvia, people are usually afraid of the risk and do not always know how to work in teams, which comes from the fact that the older generation in particular has never been taught, for instance, to become entrepreneurs. There is a tendency that the new generation is changing in this regard.' This confirms the necessity of educating future entrepreneurs from an early age. Altogether, however, the interviewees indirectly point to the often conflicting formal and informal institutions (North 1990) which seem to be a serious challenge even during an advanced stage of transition in Latvia.

Furthermore, as emphasized by the representative of the Academy of Sciences of Latvia, the major problem with entrepreneurs in general in Latvia is that when starting a business they do not have a vision about the future. 'Companies do not know whether they want to remain small, become middle-sized or perhaps grow to large internationals. In each stage there are different requirements and also policy makers can provide support in a number of ways. But this support, regardless of whether we are talking about financial assistance or the provision of specific knowledge necessary for business development, should come as a consequence of previous achievements.' Still, not everything can be achieved by entrepreneurs themselves, and there are a number of ways in which policy makers can support them. But what support do entrepreneurs need? According to representatives of business support organizations and associations, they do not need much.

First, the lack of appropriate education is emphasized and in the light of the arguments expressed previously in the chapter, we are talking about the necessity to improve the education system. If more entrepreneurship is better for the country (Reynolds et al. 2005), perhaps more entrepreneurship-related education, including teaching the basics of entrepreneurship to engineers, chemists, artists and people from other professions, could help. Secondly, successful entrepreneurship activities face difficulties if there is no market for products and services. In this light, policy makers could assist local entrepreneurs in their efforts to enter new markets. And we are not talking about the organization of trade fairs and international meetings; the issue is much deeper than that. Apart from investing in the development of a 'Latvia brand', thus promoting the recognition of Latvia across its borders, government should also promote competitiveness through focusing on fostering innovations in products and services, research and development, specific and unique knowledge developed as a result of successful interaction between educational and research institutes and entrepreneurs. Hand in hand with support for expansion in the international markets, it is also important to provide general assistance for investments, regardless of whether a company is locally or internationally oriented. This is especially important for small companies, in particular those in peripheral regions, that are willing to grow; and it could in fact help reduce shadow and illegal activities (Baumol 1990). For example, a small company can use 'under-the-table money' to buy a sewing machine for manufacturing purposes, but if such investment in manufacturing was tax deductible, companies would be more willing to report such investments as well as the resources necessary to acquire them.

Furthermore, as highlighted throughout the chapter, the engagement and consultation process between policy makers and entrepreneurs needs to be improved. This also includes ensuring that entrepreneurs perceive policy makers as partners in developing their businesses and trust that policy makers 'really care' and are able to help. In this regard, a better understanding of the diverse challenges faced by entrepreneurs through their involvement in the various stages of the policy making process is recommended. Furthermore, investment in academic and applied research in order to get a more in-depth picture with regard to various aspects of entrepreneurship promotion can only help. At least the experience from 'old EU' countries shows that these efforts create positive output: the 'reward' will be more competitive products representing Latvia on the international arena as well as new jobs, possibly also reducing migration from Latvia to 'old EU' countries.

And finally, as mentioned earlier, one of the problems still unsolved in Latvia is the huge difference in entrepreneurship activities across regions. More specifically, as many as one third of all companies are located in the capital city of Latvia, Riga, with some regions having very low entrepreneurship rates. Negative tendencies can also be observed with regard to the regional development of entrepreneurship. For example, as the entrepreneurial activity in Riga increased by approximately ten entrepreneurs per 1000 inhabitants from 1999 to 2004, the increase outside of Riga was only by about two entrepreneurs (http://www.lursoft.lv). In this light, it would be appropriate to actively continue work on establishing the appropriate infrastructure, including better quality roads and the general business support infrastructure, and on supporting education centres in the regions. These activities in turn could help to attract investments, for example, from large multinationals interested in establishing a factory – and although they are still uncommon, there are already success stories in this regard in Latvia.

To sum up, considerable effort has been made both by policy makers and society in general during the last 20 years. As exemplified by this chapter, however, it is too early to rest on the previous achievements as a number of problems desperately need serious attention both from policy makers and entrepreneurs themselves. Our interviews suggest that in order to solve these problems, it is of crucial importance for policy makers and entrepreneurs to critically assess their existing norms and values. After this, perhaps it would also help policy makers to think about what it is like to be an entrepreneur and vice versa, and to start developing communication based on these conclusions. After all, communication is a tool which can help solve various problems. In this light, we should hope for consistency, persistence, mutual understanding, tolerance and above all, the best of luck to both sides.

NOTES

1. 'Knightian uncertainty' and 'framework uncertainty' are two major forms of uncertainty characterizing transition countries. While Knightian uncertainty is associated with unpredictability about the future, framework uncertainty arises as a consequence of the collapse of previous legal framework (Aidis 2006). In this light, as Earle and Sakova have

noted, 'It is difficult to imagine a regime more hostile towards entrepreneurship than the centrally planned economies of Eastern Europe' (2001, p. 6).
2. See Aidis and Sauka (2005) for an overview.
3. These include the Law on Individual (Family) Business, Farms or Fishing Companies and Individual Work (1992), the Law on Limited Liability Companies (1991), the Law on Joint Stock Companies (1993), the Law on Co-operatives (1991), the Law on Government Companies (end of 1990), the Law on Company Register (end of 1990) and a few others.
4. Latvian Chamber of Commerce and Industry (LCCI) is a non-governmental, voluntary organization uniting approximately 800 Latvian companies. The organization aims to create a favourable business environment by representing the interests of Latvia's entrepreneurs and offering business promotion services. LCCI represents business interests through a dialogue with national and local governments and participates in the drafting of commercial legislation in Latvia (see http://www.chamber.lv/en for more information).
5. The Investment and Development Agency of Latvia (LIAA) is a state institution reporting to the Ministry of Economy of Latvia. While focusing on promoting business development and competitiveness of Latvian companies, LIAA acts as one of the institutions implementing state support programmes, advancing grants to entrepreneurs to increase their competitiveness. LIAA is also involved in the implementation of national programmes on export and innovation promotion (see http://www.liaa.gov.lv for more information).
6. The Latvian Technological Center (LTC) is an innovation and technology-oriented business support structure aiming to stimulate emergence and growth of knowledge-based SMEs in Latvia by promoting relationships between research and industry as well as encouraging SMEs for transnational cooperation. LTC was founded in 1993 by Riga City Council, Latvian Academy of Sciences, Institute of Physical Energetics and Latvian National Society for Quality (see http://www.innovation.lv for more information).
7. The introduction of Commercial Law in early 2002 has to be mentioned as the most important amongst those activities.

REFERENCES

Aidis, R. (2006), *Laws and Customs: Entrepreneurship, Institutions and Gender During Transition*, SSEES Occasional Series, London: University College London.
Aidis, R. and A. Sauka (2005), 'Entrepreneurship in a changing environment: analyzing the impact of transition stages on SME development', in F. Welter (ed.), *Challenges in Entrepreneurship and SME Research*, Inter-RENT 2005 online-publication, available at http://www.ecsb.org, pp. 5–36.
Baumol, W. (1990), 'Entrepreneurship: productive, unproductive and destructive', *Journal of Political Economy*, 98, 893–921.
Chrisman, J. and W. McMullan (2002), 'Some additional comments on the sources and measurement of the benefits of small business assistance programs', *Journal of Small Business Management*, **40** (1), 43–50.
Davidsson, P. (2004), *Researching Entrepreneurship*, New York: Springer.
Earle, J. and Z. Sakova (2001), 'Entrepreneurship from Scratch', IZA discussion paper No. 79, Bonn: Institute for the Study of Labour.
European Bank for Reconstruction and Development (1995), *Transition Report 1995*, London: EBRD.
European Bank for Reconstruction and Development (2005), *Transition Report 2005*, London: EBRD.
Kuzmina, I. (1999), 'Economic and social aspects of entrepreneurship in Latvia during transition to the market economy', Doctoral Dissertation (in Latvian), University of Latvia.

North, D. (1990), *Institutions, Institutional Change, and Economic Performance*, Cambridge: Cambridge University Press.

Raiser, M. (1999), 'Trust in transition', European Bank of Reconstruction and Development working paper No 39, London: EBRD, available at http://www.ebrd.org.

Reynolds, P., R. Thurik, A. van Stel and S. Wennekers (2005), 'Nascent entrepreneurship and the level of economic development', *Small Business Economics*, 24, 293–309.

Sauka, A. and F. Welter (2010), 'Business insolvencies in Latvia', TeliaSonera Institute Discussion Paper No. 7. Riga: Stockholm School of Economics.

Smallbone, D. and F. Welter (2001), 'The distinctiveness of entrepreneurship in transition economies', *Small Business Economics*, **16** (4), 249–62.

Smallbone, D. and F. Welter (2006), 'Conceptualising entrepreneurship in a transition context', *International Journal of Entrepreneurship and Small Business*, **3** (2), 190–206.

Smallbone, D. and F. Welter (2009), *Entrepreneurship and Small Business Development in Post-Socialist Economies*, Routledge Studies in Small Business, London and New York: Routledge.

Van de Mortel, E. (2002), *An Institutional Approach to Transition Processes*, Hants, UK: Ashgate.

Welter, F. and D. Smallbone (2006), 'Exploring the role of trust for entrepreneurial activities', *Entrepreneurship Theory & Practice*, **30** (4), 465–75.

Welter, F., T. Kautonen, A. Chepurenko, E. Malieva and U. Venesaar (2004), 'Trust environments and entrepreneurial behavior – exploratory evidence from Estonia, Germany and Russia', *Journal of Enterprising Culture*, **12** (4), 327–49.

Wood, W. (1999), 'Benefit measurement for small business assistance: a further note on research and data collection', *Journal of Small Business Management*, **37** (1), 75–8.

Webpages

http://www.chamber.lv/en, accessed 10 March 2009.
http://www.innovation.lv, accessed 22 April 2009.
http://www.liaa.gov.lv, accessed 22 April 2009.
http://www.lursoft.lv, accessed 3 April 2009.

6 University-level entrepreneurship education in Poland[1]
Jerzy Cieślik

INTRODUCTION

The collapse of the Soviet bloc in the last decade of the twentieth century coincided with the global explosion in information and communication technologies (ICT), which has had a tremendous and widespread impact on virtually all spheres of human life. With respect to entrepreneurship, the ICT revolution has been reflected in the emergence of a dynamic, innovative segment within the traditional small business sector. Strong interrelationships between entrepreneurship, innovation and higher education are fundamental for achieving long-term socio-economic goals, so they have attracted the attention of policy makers.

In Central and Eastern Europe (CEE), particularly in Poland, the end of the twentieth century also brought a rapid expansion in the tertiary-level education sector. This chapter addresses the role of educational programmes in transition economies, as exemplified by Poland, in enhancing an entrepreneurial spirit among students and in developing the skills necessary for launching dynamic, knowledge-based businesses. As background, we outline key directions in entrepreneurship education at the university level in Poland after 1989. Next, we review principal lessons derived from teaching entrepreneurship in western (mostly US) academic institutions and then summarize our experiences in launching the 'Dynamic Entrepreneurship Programme' in Poland, which is aimed at accelerating entrepreneurship education at Polish universities. The succeeding section identifies barriers and success factors in launching entrepreneurship programmes at the university level in a transition context. Key findings and recommendations that can be particularly relevant for transition economies are summarized in the final section.

TRENDS IN ENTREPRENEURSHIP AND HIGHER EDUCATION IN POLAND AFTER 1989

The expansion of the private segment of the higher education system in Poland after 1990 has been equally dramatic as the growth of the small business sector. In 1990–91 there were 112 institutions of higher education, the vast majority of which were public, serving 404 000 students. By 2006–07 this number had increased to 455 institutions, with all but a few of the newly established institutions being private. The number of students reached 1 941 000 in 2006–07 and was 4.8 times higher than the number of students served in 1990–91. The increase in institutions of higher education helped to increase the very low scholarization index (gross) in tertiary education from 12.9 per cent in 1990–91 to 49.9 per cent in 2006–07, which is high even compared with the levels achieved by more mature economies (GUS 2008). The rapid expansion of the higher education sector in Poland reflected the unrealized demand for university-level education during the communist era, when a maximum quota for students in public universities was imposed. After 1990, not only the younger generations but also more mature people took advantage of the opportunity for higher education. Students correctly perceived earning a higher education diploma as the path to increasing employment opportunities and future incomes while, at the same time, entrepreneurial members of the academic community embarked on founding new private schools.

A particularly important development in entrepreneurship education in the Polish education system was the introduction of an obligatory course 'Basics of Entrepreneurship' in secondary schools in 2002. While its implementation has been hampered by a shortage of teachers with proper qualifications and attitudes, it opens the door for proactive teachers to implement additional initiatives aimed at building entrepreneurial spirit among students in the secondary schools. The institutions of higher education in Poland enjoy much greater freedom than do the secondary schools regarding the structure and content of courses offered; however, they must follow some specific guidelines outlined by the Ministry of Science and Higher Education. According to these guidelines, a course on entrepreneurship is obligatory in only one field of study, that is Management (for a detailed presentation see Wach 2008). Within their own jurisdictions, however, institutions of higher education have taken various measures to introduce entrepreneurship courses in their curricula. Among private business schools established during the 1990s, about 20 incorporated 'entrepreneurship' into their names, with a clear intention to emphasize their strategic orientation towards the small business sector.

Some of the public economic universities as well as the private business schools have introduced entrepreneurship as a specialization at the master level in the economics and management fields of study. However, such teaching initiatives have brought mixed results because of weaknesses in course designs and methodologies, leading to a declining trend in offering entrepreneurship courses in recent years. One of the weaknesses was that instruction more often dealt with entrepreneurship in the traditional small business environment, rather than stimulating entrepreneurial initiatives of students in the modern sectors of the economy.

Thus far, the initiatives to introduce entrepreneurship into the curricula of Polish higher education institutions have been almost exclusively confined to business schools and economic universities so, despite some shortcomings, those institutions have recognized the importance of the field. However, the hard sciences, technical, agricultural, medical disciplines, and so on are offered almost exclusively at public universities, where entrepreneurship courses were, until recently, almost non-existent. Therefore non-business universities became the primary domain of the 'Dynamic Entrepreneurship Programme' presented below.

WHAT CAN BE LEARNED FROM THE EXPERIENCES ACCUMULATED IN MATURE MARKET ECONOMIES

Although the origins of entrepreneurship education in the US can be traced back to the nineteenth century (Katz 2003, Kuratko 2005), its widespread presence in university-level institutions is more recent, encompassing only the last 30 years. Lessons derived from the accumulated experiences of teaching entrepreneurship courses relate to the overall role of education within the broader framework of academic entrepreneurship, the course content and teaching methodologies.

(Entrepreneurship) Education Within a Broader Framework of Academic Entrepreneurship

Entrepreneurship education must be viewed as an integral part of a broader effort to promote and support academic entrepreneurship initiatives, not only by academic staff but also by students and graduates. This approach is illustrated in Figure 6.1. Various entrepreneurship courses available to all students form the base for more advanced support measures for smaller groups with specific interest in and drive towards entrepreneurship. These measures include participation of industry representatives in the teaching process, coaching and counselling, networking with the business community, and pre-incubation and incubation of entrepreneurial ventures. The most advanced level – academic entrepreneurship per se, which involves support measures addressed to academic staff – requires assistance in resolving intellectual property issues, setting up spin-off/spin-out companies, facilitating access to financing, and so on.

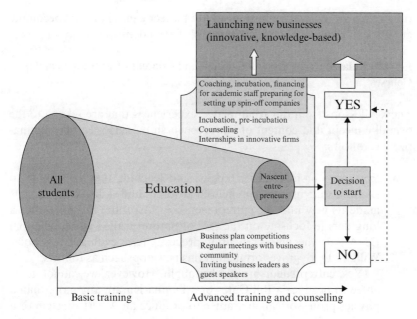

Launching new businesses (innovative, knowledge-based)

Coaching, incubation, financing for academic staff preparing for setting up spin-off companies

Incubation, pre-incubation
Counselling
Internships in innovative firms

All students

Education

Nascent entre-preneurs

YES

Decision to start

NO

Business plan competitions
Regular meetings with business community
Inviting business leaders as guest speakers

Basic training   Advanced training and counselling

Source: Author.

Figure 6.1   Education within a broader framework of academic entrepreneurship

Such an integrated framework provides for positive synergies and efficient allocation of resources. The education programmes, which are relatively less expensive than the advanced support measures, are addressed
to a broad student base. Smaller groups presenting the most promising
business ideas shall qualify for more sophisticated and costly support.
Those students who eventually become members of academic staff or enter
PhD programmes will be much better equipped to launch ambitious start-
ups. The proposed approach also calls for broadening the definition of
expected outcomes, since success in the field of academic entrepreneurship
is typically measured by the number of spin-off/spin-out companies by
academic staff and the number of student firms established in incubators.
However, a capable student who takes a high-quality entrepreneurship
course seldom seeks additional support but goes directly into business,
sometimes after first taking employment for a short period in order to
gain useful experience, obtain industry contacts, and to earn some start-up
capital. Identifying such instances in order to measure the course's impact
may not be easy in a university context because it requires close links with
the alumni. The effort is worth undertaking, however, as the alumni who

run their own innovative businesses are perfect candidates for becoming guest speakers and serving as role models for students.

Lessons Related to the Overall Concept and Content of Entrepreneurship Courses

The key lessons from the accumulated experiences that are related to the overall concept and content of entrepreneurship courses can be summarized as follows:

- Entrepreneurship can be taught, and teaching may contribute to shaping students' entrepreneurial attitudes and skills. This view has made its way into the entrepreneurship literature, but only after a long debate focusing on the role of natural traits ('entrepreneurial DNA') in the entrepreneurial process. The leading US scholar William D. Bygrave formulated this new approach as follows:

  'Yes, entrepreneurship can be taught. However, we cannot guarantee to produce a Bill Gates or a Donna Karan, any more than a physics professor can guarantee to produce an Albert Einstein or a tennis coach a Serena Williams. But give us students with the aptitude to start a business, and we will make them better entrepreneurs.' (Bygrave 2004, p. 2)

- Entrepreneurship is predominantly reflected in the launching of new businesses. Distinct features of the start-up process and the early expansion stage justify focussing on this phase while teaching entrepreneurship.[2] However, launching a new business is a much broader concept than merely the registration of a new business establishment. It starts with the identification and evaluation of business opportunities, the most promising of which are developed in the form of business plans, although not all of these will come to fruition, and leads finally to the implementation of a business plan.

- Entrepreneurship is not only for business students but is also appropriate for non-business students, such as those in engineering, the natural sciences, medical fields, and the arts. This view contradicts the still frequently prevailing view, particularly in Europe, that entrepreneurship should be confined to business studies. The apparent success of many US technology, agricultural and medical universities in running such courses and promoting entrepreneurial attitudes among their students has paved the way for new policy measures in the European Union. The set of initiatives launched recently by the European Commission focuses specifically on entrepreneurial education within non-business studies (European Commission 2008).

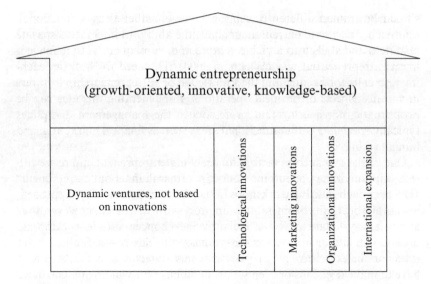

Source: Author.

Figure 6.2 Dimensions of dynamic entrepreneurship

- The pursuit of dynamic (high-potential, ambitious) entrepreneurship should be seen as a distinct segment calling for different teaching concepts and methodologies, as compared to the majority of start-ups in the traditional small business sector, with no plans to grow (Shane 2008, p. 7). Dynamic, growth-oriented undertakings typically account for a few per cent of new businesses and they seldom exceed 10 per cent of business start-ups (Autio 2007). It is important to attract university-level students to starting more ambitious ventures where they can use the knowledge and skills they acquire during the course of their studies. This approach is particularly relevant in Europe, where there is a traditional focus on small business training (Wilson 2004). However, dynamic entrepreneurship should not be confined to high-tech businesses only; in fact, many successful dynamic ventures are not based on technological innovations (Bhide 2000, pp. 29–36). Figure 6.2 illustrates the concept of dynamic entrepreneurship.

Lessons Related to Teaching Methodologies

The most important conclusion derived from accumulated experiences of other countries is that entrepreneurs are different from managers and should be trained differently using a holistic, rather than a functional, approach. Successful entrepreneurs have the ability to integrate disparate resources and skills into a viable venture and, subsequently, to manage it in an entrepreneurial way (Wickham 2004). The need for holistic teaching also calls for broadening the knowledge of entrepreneurship lecturers in various aspects of business operations. Implementing this idea can be problematic, considering that professors in the management disciplines typically specialize within functional areas such as finance, marketing, and human resources.

One of the key success factors for teaching entrepreneurship rests with the adoption of the 'for entrepreneurship' rather than 'about entrepreneurship' approach. During workshops in the 'for entrepreneurship' approach, issues relating to the business start-up process are discussed; however, they almost always relate to the particular business concepts students elaborate on (individually or in small groups) outside the classroom. Students who take part in exercises, even if they are only didactic games, where they have to make decisions or even set up a real business will learn much more than those who passively listen to traditional classroom lectures (Solomon 2008; Wissema 2005).

Even from the accumulated teaching experiences, it is difficult to point out methods that are universally effective; instead, mixed methods and tools for teaching entrepreneurship have proven to be the most effective. Direct classroom sessions can be combined with web-based tools and supporting materials. However, the latter does not eliminate the 'paper' textbook. Direct contact with real business through, for example, inviting entrepreneurs as guest speakers and arranging visits to existing firms is also important.

THE 'DYNAMIC ENTREPRENEURSHIP PROGRAMME' IN POLAND

The initial impulse to implement the 'Dynamic Entrepreneurship Programme' (the Programme in the following) came from analysing the experiences and progress achieved by leading western universities in launching entrepreneurship education programmes for their students as outlined in the previous section. Given the present situation in Poland, it became clear that waiting for bottom-up initiatives by individual universities and lecturers would not yield meaningful progress in the short- or even mid-term toward the goal of catching up. There was a need for a nationwide coordinated effort similar to that undertaken in some western European countries, with the aim of narrowing the gap in entrepreneurship education between European institutions of higher learning and those in the US. Such nationwide initiatives have included, for example, the UK National Council for Graduate Entrepreneurship; the FGF, an association founded for the purpose of supporting entrepreneurship research and education in German-speaking Europe; the Danish IDEA Network; and the Öresund Entrepreneurship Academy, a Danish–Swedish cooperative project.

Key Features

An important feature of the Programme is its 'latecomer advantage' conceptual foundation (Veblen 1915), which seems to be particularly relevant to entrepreneurship education in an emerging economy that is undergoing systemic transformation. Being late and underdeveloped is obviously a disadvantage in most respects but, at the same time, the latecomer can learn from others' mistakes, assimilate best practices quickly, and make progress much faster than the leaders in a field were able to do. Entrepreneurship education in emerging economies can greatly benefit from accumulated know-how, particularly that from US academic institutions, about course content, teaching methodologies and tools. This dispersion of know-how has been greatly facilitated in a recent trend by leading academic institutions to make freely available via Internet their teaching materials, as illustrated by the MIT OpenCourseWare initiative (OCW, see http://ocw.mit.edu.pl).

The Programme is based on the principles of social entrepreneurship, that is, the achievement of important social objectives through proactive, innovative and risk-taking initiatives.[3] Although the Programme was designed from the beginning with a view to resolving the issue of insufficient entrepreneurship education at the country level, it was started on a smaller scale because it was an individual initiative. Once the key elements were implemented some governmental agencies and non-governmental organizations were approached to secure financing and establish collaborative links as a step to expanding the Programme.

The focus of the Programme is on non-business-oriented academic institutions, although entrepreneurship has typically been perceived as the domain of people with business education backgrounds. However, the actual experiences of successful entrepreneurs, particularly in the US, have proven that engineering or IT students are just as capable of starting successful businesses if their engineering background is strengthened by a broad and general understanding of certain business subjects, particularly marketing, finance, and legal issues, including IP protection.

Another important feature of the Programme is its network approach where, rather than waiting for each university to make individual efforts, the Programme established a nationwide network platform to provide tools and teaching materials for the accelerated implementation of entrepreneurship courses by educators from an array of academic institutions. Since 2007, a training the trainers' component has been added to the Programme. With the financial support of Poland's Ministry of Science and Higher Education, 20 entrepreneurship lecturers from polytechnics, universities, and agricultural schools received ongoing methodological support and training in launching pilot courses in entrepreneurship. Later, this training will constitute an integral part of the teaching curricula of participating academic institutions. In November 2008, a new grant was received from the Ministry of Science and Higher Education that will provide for the continuation and the formalization of the Polish Network of Academic Entrepreneurship Educators (Polish acronym: SEIPA). The financing for 2009 and 2010 provided ongoing support for the lecturers who were already part of the network, as well as training for 20 new lecturers who will then run pilot entrepreneurship courses for students in their universities. In addition, advanced courses on Technology Entrepreneurship for PhD students and academic staff will be launched in five academic institutions.

Tentative Results

Since the beginning of 2006, when the Programme became fully operational, our own experiences have added to those we accumulated from other countries. So far, the Programme has achieved the following results:

- Over 1600 students have been trained in entrepreneurship with the use of the methodology, tools, electronic platform and textbook developed within the framework of the programme.
- Pilot entrepreneurship courses have been launched in 25 institutions of higher education (mostly non-business) throughout Poland that did not have prior experience in teaching entrepreneurship.
- A network of lecturers from polytechnics, universities and agricultural schools has been firmly established. At present, there are some 50 members in the network.
- The accumulated teaching experiences facilitated the preparation of a modern-style textbook on *Dynamic Entrepreneurship: How to start your own business*, which was addressed primarily to the academic community and was published in 2006, with a second edition in 2008 (Cieślik 2008). The textbook and the dedicated portal 'http://www. cieslik.edu.pl', which offers supplementary materials and tools for

students, provided a new dimension to entrepreneurship education at the university level in Poland, which has traditionally concentrated on the management of the small business firms (Piasecki 2001, Targalski 2003).

- A separate portal SEIPA which is addressed to entrepreneurship educators (http://www.seipa.edu.pl), features teaching tips and materials for lecturers, serves as a database for teaching materials and cases, and provides a facility with which to run courses (blended learning) by lecturers from various universities who do not run their own websites. The SEIPA portal streamlines the exchange of experiences, materials, and other resources among lecturers who join the network.
- In addition to the basic course in entrepreneurship, new specialized educational initiatives have been developed. During 2006–07 an advanced programme was implemented for 120 students from 32 institutions of higher education, mostly non-business, in the central Mazovia region. In addition to training and advisory support, the students with the best business projects received 6000 € each. The project has been financed by the European Union (EU) Structural Funds. Thanks to financial support from the Foundation for Polish Science (FNP) in 2007, a pilot course on 'Technology Entrepreneurship' was conducted for PhD students from polytechnics and hard science departments from universities across Poland. The course was run twice more in 2008, with approximately 60 PhD students participating.

Lessons Learned from the Programme

The results achieved during the implementation process have generally confirmed the experiences accumulated from the academic institutions in the United States and Western Europe. In fact, one of the key issues was the apparent diversity of such experiences, particularly with respect to the variety of course offerings. In the Programme, the decision was made to offer only a limited number of courses, at least during the initial stage, in order to achieve scale economies and tangible results. Second, certain formal and organizational requirements must be taken into consideration, particularly those reflecting the Bologna System that defines the bachelor, master and PhD levels of tertiary education. Based on these prerequisites, the initial course offering promoted under the Programme framework consisted of three categories of entrepreneurship courses. The proposed positioning of each course, in line with the Bolonia System, is presented in Figure 6.3.

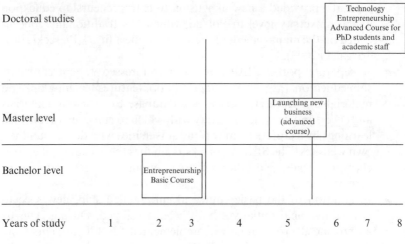

Source: Author.

Figure 6.3   Initial course offer in entrepreneurship for students and academic staff

The cornerstone of the entrepreneurship teaching is the basic course in entrepreneurship, which, following the recommendations of the European Commission (2008), should be included in the curricula relatively early in the study programmes – no later than the bachelor level. This basic course should provide students with a general understanding of the entrepreneurship and business start-up process, not necessarily with the objective of starting a new venture, but preparing students for such a career option.

The second, more advanced, course, 'Launching New Businesses', targets the master level, particularly last-year students who have plans to set up their own businesses. After intensive training and coaching, students present their business plans, and the most promising projects receive some financial support. Needless to say, securing that external funding is critical to the success of this course offering.

The most advanced course, 'Technology Entrepreneurship', is primarily addressed to academic staff and PhD students as a preparation for setting up spin-off companies. The programme is heavily blended with issues relevant to technology-based ventures. Additional funding is also crucial because, in addition to the lecturer, a professional consultant is also involved in the course implementation.

Another critical issue that had to be resolved was related to the use of specific teaching tools and materials, such as the choice of cases that are readily available through case repositories. Cases are widely used in teaching management disciplines in CEE business schools and economic universities. But the initial experiences with Western cases used for teaching entrepreneurship brought mixed results because students felt that these cases did not address the problems and business realities with which they are confronted. Consequently, we have compiled our own illustrative mini-cases that reflect the Polish business operating environment.

The idea of launching entrepreneurship courses in non-business fields, particularly engineering and hard sciences, proved to be particularly relevant in Poland. The students reacted very favourably, even though the courses offered were typically electives. However, implementing entrepreneurship programmes in non-business academic institutions involves deeper adjustments of attitudes and perceptions among students since many of them typically associate entrepreneurship with small businesses, which may be viewed as a less attractive career option for university graduates in non-business fields.

The reaction of PhD students to an advanced course in 'Technology Entrepreneurship' was also favourable; however, only a few participants embarked on launching spin-off companies, which was the key objective of the Programme funded by the Foundation for Polish Science (FNP). For most of the students, the course was their first encounter with marketing, financial and business issues in general, and it was too late in their academic careers to overcome technology-based rigidity in their overall thinking about the innovation process. This situation may change when future PhD students have the opportunity to enter the 'entrepreneurship funnel' at an earlier stage by taking the basic entrepreneurship course at the undergraduate level.

Some necessary changes to the content of basic entrepreneurship course in technical universities are also worth mentioning: While there are basic rules of starting a business which must be conveyed to all students, irrespective of their specialization, for engineering, IT, and hard science students, the course content should be blended towards their core subjects and should include topics such as:

- identifying business opportunities based on technological innovations
- characteristics of technology entrepreneurs and functioning of entrepreneurial teams
- financing of technology businesses, including venture capital
- marketing of innovative products and services
- intellectual property protection as a strategic business issue.

One important observation derived from the initial courses, which was, to some extent, transition-specific, was that students came to the workshops with the strong built-in perception of entrepreneurship as confined to small businesses and self-employment (under communism private businesses were allowed to operate, albeit on a very small scale). Therefore, the course laid substantial emphasis on building a 'think big' culture among students, even if they had planned business activities in the traditional sectors. In some cases, such efforts were quite rewarding. For example, a student of music who enrolled in a programme financed by the EU structural funds during 2006–07 planned to become a professional wedding consultant. In the course of training and with the assistance of a professional consultant, her initial single-outfit concept turned into a franchise network with six franchise units in major cities in Poland and one recently opened in London. Moreover, with the larger scale she was able to fully exploit her natural organizational and negotiating skills and her true talent in coping with media, which a smaller-scale operation would not have used to as great a degree.

Discussions and interviews with students also helped to modify the initial focus on the start-up phase only. Among Kozminski University students, approximately 20 per cent have family business traditions, yet few intend to work for their family businesses after graduation. Parents prefer that their children find a 'better life' by seeking employment in large banks, foreign-controlled corporations, consulting firms, and so on. The roots of this attitude originate in the particular characteristics of the transition process, specifically the hardships of and barriers to running one's own business during the 1990s. During that period, many firms with high growth potential scaled down their ambitions and remained very small. To address this issue, a new training and consultancy project idea has been developed called 'Accelerating growth of small family businesses', in which students, together with their entrepreneurial parents, attend a series of workshops and develop a restructuring plan for their businesses, supervised by a project leader and a professional consultant. The pilot implementation of this offspring of the Dynamic Entrepreneurship Programme began in autumn 2009.[4]

With respect to teaching methodologies, the 'for entrepreneurship' methodology proved to be particularly useful, as did mixing class workshops with web-based learning and a standard entrepreneurship textbook. The initial reaction of the lecturers who underwent training in using this methodology was somewhat restrained but, later, they found it much more effective and rewarding than the traditional classroom lecture approach.

One essential adjustment of the 'for entrepreneurship' methodology was intended to cope with the 'business plan obsession' that makes the preparation of a formal business plan document compulsory even if the business idea development did not justify it. For the course assessment, it is sufficient to elaborate a shorter document called the 'initial business concept'.

One surprising finding was that adopting the holistic approach to teaching entrepreneurship (that is, addressing issues pertaining to finance, legal aspects, marketing, human resource management, and so on in an integrated way) makes it more difficult to expand entrepreneurship training to state economic universities and private business schools. This is because a professor of economics or management, running this course in entrepreneurship and following the holistic way would need to take up subjects in which he or she does not specialize, which contradicts the principle of narrow specialization generally followed by the academic community in the management disciplines, both in research and teaching.

KEY BARRIERS AND SUCCESS FACTORS

Figure 6.4 presents the key success factors for launching entrepreneurship programmes at academic level. First, lecturers in entrepreneurship must themselves be 'entrepreneurial' in the sense that, in their teaching

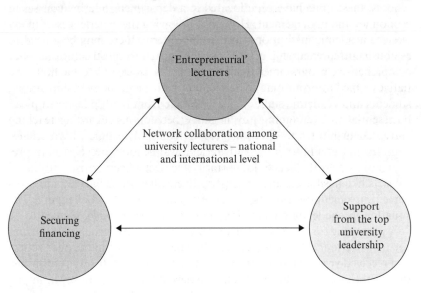

Source: Author.

Figure 6.4   *Accelerating entrepreneurship education at the academic level: key success factors*

activities, they are proactive and innovative, and are willing to accept some risks. In addition to a sound academic background, these lecturers need to have good relationships with students, along with the organizational skills that will help them with auxiliary support initiatives, like coaching, regular meetings with entrepreneurs and, at the advanced stage, setting up business incubators. Maintaining good relationships with the local business community is also of particular importance. The key barrier is that lecturers with the required skills and attitudes are rare in the academic community. Moreover, when they are occupied with assisting students in their business undertakings, inviting guest speakers and organizing business plan competitions and promotion events, they do not have much time left for the research and publication necessary for advancement up the academic career ladder. This is a widespread condition in many higher education institutions throughout Europe (European Commission 2008).

Second, the support of the top leadership of the institution is critical, particularly during the initial stages of the Programme because there are a number of sensitive issues, going beyond teaching as such, which are to be addressed. For example, the choice of the department in which the teaching unit offering entrepreneurship courses is located, can be a highly political decision. In the case of Polish polytechnics, universities, and agricultural schools, these units have been located in a department offering courses in economics and management. However, following the experiences of many western academic institutions, in the longer-term, there may be a need to establish entrepreneurship centres outside departmental structures to offer comprehensive programmes to all departments, as well as to facilitate initiatives aimed at promoting dynamic, innovative entrepreneurship among students and academic staff. A clear message from the top leadership can be essential to overcoming any negative perceptions regarding teaching entrepreneurship since, often, professors from polytechnics, hard science departments at universities, and agricultural schools perceive entrepreneurship as a 'soft' (hence, low-priority) subject in comparison to 'hard' subjects like mechanics and chemistry. Even when these barriers are overcome, implementation of the necessary changes can be challenging. The situation in one leading technology university, for example, seemed to be very promising for launching entrepreneurship courses throughout the university: a lecturer in entrepreneurship had been trained and the pilot course had received very high notes from the students. The Rector was enthusiastic and they were able to secure initial external financing. However, implementation has been delayed as a result of prolonged consultations with the deans of various departments where the courses were to be implemented.

The third key success factor relates to securing external financing for supporting entrepreneurship projects developed by students at the master level. This financing does not have to involve large amounts; for example, under a regional programme for 120 students and financed from EU Structural Funds, only 12 'finalists' obtained financial support amounting to 6000 € each. (Needless to say, this was a strong motivating factor for the students participating in the project.) For the 'training the trainers' component, the financing provided by the Polish Ministry of Science and Higher Education paid for the training, teaching materials and ongoing support of 20 lecturers from non-business schools for less than 2500 € per lecturer. As with the university students, this 'triggering factor' was key to attracting polytechnics, universities and agricultural schools with no prior experience in entrepreneurship education to join the network initiative.

The EU Structural Funds allocated in the 2007–13 budget seem to be a particularly appropriate source for financing entrepreneurship training in the new EU member states. One important barrier stems from the traditional policy approach in Poland, which primarily links entrepreneurship with self-employment and the small business sector in general. For example, the EU Operating Programme 'Human Capital' that is currently being implemented in Poland, has allocated substantial funds to support the unemployed. In addition to training and coaching, they receive financial support to cover their initial investments in launching new businesses. Similar projects addressed to the academic community are confined to training and coaching, not direct financial support.

Finally, networking among entrepreneurship lecturers is essential in alleviating start-up barriers and making the implementation process more efficient. The preparation of the course design, teaching materials, tools, and case studies is costly and time-consuming, and sharing resources, methodologies, and tools among lecturers can greatly reduce such costs. The Polish lecturers who introduced entrepreneurship courses for the first time greatly appreciated the opportunity to get ongoing support and advice on practical issues from the network, and the dedicated electronic platform (portal) proved to be very useful here.

CONCLUSION

The experiences with a particular bottom-up initiative aimed at fostering entrepreneurship education in the Polish universities outlined in this chapter were accumulated during a brief implementation period in 2005–08, so the conclusions and lessons drawn are tentative. However, the general reflection is an optimistic one. While climbing up the developmental ladder, universities – as well as nations and companies – can benefit from the wealth of accumulated knowledge and experience of advanced economies. The 'latecomer advantage' concept became particularly relevant in the era of the ICT revolution, since access to the pool of global knowledge was easier, faster and more cost-efficient for latecomers. The transition economies in the CEE region thus could take advantage of the historic coincidence of the move from a centrally planned economy to a market economy system and the ICT revolution that began in the early 1990s.

However, the initial Polish experiences in fostering entrepreneurship education at the university level points to several problems and contradictions. Even if accumulated knowledge, best practices, and so on become easily accessible, particular skills are needed to ensure the efficiency of the assimilation process. First, even with the wealth of available knowledge, it is important to assess its relevance to a particular socio-economic context. Second, it is not realistic to assume that the required know-how can be simply picked 'from the shelf' and be ready to use because it typically requires considerable adaptation to the local environment.

Thus far, accumulated experiences relate primarily to the initial assimilation of western know-how and best practices in teaching entrepreneurship in Poland. Its effective transfer to the higher education institutions participating in the Programme will take some time. What is already evident, however, are the benefits of the collaborative implementation scheme. From the perspective of an inexperienced lecturer in a small university located outside the major academic centres in Poland, launching an entrepreneurship course for students at a reasonably advanced level would be extremely difficult and time-consuming. The power of the network as developed in the Programme makes the whole process faster and more efficient. The planned creation of a European Network of Entrepreneurship Educators shall add an international dimension and strengthen the national collaborative efforts.

NOTES

1. This chapter draws on a paper which was presented at the Third International Conference on Economics, Law and Management, ICELM-3, 'Petru Maior' University of Tirgu-Mures, Romania, 4–6 June, 2008.
2. Both researchers and lecturers have struggled for many years with defining the borderline between the start-up phase and the day-to-day management of the young firm. The concept of the business platform, introduced by Davidsson and Klofsten, provide a way to measure the level of a newly established firm's maturity and helps to resolve this issue (Davidsson and Klofsten 2003).
3. The Programme was initiated by the author in 2004 after he resumed an academic career that had been interrupted by a business engagement lasting 14 years. During 1990–2003, the author was engaged in establishing Ernst & Young, an audit and consultancy firm,

in Poland. During 1996–2000, he served as the managing partner of Ernst & Young Poland.
4. The issue of smaller firms which, due to various circumstances, at certain stages have tempered their ambitions despite existing growth potential, calls for greater attention of both researchers and the policy makers, particularly with the view of implementing effective policy measures aimed at combating unemployment.

REFERENCES

Autio, E. (2007), *GEM 2007 Global Report on High-Growth Entrepreneurship*, Babson Park MA.
Bhide, A.V. (2000), *The Origin and Evolution of New Business*, Oxford: Oxford University Press.
Bygrave, W.D. (2004), 'The entrepreneurial process', in W.D. Bygrave and A. Zacharakis (eds), *The Portable MBA in Entrepreneurship*, Hoboken: John Wiley & Sons, pp. 1–27.
Cieślik, J. (2008), *Dynamic Entrepreneurship. How to Start Your Own Business*, Warsaw: Wydawnictwa Akademickie i Profesjonalne.
Davidsson, P. and M. Klofsten (2003), 'The business platform: developing an instrument to gauge and to assist the development of young firms', *Journal of Small Business Management*, **41** (1), 1–26.
European Commission (2008), *Entrepreneurship in Higher Education, Especially in Non-Business Studies. Final Report of the Expert Group*, Brussels, available at http://ec.europa.eu/enterprise/entrepreneurship/support_measures/training_education/entr_highed.pdf.
GUS (2008), *Szkoły wyższe i ich finanse w 2007 r.*, Warsaw: GUS.
Katz, J.A. (2003), 'The chronology and intellectual trajectory of American entrepreneurship education 1876–1999', *Journal of Business Venturing*, **18**, 283–300.
Kuratko, D.F. (2005), 'The emergence of entrepreneurship education: development, trends, and challenges', *Entrepreneurship Theory & Practice*, 577–97.
Lundström, A. and L. Stevenson (2005), *Entrepreneurship Policy Theory and Practice*, New York: Springer.
Piasecki, B. (ed.) (2001), *Ekonomika i zarządzanie małą firmą*, Warsaw: PWN.
Shane, S.A. (2008), *The Illusions of Entrepreneurship*, New Haven and London: Yale University Press.
Solomon, G. (2008), 'Entrepreneurship education in the United States', in J. Potter (ed.), *Entrepreneurship and Higher Education*, Paris: OECD, pp. 95–118.
Targalski, J. (2003), *Przedsiębiorczość i zarządzanie*, Warsaw: C.H. Beck.
Veblen, T. (1915), 'The opportunity of Japan', *Journal of Race Development*, 6, June, reprinted in L. Ardzrooni (ed.) (1964), *Essays in Our Changing Order*, New York: Augustus M. Kelly, pp. 248–66.
Wach, K. (2008), 'Entrepreneurship education in Poland', *ERENET Profile*, III, **3** (11), 36–45, available at http://www.erenet.org/publications/profile11.pdf, (accessed 15 December 2009).
Wickham, P.A. (2004), *Strategic Entrepreneurship*, 3rd edn, Harlow: Prentice Hall.
Wilson, K. (2004), *Entrepreneurship Education at European Universities and Business Schools. Results of a Joint Pilot Study*, Brussels: European Foundation for Management Development.
Wissema, J.G. (2005), *Technostarterzy dlaczego i jak?*, Warsaw: Polish Agency for Enterprise Development.

7 Creating a regional innovation system: the case of Lodz in Poland
Anna Rogut and Bogdan Piasecki

INTRODUCTION

Growing globalization is a phenomenon that is not to be ignored, especially as it may potentially hamper the development of poorer regions (ESPON 2007), including Lodz Province. The region covers an area of 18 219km^2 and has 2 630 400 inhabitants. It is located in the geographical centre of Poland. The disadvantageous position of the region is reflected, first of all, in the traditional industries, a low level of innovation and development in the advanced technology sectors, a relatively low level of foreign capital investment and the flow of highly qualified workers to the strongest economic areas. Thus, the macroeconomic conditions provide a less favourable climate for SME development. At the same time, the region possesses a number of strengths opening new opportunities. In order to take advantage of them, one solution would be to strengthen the regional innovation system in order to help smaller companies face the challenges and opportunities arising out of globalization (Devi and Thangamuthu 2006; Holmes and Schmitz 2001; Thukral et al. 2008).

The subject matter of this chapter is to characterize the evolution of the approach to creating such a system in the region. The empirical evidence on which it is based was gathered between 2005 and 2007. The research comprised of four directions of analysis, and focused on the following issues: clusters, regional benchmarking, technological and innovation audit, and regional foresight. In the remaining part of this chapter, a brief account will be given of the changes in the approach to entrepreneurship policy in Poland that have taken place since the early 1990s. Although this policy has never been purely oriented towards individuals and individual behaviour (Lundström and Stevenson 2002), it has always tried to meet the actual needs of the dynamically developing private sector. In subsequent years, the character of the entrepreneurship policy changed with the role of entrepreneurship and the shift from an economic and political transition (Zecchini 1997) towards a transformation into a more entrepreneurial economy (Acs and Szerb 2007). Furthermore, this chapter briefly presents the developments in entrepreneurship and small business in Poland. The last part of the chapter, based on the experiences of the Lodz Region, is devoted to the first Polish steps towards the development of regional innovation systems.

ENTREPRENEURSHIP IN POLAND

Entrepreneurship is a multidimensional concept (Audretsch 2002; Ireland and Webb 2007; Low and McMillan 1988). Therefore, in practice there exist both a narrow understanding of entrepreneurship as limited to the pre-start, start-up and early phases of business development (Hart 2003; Lundström and Stevenson 2002) as well as a broader understanding that encompasses the established phase of businesses and their possible discontinuation (Bosma et al. 2008).

A more universal approach defines entrepreneurship as 'the mindset and process of creating and developing economic activity by blending risk-taking, creativity and/or innovation with sound management, within a new or existing organisation' (European Commission 2003, p. 6). However, it does not take a definite stance as to its position and role in wealth creation and distribution. As a result, authors tend to distinguish productive (rent-creating), unproductive (rent-seeking) and destructive (rent-destroying) entrepreneurship, with different effects on economic growth (Baumol 1990; Desai and Acs 2007; Douhan and Henrekson 2008).

Yet another approach defines entrepreneurship as the perception of opportunities, their discovery and exploitation. Still, even this approach is not free of discrepancies, mostly related to the different assessment of the character of opportunities, and the role of the entrepreneur (Buenstorf 2007; Casson and Wadeson 2007; Companys and McMullen 2007; Eckhardt and Shane 2003; OECD 1998; Phillips and Tracey 2007; Plummer et al. 2007; Sanders 2007; Spencer et al. 2008). The development of a knowledge-driven economy favours the endogenization of the sources of opportunities (Alvord et al. 2004; Dess et al. 2003; Garud et al. 2007; Goss 2005; Leca and Naccache 2006; Wijen and Ansari 2007) and perceives them 'as an objective construct visible to or created by the knowledgeable or attuned entrepreneur' (McMullen et al. 2007, p. 273).

Similar differences in interpretation occur also in Poland (Sudoł 2008), where entrepreneurship has a long tradition, cultivated even under the socialist system (Piasecki and Rogut 1994). However, while under socialism it was (most often[1]) perceived as an enemy of the system, during the period of transformation, it advanced to the role of a positive protagonist (Piasecki 2002b). At the bottom of understanding of entrepreneurship, there has always been a firm belief that it is a certain set of features that enable particular individuals to undertake profitable business initiatives

Table 7.1   Number of active SMEs in Poland in the main stages of entrepreneurship development

Stage of entrepreneurship development	Number of SMEs
Entrepreneurial boom	
1989	572 451
1991	1 496 797
Phase of slow down	
1994	1 110 600
Pre-accession phase	
1995	1 136 808
1999	1 758 100
2004	1 689 100
After accession phase	
2005	1 674 694
2006	1 712 664
2007	1 773 831

Sources: Based on Chmiel (2001), Łapiński (2009), Piasecki (2002b), Piasecki et al. (1999) and Pyciński and Żołnierski (2007).

(Doroszewski 1965). However, with the beginning of the transformation (latter half of 1989 and first half of 1990), a narrower understanding of entrepreneurship became prominent that defined it as starting and developing private business activity, which entailed the necessity of prompt privatization of the economy and creating mature market structures (Rogut 2002a). Since 1995, the focus started to gradually shift towards an understanding of entrepreneurship as the perception of opportunities, their discovery and exploitation, which called for analysis of opportunities and threats connected to future integration with the European Union and the necessity to face global competition (UKIE 2003). The early 2000s saw a renewed interest in start-up processes, this time, however, primarily from the point of view of the development of knowledge-intensive and technologically advanced areas (Wissema 2005). The current economic crisis may trigger a discussion around productive entrepreneurship, but so far it has not met with broader interest, especially that in practice entrepreneurship is equated with the sector of small and medium-sized enterprises (SME).

The development of entrepreneurship thus understood has had its ups and downs in Poland. One of the most spectacular surges was the entrepreneurial boom in the years 1989–91, coinciding with the beginning of economic and political transformation (Table 7.1). The development of enterprises in this period seems to confirm the complementary nature of the Schumpeterian and Kirznerian views on entrepreneurship. 'After the Schumpeterian entrepreneur disturbs the existing equilibrium, creating disequilibrium, the Kirznerian entrepreneur takes over, making corrections that initiate convergence towards a new equilibrium in which all actors' plans are fully coordinated.' (Chiles et al. 2007, p. 469).

In the following years, the pace of SME growth decreased reaching a minimum in 1994. A breakthrough came in 1995 with the exceptionally favourable macroeconomic situation (Piasecki et al. 1999), and the beginning EU integration efforts. This reinvigorated entrepreneurial activities, in particular starting with 1996, when the number of active SMEs began to incessantly grow to reach maximum in 1999. The subsequent years, however, saw a drop in the number of active SMEs. The year 2004 was still an important milestone. That year Poland was granted membership in the EU and all companies gained access to an immense land of integration opportunity. Nevertheless, the benefits came bundled with a range of possible threats, which involved the costs of adjustment to the internal market and, in the long term, the relocation of industries and resources, as it was the case in the EU in years past (Rogut 2002b). Poland's membership in the EU has two aspects: a positive and negative one. The advantages of EU membership include a lack of major crises in the first period of membership and an increase in the number of active SMEs. Although the first signs of the liquidation of the weakest companies (marginal producers) are observed, it is still too early for the full consequences of the internal market to appear. On the other hand, the bad points are the low level of exports and a lack of more substantial changes in the competitive advantages of Polish SMEs (Rogut 2008). This is due to the fact that Polish SMEs are still too attached to (transient) lower order advantages, including low cost of labour, and underrate the need to invest in higher order advantages. And it is the latter that decide the balance of integration benefits in the long term. The creation of these advantages is tied to the level of innovation, which is generally low. This is reflected by the fact that Poland is classified in the class of catching-up countries for which the Summary Innovation Index is substantially below the EU-27 average. Even though recently a process of convergence has become apparent, it is estimated that it will take at least 60 years to bridge the gap between Poland and innovation leaders (European Commission 2008).

The length of the convergence period is a gauge of the technological gap that characterizes the Polish economy and Polish SMEs. The technological gap, in turn, has an impact on foreign direct investment (FDI) and the pace of technology diffusion. The volume and directions of FDI reflect more profound reorganization processes in the European value chain (changes in the specialization profile of particular countries, localization of the research and development sector, relocation of industries, and so on). Thanks to FDI and the cooperation of domestic organizations with foreign companies it may be possible to develop new fields of competence and specialization. However, as a result of the low technological intensity and relative backwardness of Polish manufacturers, most FDI has so far concentrated on assembly, which significantly decreases the pace of modernization of the technical and technological base (European Commission 2006a). On the other hand, there are first harbingers of reversing this tendency, but it is necessary to take more decisive actions in order to attract more FDI to research and development activities (United Nations 2005). Many studies show that the acquisition and use of new technologies (imported either through FDI or through the purchase of know-how licenses) is not an automatic cost-free process. Enterprises and states need to invest in the development of capacity for knowledge absorbance or national readiness for assimilating knowledge, which in turns depends on expenditures on research and development (Goldberg 2004).

THE PAST AND PRESENT OF ENTREPRENEURSHIP POLICY

The development of entrepreneurship and SMEs was accompanied with an evolution in public policy. And although this was never given its pure form of a narrowly defined entrepreneurship policy (Audretsch 2002; Gilbert et al. 2004; Hart 2003; Lundström and Stevenson 2002), it was always meant to meet the actual needs of the robustly growing private sector (Piasecki 1997, 2002a). An exception in this respect was the first period of post-communist transformation (Balcerowicz 1994; World Bank 1996; Zecchini 1997) focused on creating 'rules of the game' for productive entrepreneurship (Baumol 1990).

The beginnings of prioritizing SMEs were related to the intensification of activities for integration with the EU (1995). That period also witnessed the creation of the first SME policy programme for the years 1995–97 aimed at setting up and developing SMEs, decreasing economic risk, increasing the competitiveness of SMEs and developing financial services (Ministerstwo Przemysłu i Handlu 1995). This programme, among others, has led to several bills (including the Business Activity Act); the establishment of the Loan Guarantee Fund; the creation of the Polish Foundation for the Promotion and Development of Small and Medium-Sized Enterprises (later transformed into the Polish Agency for Entrepreneurship Development); and support for regional development as well as to local organizations promoting SMEs (Ministerstwo Gospodarki 1999).

The first policy programme was followed up by a second, which was prepared specifically for the pre-accession period and focused on creating conditions for making full use of the development potential of SMEs, and especially with a view to increasing the competitiveness of SMEs, boosting exports and stepping up SME investment expenditures (Ministerstwo Gospodarki 1999). Since 2002, more initiatives have been taken, such as the adoption of the European Small Business Charter, the preparation of Priorities for the 'First of All Entrepreneurship' package, the implementation of the 'Anti-crisis action plan for the protection of the labour market and workplaces' (strengthening the system of guarantees and credit flow for SMEs). The above-mentioned activities were complemented by SME participation in pre-accession programmes (for the most part PHARE[2] and SAPARD[3]), in EU programmes as well as programmes financed by other donors. However, it was not possible to systematically monitor the sensitivity of SMEs to the type and scope of the instruments used, which decreased the effectiveness of the activities undertaken.

Poland's integration with the EU and broader global trends (Pilat et al. 2006) confronted the country (and Polish SMEs) with a double challenge, namely to effect significant structural changes and bridge the technological gap. In the latter case, there was a possibility for a two-speed catch-up process, with the non-Baltic new Member States (including Poland) underperforming (Bureau of European Policy Advisers and Directorate-General for Economic and Financial Affairs 2006). Therefore, it was critical to create and maintain a competitive advantage. That could have been achieved by two different approaches: the Low Road Approach (based on lowering production costs, especially wage rates) and the High Road Approach (Davies 1995). The former entailed the danger of 'downgrading', attracting 'not very loyal' foreign investors who are ever ready to move on to even cheaper locations and reluctant to make larger investments in the local environment. The latter approach is aimed at increasing the effectiveness of the use of funds through investments in products, processes, technological innovations, and the development of employee qualifications (Crespi et al. 2007). This road stimulates and modernizes local resources and leads to a sticky economy having a considerable power of attraction and retention of companies and industries (Davies 1995). In the case of Poland, the actual structural changes were closer to the Low Road Approach (Rogut 2008; Rogut and Piasecki 2008a), at least in the beginning. The willingness to follow the High Road Approach, and thus a transformation towards a more entrepreneurial economy (Acs and Szerb 2007), shifts the emphasis of public policy from SME policy to support for competitiveness, innovativeness and productivity (innovation policy) as well as from sector policies to horizontal policy. The first step in that direction was taken by the Third Support Programme for SMEs for the years 2003–06 and its goal to boost the competitiveness of SMEs and their capacity to operate in the Single European Market (Ministerstwo Gospodarki, Pracy i Polityki Społecznej 2003). In the first years of Poland's membership in the EU (2004–06) the programme was supported with structural funds. Sectoral operational programmes (SOPs) played a major role in this respect, including SOPs for 'Improvement of the Competitiveness of Enterprises', the Sectoral Operational Programme on Human Resources Development and the Integrated Regional Operational Programme (IROP). The IROP's effectiveness was meant to be increased by regional innovation strategies which will be reviewed for the case of Lodz region in the next sections.

The approach to science and technology policy was also modified with a view to boosting company innovativeness, with the new version being called 'Priorities for Polish Scientific, Technological and Innovative Policy'. At the same time, new versions of innovation policies appeared, crowned with the programme 'Increasing economic innovativeness in Poland by the year 2006' and a 'Strategy for increasing research and development expenditure to meet the objectives of the Lisbon Strategy' (Rogut 2008). From 2007 onwards, innovation policy has replaced the previously formulated SME policy. Its objective is to enhance enterprise innovation to keep the economy in the fast lane of development. This goal is to be attained through activities in the fields of human resources, research, intellectual property, as well as finances and infrastructure for innovation (Ministry of Economy 2006). Since 2007, new operational programmes have been implemented, the most important ones being 'Innovative Economy' and 'Human Capital'.

The recent years have been additionally characterized by a shift from sectoral to horizontal instruments developed in the field of research and development, innovation, human capital, access to capital and sales markets, information technologies, industrial property protection and environmental protection (Ministerstwo Gospodarki 2007). This was accompanied by increasing the competence and independence of regions in terms of the directions of spending state funds. This trend was initiated in 1999 with a new administration division (administrative regionalization) and the establishment of regional self-governments. This was accompanied by redefining regional development as a field of government administration and in 2000 providing the new regions with competences with respect to carrying out regional policy (Ministerstwo Rozwoju Regionalnego 2007). The regional policy is based on strategies developed over many years, programmes, and development plans. The governing documents are National Strategies for Regional Development (NSRD). The main aim of the NSRD 2001–06 was to create conditions conducive to the enhancement of competitiveness and counteraction of marginalization in some areas, in favour of promoting the long-term economic development of the country, economic, social and territorial cohesion, and integration with the EU. The NSRD 2007–13 has similar goals, although in this case emphasis is placed on the improvement of economic competitiveness of all the regions through initiating regional development that would make better use of regional endogenous potential while preserving diversity, rationally managing resources and ensuring a greater cohesion of Poland. Some of the instruments designed to achieve such goals are regional strategies and innovation systems initiated on a wider scale in 2002, which will be reviewed in the case of the Lodz region in the next section.

THE DEVELOPMENT OF REGIONAL INNOVATION SYSTEMS: A CASE STUDY OF THE LODZ REGION[4]

The Starting Point

Even though there is no universal consensus as to the definition of a regional innovation system, it is usually assumed to be 'a set of interacting private and public interests, formal institutions and other organizations that function according to organizational and institutional arrangements and relationships conducive to the generation, use and dissemination of knowledge' (Doloreux and Parto 2004, p. 9). The creation of such a system in the Lodz Province was initiated in 2004 by the adoption of the first regional innovation strategy (RIS LORIS), which provided a strategic framework for a flexible innovation system in the Lodz Region. Emphasis was placed on the compatibility of the regional innovation strategy with existing regional socio-economic policies and priorities (Piasecki et al. 2004). Meanwhile, the Strategy for the Development of the Lodz region was amended, the Regional Operational Programme for the years 2007–13 was approved, as were several essential programme documents related to some of the RIS LORIS objectives. The studies presented in the following section were designed to update the diagnostic and increase the effectiveness of the regional innovation policy (Table 7.2).

Redefining the Regional Innovation Strategy

Despite the above-mentioned efforts, the Lodz Province has not been able to accumulate the critical mass indispensable for the acceleration of development of a knowledge-based economy in the region. This is why in

Table 7.2   Key milestones in developing the regional innovation systems for the Lodz region

Period	Milestone	Areas
2004	Regional Innovation Strategy RSI LORIS	• Knowledge-based economy (intensity of R&D expenditures; regional R&D potential; framework conditions conducive to medium and high tech industries; knowledge intensity in traditional industries; services for information society and knowledge-based economy) • Innovation culture (promotion of innovation and entrepreneurship; education for innovation) • Innovation regional management (durable partnership; anticipation of the future; efficient RIS implementation instruments)
2006	The Development Strategy for the Lodz Region for the years 2007–20	• Social sphere (knowledge and skills; life quality; social policy; civil society) • Economic sphere (availability; economic base; information society; rural areas; labour market; image of the region) • Functional and spatial sphere (settlement system; spatial order; regional identity; environmental protection)
2007	Regional Operational Programme for the Lodzkie Voivodship for the years 2007–13	• Transport infrastructure (improvement of the transport accessibility of the Lodzkie Voivodship) • Environmental protection, risk prevention and power engineering (improvement of the state of natural environment and energy security) • Economy, innovativeness, entrepreneurship (development of the innovative and competitive economic sector in the region) • Information society (development of the information society) • Social infrastructure (creation of favourable conditions for development of human resources) • Revitalization of urban areas (economic and social revival in degraded urban areas)
2008	Second generation of Regional Innovation Strategy RSI LORIS PLUS	• Qualifications/skills/competencies (development of human capital in the region as a prerequisite condition of a substantial growth in the absorption capacity of companies) • Radical innovations (development of the R&D and innovation potential of regional companies)

Table 7.2 (continued)

Period	Milestone	Areas
		• Cooperation/clusters/research and development networks (increasing openness to regional clusters and R&D networks, and creating favourable conditions for their development) • Services for innovation (development of the services market, especially those highly specialized and supporting company operations) • Finances for innovation (development of regional financial institutions helping the economy in the process of transformation) • Transformation management (development of qualifications and skills of regional authorities in terms of supporting economic transformations both at the conceptual and implementation levels)

Sources: Based on Piasecki et al. (2004), Rogut and Piasecki (2008b), Sejmik Województwa Łódzkiego (2006) and Urząd Marszałkowski (2007).

the years 2005 to 2007 further research was initiated in order to obtain a better understanding of the determinants of successful transformation of the region. Their results have been employed for the preparation of the second generation regional innovation strategy.

Relevant studies focused on four aspects, namely cluster analysis, regional benchmarking, a technological and innovation audit, and regional foresight. The objective of the first study was to identify regional clusters and determine their innovation potential and needs in terms of support mechanisms. The objective of benchmarking was to determine the convergence of demand and supply for information, training, advisory and consulting services, as well as to compare the quality of services provided by various institutions. Within each group of services, those connected with outside sources of funding, technological research/development, legal problems, company management, quality/certification management, environmental protection, information and communication were singled out. The technological audit was focused on stimulating entrepreneurs' awareness regarding the need for technological and innovation development as well as improving their abilities to independently perform simple technological audits and determine the main trends, technological possibilities, procedures and needs of support. The aim of the innovation audit was to determine the level of openness to effective management of innovation processes as well as the ability to effectively manage innovation processes. Finally, the aim of foresight was to outline the main directions of the development of the region as a knowledge-based one as well as to identify transformation areas for the regional industry.

As far as *clusters* are concerned, they are usually defined as groups of companies located in geographical proximity. But in their mature form clusters usually comprise a whole spectrum of external advantages resulting from connections of these companies with specialized suppliers and service providers, with companies from related sectors and with other specialized institutions operating in various areas (Porter 1998, 2003). In this case, the concept of clusters overlaps with the sectoral innovation system, comprising knowledge, skills, technology, expenditures as well as (actual and potential) demand (Adame-Sanchez and Escrig-Tena 2001; Asheim and Coenen 2004; Breschi and Lissoni 2000; Malerba 2004; OECD 2001, 2007; Smith 2000). The participants of this system are individuals and organizations that operate at various levels of learning, competence, organizational structures, beliefs, objectives and behaviour. Interactions between the participants take place during the processes of communication, exchange, cooperation, and competition, all of these being shaped by system-specific institutions. Such a system undergoes constant transformations inspired by the co-evolution of its elements. This co-evolution affects the shape of the innovation model which may take the form of creative destruction or creative accumulation (Malerba 2003).

For the Lodz region, research results revealed that the process of the creation and development of cooperation networks faced a number of barriers, particularly in the case of smaller companies. The following problems have been identified: the lack of a strategic participant that would play the role of a 'network integrator', a trust deficit, lack of time for cooperation, low awareness of the opportunities and advantages of cooperation as well as limited resources. All of this explains why actual cooperation between companies of various sizes, universities and R&D units occurs so rarely. Recently, though, there have emerged several interesting cluster initiatives which are, for the time being, at the stage of developing organizational structures in order to prepare joint strategies and obtain financial resources in the future.

The *regional benchmarking* draws on the achievements of evolutionist theories, which emphasize the role of the institutional environment as the key factor deciding the success of individual companies and the growth dynamics of the whole economy. As a result, a new outlook on political goals and the role of public authorities has emerged. Above all, they are now supposed to create and develop an institutional environment which would be friendly to companies rather than use direct intervention, as was previously the case (European Commission 2001; Kuusi 1996; Navarro 2003; Quéré 2004). In the Lodz region, such an institutional environment has been developed since the beginning of the 1990s. However, benchmarking results have revealed two characteristic deficits of the environment:

- Market failure, for the most part affecting information and training services, which is characterized by the unwillingness of companies to pay in part or in full for using such services. The present market failure seems to stem from the support offered that favoured financing business support organizations, and from the creation of a large base of services which is but poorly correlated with the demand for support, both from the point of view of content and quality ('market spoiling').
- So called interaction or connectivity deficits within the innovation system (European Commission 2006b), reflected in the lack of systematic interaction between the various actors.

In turn, the *innovation and technological audits* have demonstrated that regional companies have poor knowledge of innovation management techniques and most of them do not have a well-developed innovation culture. Finally, *foresight studies* outlined two possible scenarios for the region's development. Both are internal convergence-oriented (catching-up effect), although the first one favours a polycentric development and the elimination of intra-regional disparities and the second favours central-peripheral development and growing intra-regional disparities. Internal convergence will be accompanied by growing wealth but also by an increase in costs of business activity (at least to match the national average). This, in turn could lead to relocating labour-intensive production to regions/ countries having lower labour costs. Alternatively, regional industries could be transformed from labour- into science- and capital-intensive. This, however, would require intensive cluster development, access to EU funds assigned to the improvement of innovativeness of enterprises and, in this way, diminishing the technological gap of regional companies, a significant increase in the share of enterprises in financing research and development activities as well as streamlining the commercialization of research results and a much better adaptation of educational services to the market needs.

As far as the transformation of regional industries is concerned, foresight studies revealed that this will be focused on two types of processes constituting four possible scenarios (Figure 7.1): either a transition from

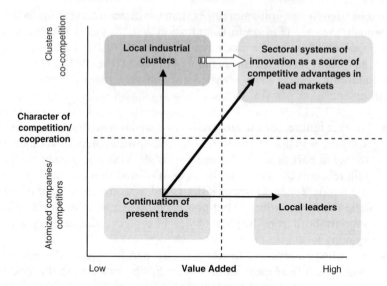

Source: Rogut and Piasecki (2008b).

Figure 7.1   Transformation scenarios for regional industries

individual to system-type (cluster) competition or moving up the value chain towards the phases generating larger value added.

The scenario of current trend continuation with possible automation and robotization as well as reorganization of the value chain (moving the most labour-intensive phases of production to regions/countries with lower labour costs) would be the most dangerous. As it was mentioned earlier, it would be a typically reactive strategy leading, in the long term, to the degradation of the region's industry.

The scenario of the development of local industrial clusters, which may later lead to the formation of sectoral innovation systems, seems to be the most likely. However, its realization requires the expansion and qualitative improvement of the services directed to the industry by the regional business support infrastructure as well as an improvement in the efficiency of the region's labour market.

New Principles for the Creation of a Regional Innovation System

The research results outlined in the previous section helped to define three basic principles for the creation of a regional innovation system: (i) an evolutionary model of changes, (ii) sectoral approach to transformation and (iii) a focus on constructed advantages.

An *evolutionary model of changes* is needed for the region to change its prevalent economic structure and build new, high-tech industries/services. The question remaining concerns the transformation path: a revolutionary path, which is focused on rapidly constructing new high-tech industries/ services 'from scratch', or an evolutionary path, which is a combination of the fastest possible transformation of the existing industries and building new high-tech industries/services. In the case of the Lodz region, the evolutionary path seems to be more appropriate, as it would ensure an adequate management of the transformation of existing resources as well as the rational use of traditions, industrial culture, intellectual and scientific and research potential as well as material potential, while avoiding the 'stuck in history' effect. Moreover, this would also help to develop a strong internal demand for products of new high-tech industries and services (bio-, nano-, materials engineering and so on), and thus favourable conditions for building new areas of regional competence. Finally, it would contribute to a decrease in the social costs of transformation and easing tensions in the local labour market.

A *sectoral approach to transformation* is an integral part of a regional innovation system, which should lead to developing strong sectoral innovation systems. These would enable a better understanding of differences and similarities of various industries/services, their organization, dynamics and pace of transformation, thus helping to successfully identify different technological regimes particular to different industries. A technological regime shows the level of maturity and the transformation path of prevailing technologies and determines the amount of innovation opportunities. Moreover, this will result in a correct description of factors determining the intensity of innovation, economic potential, and international competitiveness of companies operating in particular industries/ services, thus allowing a reliable definition of the intensity, directions and scope of public assistance (support policy), which would be more exact and adequate to the needs and possibilities of sectors.

Globalization has led to a shift from the economy of regions based on competitive advantages to one based on *constructed advantages* (Cooke and Leydesdorff 2006; Furman et al. 2002). Such an approach sheds new light on the role of policy and regional authorities. Their intervention is necessary if the market fails or if there is a deficit of interaction or connectivity within innovation systems. However, the essence of this intervention should be to complement, and not to replace or duplicate, market mechanisms. An intervention should always follow from a systematic diagnosis and response to an actual problem (beneficiary-oriented). This means that policy decision-makers have (or may create) a (competence, qualification, organizational, financial) potential that would ensure that the problem is solved both at the conceptual and implementation levels.

These rules gave rise to a redefinition of the regional innovation strategy in order to readjust it to the requirements of a prompt reaction to the challenges and opportunities arising out of globalization. This was attained through the prioritization of six areas of action:

- Qualifications/skills/competencies aimed at the development of human capital in the region as a prerequisite for a substantial growth in the absorption capacity of companies.
- Radical innovations, meant to develop R&D and the innovation potential of regional companies.
- Cooperation/clusters/research and development networks focused on increasing openness to regional clusters and R&D networks, as well as at creating favourable conditions for their development.
- Services for innovation designed to develop the services market; in particular services that are highly specialized and support company operations (information, training, advisory, and consulting; services related to knowledge and technology transfer; increasing the quality of services).
- Finances for innovation meant to develop regional financial institutions helping the economy in the process of transformation. And last but not least,
- Strengthening appropriate RIS management structures (the development of qualifications and skills of the region's authorities in terms of supporting economic transformations both at the conceptual and implementation levels).

CONCLUSIONS

The report of the High Level Group on Key Technologies (European Commission 2006c) states that Europe faces the necessity to revise and restructure its economic model because the European economy is based on old paradigms and its research and development is insufficiently commercialized. Going forward requires 'a creative system disruption' based on long-term coherent investments in key technologies (European Commission 2006b, p. 5).

The same pertains to the Lodz Province, which is still a region with a relatively poor presence of medium and high technologies or technologically advanced services. Its economic structure is dominated by industries traditionally classified as low-technology and often defined as 'declining' industries threatened with a gradual elimination and moving to regions/ countries with lower labour costs. A low level of innovative activity of regional companies makes the situation even worse. The change of the prevalent economic structure and building new high-tech industries/ services is an inevitable necessity for the Province; transformation must be conducted simultaneously in a number of areas, including knowledge and competences; cooperation and networks; science and business support infrastructure (transfer of knowledge and technologies, other institutions and organizations determining the extent, pace and efficiency of the innovation process); financial institutions and public assistance management.

It is possible to carry out such fundamental changes (or at least achieve some significant success in the course of the pursuit of the desired transformations) in the present programming period (2007–13), when the local authorities have at their disposal – thanks to the structural funds – substantial financial means (the largest to date). Therefore, it is important for these means to be invested mostly in the weakest links of the regional innovation system, which are now barriers to desired transformations. They include:

- in terms of the industries in the process of transformation: a relatively low absorption potential mostly resulting from insufficient financing and staff for transformation. Consequently, there is a relatively low potential for introducing more radical innovations and, in the case of clusters and cooperation networks, a lack of leading companies/organizations that could be network integrators,
- in terms of services: decline of the services market and a poor accessibility of finance resources, especially high-risk capital,
- in terms of regional management: an insufficient information basis and transformation strategy.

The new definition of a regional innovation strategy is meant to help overcome these barriers; making it possible to achieve a greater balance between the regional potential of creating new knowledge, its transfer and absorption (Sharpe and Guilbaud 2005).

NOTES

1. The first changes date back to the 1980s, when entrepreneurship became a cautious instrument for increasing the effectiveness of a centrally planned economy. Back then, the first reforms were introduced (for example, a change in the Public Enterprise Act in June 1981 permitting state-owned enterprises to sell part of their assets to individual persons; adopting, in February 1982, the new Price Act reducing the state intervention in

price fixing; adopting, in July 1982, the Act of Small Scale Foreign Enterprises permitting for foreign capital investments; legal sanctioning, in June 1983, of a possibility of the state-owned enterprise bankruptcy and specifying the ways of using assets of insolvent enterprises; opening, in September 1983, access for private firms to foreign exchange loans for purchases of machines, equipment and supplies; passing, in April 1986, new laws permitting the establishment of companies with foreign partners; liberalization, in October 1987, of regulations concerning business activity of private firms in international trade) stimulating the development of the private sector in Poland.
2. Poland and Hungary Assistance for Reconstructing of their Economies, a pre-accession fund which was meant to prepare new countries to become members of the European Union and help to reduce economic disparities.
3. Special Accession Programme for Agriculture and Rural Development, an EU programme of financial support for programmes adjusting agriculture to a market economy in countries applying for EU membership.
4. This part of the chapter draws on Rogut and Piasecki (2008b).

REFERENCES

Acs, Z.J. and L. Szerb (2007), 'Entrepreneurship, economic growth and public policy', *Small Business Economics*, **28** (4), 109–22.
Adame-Sanchez, C. and A.B. Escrig-Tena (2001), 'Innovating behaviour in local productive systems based on SMEs', *International Journal of Innovation Management*, **5** (1), 1–20.
Alvord, S.H., L.D. Brown and C.W. Letts (2004), 'Social entrepreneurship and societal transformation. An exploratory study', *Journal of Applied Behavioral Science*, **40** (3), 260–82.
Asheim, B.T. and L. Coenen (2004), 'The role of regional innovation systems in a globalizing economy: comparing knowledge bases and institutional frameworks of nordic clusters', DRUID Summer Conference 2004 on Industrial dynamics, innovation and development, Elsinore, Denmark, June 14–16, available at http://www.druid.dk/uploads/tx_picturedb/ds2004-1370.pdf (accessed 17 June 2005).
Audretsch, D.B. (2002), 'Entrepreneurship: a survey of the literature', available at ec.europa.eu/enterprise/entrepreneurship/green_paper/literature_survey_2002.pdf (accessed 15 February 2004).
Balcerowicz, L. (1994), 'Understanding postcommunist transitions', *Journal of Democracy*, **5** (4), 75–89.
Baumol, W.J. (1990), 'Entrepreneurship: productive, unproductive and destructive', *Journal of Political Economy*, **98** (5), 893–921.
Bosma, N., K. Jones, E. Autio and J. Levie (2008), *Global Entrepreneurship Monitor. 2007 Executive Report*, Babson Park, US and London UK: Babson College, London Business School, and Global Entrepreneurship Research Consortium (GERA).
Breschi, S. and F. Lissoni (2000), 'Geographical boundaries of sectoral systems. Final report', Working Paper ESSY, available at http://www.cespri.unibocconi.it/essy/wp/bresliss.pdf (accessed 20 August 2007).
Buenstorf, G. (2007), 'Creation and pursuit of entrepreneurial opportunities: an evolutionary economic perspective', *Small Business Economics*, **28** (4), 323–37.
Bureau of European Policy Advisers and Directorate-General for Economic and Financial Affairs (2006), 'Enlargement, two years after: an economic evaluation, European economy', Occasional Papers No. 24, available at http://europa.eu.int/comm/economy_finance/index_en.htm (accessed 22 February 2007).
Casson, M. and N. Wadeson (2007), 'The discovery of opportunities: extending the economic theory of the entrepreneur', *Small Business Economics*, **28** (4), 285–300.
Chiles, T.D., A.C. Bluedorn and V.K. Gupta (2007), 'Beyond creative destruction and entrepreneurial discovery: a radical Austrian approach to entrepreneurship', *Organization Studies*, **28** (4), 467–93.

Chmiel, J. (ed.) (2001), *Stan sektora MSP w 1999 r. Tendencje rozwojowe w latach 1994–1999*, Warsaw: Polska Agencja Rozwoju Przedsiębiorczości.

Companys, Y.E. and J.S. McMullen (2007), 'Strategic entrepreneurs at work: the nature, discovery, and exploitation of entrepreneurial opportunities', *Small Business Economics*, **28** (4), 301–22.

Cooke, P. and L. Leydesdorff (2006), 'Regional development in the knowledge-based economy: the construction of advantage', *Journal of Technology Transfer*, **31** (1), 5–15.

Crespi, G., P. Patel and L. Besta (2007), 'Sectoral knowledge production function in OECD countries', available at http://www.europe-innova.org/index.jsp?type=page&lg=en&from=child&classificationId=8433&classificationName=Draft%20Research%20Reports&cid=8434&parentClassificationId=4963&parentClassificationName=Innovation%20Wat ch&parentContentId=507 (accessed 7 March 2008).

CSO (2008), *Regions of Poland*, Warsaw: Central Statistical Office.

Davies, A. (1995), *Local Economies and Globalisation*, Leed Note Book No. 20, Paris: OECD.

Desai, S. and Z.J. Acs (2007), 'A theory of destructive entrepreneurship', *Jena Economic Research Papers*, 2007-085, Jena: Max Planck Institute.

Dess, G.G., R.D. Ireland, S.A. Zahra, S.W. Floyd, J.J. Janney and P.J. Lane (2003), 'Emerging issues in corporate entrepreneurship', *Journal of Management*, **29** (3), 351–78.

Devi, S. and C. Thangamuthu (2006), 'A new paradigm of entrepreneurship vis-à-vis liberalisation and globalisation', *Global Business Review*, **7** (2), 259–69.

Doloreux, D. and S. Parto (2004), *Regional Innovation Systems: A Critical Synthesis*, UNU-INTECH Discussion Papers, Maastricht: United Nations University, Institute for New Technologies.

Doroszewski, W. (1965), *Słownik języka polskiego*, Warsaw: PWN.

Douhan, R. and M. Henrekson (2008), 'Productive and destructive entrepreneurship in a political economy framework', IFN Working Paper No. 761, available at http://www.ifn.se/web/761.aspx (accessed 30 November 2008).

Eckhardt, J.T. and S.A. Shane (2003), 'Opportunities and entrepreneurship', *Journal of Management*, **29** (3), 333–49.

ESPON (2007), 'Scenarios on the territorial future of Europe', ESPON Project 3.2, Belgium, May 2007, available at http://www.espon.eu/mmp/online/website/content/pub lications/98/1378/file_2995/espon3.2_60p._final_16-7-2007-c.pdf (accessed 14 September 2007).

European Commission (2001), *European Competitiveness Report 2001*, Luxemburg: European Commission.

European Commission (2003), *Green Paper. Entrepreneurship in Europe*, Brussels: European Commission.

European Commission (2006a), 'Enlargement, Two Years After: An Economic Evaluation', European Economy, Bureau of European Policy Advisers, Directorate-General for Economic and Financial Affairs Occasional Papers, No. 24. Brussels: European Commission.

European Commission (2006b), *Constructing Regional Advantage, Principles – Perspectives – Policies*, Brussels: European Commission.

European Commission (2006c), *Creative System Disruption: Towards a Research Strategy Beyond Lisbon. Key Technologies Expert Group*, Brussels: European Commission.

European Commission (2008), 'European Innovation Scoreboard 2007. Comparative analysis of innovation performance', PRO INNO Europe Paper No 6, 2008, available at http://www.proinno-europe.eu/admin/uploaded_documents/European_Innovation_Scoreboard_2007.pdf (accessed 30 April 2008).

Furman, J.L., M.E. Porter and S. Stern (2002), 'The determinants of national innovative capacity', *Research Policy*, **31**, 899–933.

Garud, R., C. Hardy and S. Maguire (2007), 'Institutional entrepreneurship as embedded agency: an introduction to the special issue', *Organization Studies*, **28** (7), 957–69.

Gilbert, B.A., D.B. Audretsch and P.P. McDougall (2004), 'The emergence of entrepreneurship policy', *Small Business Economics*, **22**, 313–23.

Goldberg, I. (2004), *Polska a gospodarka oparta na wiedzy. W kierunku zwiększania konkurencyjności Polski w Unii Europejskiej*, Washington: Bank Światowy.
Goss, D. (2005), 'Entrepreneurship and 'the social': towards a deference-emotion theory', *Human Relations*, **58** (5), 617–36.
Hart, D.M. (2003), 'Entrepreneurship policy. What it is and where it came from', in D.M Hart (ed.), *The Emergence of Entrepreneurship Policy. Governance, Start ups, and Growth in the U.S. Knowledge Economy*, Cambridge: Cambridge University Press, pp. 3–19.
Holmes, T.J. and J.A. Schmitz (2001), 'A gain from trade: from unproductive to productive entrepreneurship', *Journal of Monetary Economics*, **47**, 417–46.
Ireland, R.D. and J.W. Webb (2007), 'A cross-disciplinary exploration of entrepreneurship research', *Journal of Management*, **33** (6), 891–927.
Kuusi, O. (ed.) (1996), *Innovation Systems and Competitiveness*, Helsinki: Taloutieto Oy.
Leca, B. and P. Naccache (2006), 'A critical realist approach to institutional entrepreneurship', *Organization*, **13** (5), 627–51.
Low, M.B. and I.C. McMillan (1988), 'Entrepreneurship: past research and future challenges', *Journal of Management*, **14** (2), 139–61.
Lundström, A. and L. Stevenson (2002), *On the Road to Entrepreneurship Policy*, Stockholm: Swedish Foundation for Small Business Research.
Łapiński, J. (2009), 'Liczba zarejestrowanych i aktywnych MSP', in A. Żołnierski (ed.), *Raport o stanie sektora małych i średnich przedsiębiorstw w Polsce w latach 2007–2008*, Warsaw: Polska Agencja Rozwoju Przedsiębiorczości, pp. 28–33.
Malerba, F. (2003), 'Sectoral systems and innovation and technology policy', *Revista Brasileira de Inovação*, **2** (2), 329–75.
Malerba, F. (ed.) (2004), *Sectoral System of Innovation. Concepts, Issues and Analyses of Six Major Sectors in Europe*, Cambridge: Cambridge University Press.
McMullen, J.S, L.A. Plummer and Z.J. Acs (2007), 'What is an entrepreneurial opportunity?', *Small Business Economics*, **28** (4), 273–83.
Ministerstwo Gospodarki (1999), *Kierunki działań rządu wobec małych i średnich przedsiębiorstw do 2002 roku*, Warszawa Ministerstwo Gospodarki.
Ministerstwo Gospodarki (2007), *Koncepcja horyzontalnej polityki przemysłowej w Polsce*, Warsaw, http://www.mg.gov.pl, 17 August 2007.
Ministerstwo Gospodarki and Pracy and Polityki Społecznej (2003), *Kierunki działań Rządu wobec małych i średnich przedsiębiorstw od 2003 do 2006 roku*, Warsaw: Ministerstwo Gospodarki, Pracy i Polityki Społecznej.
Ministerstwo Przemysłu i Handlu (1995), *Małe i średnie przedsiębiorstwa w gospodarce narodowej. Polityka wobec MSP*, Warsaw: Ministerstwo Przemysłu i Handlu.
Ministerstwo Rozwoju Regionalnego (2007), *Raport o rozwoju i polityce regionalnej*, Warsaw: Ministerstwo Rozwoju Regionalnego.
Ministry of Economy (2006), *Strategy for Increasing the Innovativeness of the Economy in the Years 2007–2013*, Warsaw: Ministry of Economy.
Navarro, L. (2003), 'Industrial policy in the economic literature. Recent theoretical developments and implications for EU policy', Enterprise Papers 12, Luxembourg: European Commission.
OECD (1998), *Fostering Entrepreneurship*, Paris: Organisation for Economic Co-Operation and Development.
OECD (2001), *Innovative Clusters. Drivers of National Innovation Systems*, Paris: Organisation for Economic Co-Operation and Development.
OECD (2007), *Competitive Regional Clusters. National Policy Approaches*, Paris: Organisation for Economic Co-Operation and Development.
Phillips, N. and P. Tracey (2007), 'Opportunity recognition, entrepreneurial capabilities and bricolage: connecting institutional theory and entrepreneurship in strategic organisation', *Strategic Organization*, **5** (3), 313–20.
Piasecki, B. (1997), *Przedsiębiorczość i małą firma. Teoria i praktyka*, Lodz: Wydawnictwo Uniwersytetu Łódzkiego.

Piasecki, B. (2002a), 'Mała firma w teoriach ekonomicznych', in B. Piasecki (ed.), *Ekonomika i zarządzanie małą firmą*, Warsaw, Lodz: Wydawnictwo Naukowe PWN, pp. 23–94.
Piasecki, B. (2002b), 'SMEs in Poland: development paradigms', in B. Piasecki (ed.), *Entrepreneurship and Small Business Development in the 21st Century*, Lodz: Wydawnictwo Uniwersytetu Łódzkiego, pp. 315–36.
Piasecki, B. and A. Rogut (1994), 'Polish craft industries in the transformation period', in W. König and K. Müller (eds), *Craft Industries in Europe. Proceedings Conference of European Institutes on Small Business*, Göttingen: Institute of Craft Industries and Small Enterprises at the University of Göttingen, pp. 145–58.
Piasecki, B., A. Rogut, A. Rostocki and P. Żuromski (2004), *Regionalna Strategia Innowacji Województwa Łódzkiego RSI LORIS 2005–2013*, Lodz: Urząd Marszałkowski w Łodzi.
Piasecki, B., A. Rogut, E. Stawasz, S. Johnson and D. Smallbone (1999), *Warunki prowadzenia działalności gospodarczej przez MSP w Polsce i krajach Unii Europejskiej*, Warsaw: Polska Fundacja Promocji i Rozwoju Małych i Średnich Przedsiębiorstw.
Pilat, D., A. Cimper, K.B. Olsen and C. Webb (2006), 'The changing nature of manufacturing in OECD economies', STI Working Papers 2006/9, available at http://www.oecd.org/dataoecd/44/17/37607831.pdf (accessed 15 April 2007).
Plummer, L.A., J.M. Haynie and J. Godesiabois (2007), 'An essay on the origins of entrepreneurial opportunity', *Small Business Economics*, **28** (4), 363–79.
Porter, M.E. (1998), 'Clusters and the new economics of competition', *Harvard Business Review*, November–December, 77–90.
Porter, M.E. (2003), 'The economic performance of regions', *Regional Studies*, **37** (6 & 7), 549–78.
Pyciński, S. and A. Żołnierski (2007), *Raport o stanie sektora małych i średnich przedsiębiorstw w Polsce w latach 2005–2006*, Warsaw: Polska Agencja Rozwoju Przedsiębiorczości.
Quéré, M. (2004), 'National systems of innovation and national systems of corporate governance: a missing link?', *Economics of Innovation and New Technology*, **13** (1), 77–90.
Rogut, A. (2002a), 'From transformation to integration – role of SMEs', in B. Piasecki (ed.), *Entrepreneurship and Small Business Development in the 21st Century*, Lodz: Wydawnictwo Uniwersytetu Łódzkiego, pp. 405–27.
Rogut, A. (2002b), *Małe i średnie przedsiębiorstwa w integracji ekonomicznej. Doświadczenia Unii Europejskiej. Lekcje dla Polski*, Lodz: Wydawnictwo Uniwersytetu Łódzkiego.
Rogut, A. (ed.) (2008), *Potencjał polskich MSP w zakresie absorbowania korzyści integracyjnych*, Lodz: Wydawnictwo Uniwersytetu Łódzkiego.
Rogut, A. and B. Piasecki (2008a), *Delphi. Technologie Przyszłości*, Lodz: Społeczna Wyższa Szkoła Przedsiębiorczości i Zarządzania w Łodzi.
Rogut, A. and B. Piasecki (2008b), *Regional Innovation Strategy for the Lodz Province*, Lodz: Społeczna Wyższa Szkoła Przedsiębiorczości i Zarządzania w Łodzi.
Sanders, M. (2007), 'Scientific paradigms, entrepreneurial opportunities and cycles in economic growth', *Small Business Economics*, **28** (4), 339–54.
Sejmik Województwa Łódzkiego (2006), 'Strategia Rozwoju Województwa Łódzkiego na lata 2007–2020', available at http://www.lodzkie.pl/export/download/bip_strategia/strategia-lodzkie-2007-2020.pdf (accessed 22 November 2006).
Sharpe, A. and O. Guilbaud (2005), 'Indicators of innovation in Canadian natural resource industries', Centre for the Study of Living Standards for Natural Resources Canada, available at http://www.csls.ca/reports/csls2005-03-Appendix1.pdf (accessed 2 April 2007).
Smith, K. (2000), 'Innovation as a systemic phenomenon: rethinking the role of policy', *Innovation Management Study*, **1** (1), 73–102.
Spencer, A.S., B.A. Kirchhoff and C. White (2008), 'Entrepreneurship, innovation, and wealth distribution: the essence of creative destruction', *International Small Business Journal*, **26** (1), 9–25.
Sudoł, S. (2008), 'Przedsiębiorczość', *Problemy Zarządzania*, **2** (20), 9–23.
Thukral, I.S., J. von Ehr, S. Walsh, A.J. Groen, P. van der Sijde and K.A. Adham (2008), 'Entrepreneurship, emerging technologies, emerging markets', *International Small Business Journal*, **26** (1), 101–16.

UKIE (2003), *Wpływ akcesji Polski do Unii Europejskiej na sektor małych i średnich przedsiębiorstw*, Warsaw: Urząd Komitetu Integracji Europejskiej.
United Nations (2005), *World Investment Report 2005. Transnational Corporations and the Internationalisation of R&D*, New York and Geneva: United Nations Conference on Trade and Development.
Urząd Marszałkowski (2007), 'Regionalny Program Operacyjny Województwa Łódzkiego na lata 2007–2013', available at www.rpo.lodzkie.pl/export/sites/rpo/RPO/Baza_plikow/ RPO_WL_sfc_09_07.pdf (accessed 13 February 2008).
Wijen, F. and S. Ansari (2007), 'Overcoming inaction through collective institutional entrepreneurship: insights from regime theory', *Organization Studies*, **28** (7), 1080–1100.
Wissema, J.G. (2005), *Technostarterzy, dlaczego i jak?*, Warsaw: Polska Agencja Rozwoju Przedsiębiorczości.
World Bank (1996), *World Development Report 1996: From Plan to Market*, Oxford UK: Oxford University Press.
Zecchini, S. (ed.) (1997), *Lessons from the Economic Transition. Central and Eastern Europe in the 1990s*, Dordrecht, Boston, London: Kluwer Academic Publishers.

8 From making the state to institutionalizing entrepreneurship policy in Slovenia
Miroslav Rebernik and Barbara Bradač

INTRODUCTION

Slovenia, once the most developed and industrialized western part of underdeveloped socialist Yugoslavia, severed its ties with socialism and Yugoslavia in 1991. By starting its independent life as a state, this country – with a population of two million people – had to make two main transitions: the transition into an independent country and the transition from socialism to capitalism. During the transition process, the privatization of socialist companies was pivotal because, aside from craft units, the majority of companies in the newly born country were state owned.

At the dawn of this new era, the economy was characterized as a 'socialist black hole' (Vahčič and Petrin 1990, p. 69) because of the almost complete absence of small companies in the range of 10 to 100 employees. By restructuring the Slovenian economy, this black hole was filled from the top down with spin-offs and the remnants of bankrupted large companies as well as from the bottom up with growing micro and small companies contributing to employment.

This chapter will introduce a brief overview of entrepreneurship development since 1990 before proceeding with a more detailed insight into the development of entrepreneurship policy and how it was institutionalized. According to the main tasks policy makers followed, this discussion will consider three characteristic periods. The first, between 1991 and 1996, was a period of establishing all the necessary institutions and subsequently introducing the legislation forming the national state and a fully fledged market economy. The second period, between 1997 and 2003, was heavily characterized by the EU accession process and harmonizing Slovenian legislation with *Aquis communitaire*. The third period, after 2004, saw the establishment of a more coherent small and medium-sized enterprise (SME) and entrepreneurship policy.

For each of these periods we will show the main tasks, policies, and institutions whose aim was to support SMEs and entrepreneurship. Taking into account general frameworks suggested by Lundström and

Stevenson (2005) as well as Audretsch et al. (2007), we will focus on entrepreneurship promotion and education, the environment for SMEs and start-ups, financial support, business support measures for SMEs and start-ups, and on-target group strategies.

ENTREPRENEURSHIP DEVELOPMENT IN SLOVENIA SINCE 1991

We will use two sources to show the development of entrepreneurship in Slovenia since 1991. One is the statistical data obtained from the Slovenian statistical office and Eurostat; the other is primary data obtained by research of the Global Entrepreneurship Monitor (GEM). The Global Entrepreneurship Monitor is a global research programme established in 1999 with the main task of collecting harmonized data to enable comparison of entrepreneurship among countries. Slovenia joined in 2002 and some valuable data have been collected that can help us better understand the development of entrepreneurship and policy issues.

Entrepreneurship Development in Slovenia According to Statistical Data

Just before the split from Yugoslavia, economic indicators for Slovenia revealed a serious underlying economic crisis. GDP was falling rapidly, inflation had skyrocketed to 550 per cent, and industrial output was declining at an annual rate of 10.5 per cent (Petrin et al. 2002, p. 49). The process of entrepreneurship development had already started in Yugoslavia thanks to the new Company Law enacted in 1988, which boosted the establishment of companies with private and mixed ownership. Other factors contributing to the increasing number of new companies included (a) low capital and legal barriers for new incorporations; (b) the slow privatization process during the early 1990s, which encouraged many managers to establish their own companies; and (c) bankruptcies of large companies, which created opportunities for small companies – especially in the service sector (Glas and Drnovšek 2003). On the other hand, numerous obstacles to new venture creation also arose, such as the lack of debt and equity financing, cultural barriers, the lack of business premises, the strong bureaucracy, and complicated registration procedures.

Nevertheless, the 1990s were significantly influenced by rapid growth in the number of SMEs, which underscored their increasing importance as well as the dynamic role of entrepreneurship. The importance of SMEs was primarily attained by the fact that, after breaking away from Yugoslavia, Slovenia lost most of the easily accessible, low-competitive, and friendly Yugoslavian market. Large, inefficient state-owned companies were forced into bankruptcy, which resulted in an increased unemployment rate. Peak unemployment – 17.7 per cent at the national level – was reached in October 1993, although some regions (for example, Podravje) recorded unemployment in excess of 24 per cent.

Despite the strong need for industrial restructuring, it is estimated that the government's role was limited to selective measures, including provisions to traditional low value-added industries and to programs for the unemployed. The government programs were 'very often simply a source of cash for specific enterprises to cover their operating costs' (Petrin et al. 2002, p. 55). Four main reasons explain such a simplified government role (Petrin et al. 2002, p. 55–57):

- The high social costs of transitioning from a socialist to a market economy;
- The understanding of policymakers (mainly academic macro-economists) that the prime competitive advantage in Slovenia is low labour costs;
- The strong influence of experts from international lending institutions, who believed that growth would follow macroeconomic stabilization – an opinion supported by Slovenia's mainstream economists, who argued that policy intervention was justified only to correct market imperfections; and
- The state's limited capacity to provide assistance to firms, together with a widespread lack of interest in monitoring the results of such policy.

The small-company sector contributed most of the new jobs during the hard times of transition and was the most dynamic sector from 1989 to 1998 not only in job gains, but also in job losses (Drnovšek 2004). SMEs were seen as the main mechanism for solving unemployment problems; their role was primarily studied through their job creation potential. In the 10-year period from 1989 to 1998, companies with fewer than 50 employees had a positive net employment rate, with the only exception being in 1993 to 1994, when a drop in employment was detected in all types of companies due to changes in Company Law (Drnovšek and Glas 2000, p. 839). The new Company Law enforced stricter rules for doing business which, together with the abolition of certain tax reliefs and some other advantages for small and micro entrepreneurs, resulted in a slowdown of entrepreneurial activities in Slovenia. During this period, SMEs not only boosted employment significantly, but the newly created firms were also more efficient in terms of revenue growth (Vahčič et al. 1998).

In the first wave of entrepreneurship development in Slovenia, the majority of entrepreneurs were recruited from the following groups (Glas and Drnovšek 2003, p. 831):

- *Former employees of medium and large state-owned companies* who established private businesses to capture business opportunities that were not financially or strategically attractive for larger companies, yet presented possibilities for smaller firms;
- *Former top and middle managers* who left state-owned companies to form their own companies;
- *Successful craftsmen* with established circles of customers and accumulated capital;
- *Graduates of self-employment programmes* run by the Slovenian Employment Service or other government-funded agencies that provided training, consulting, and financial funds for the unemployed interested in starting their own businesses; and
- *Free professions*, such as accountants, lawyers, and business consultants, who decided to obtain legal status as entrepreneurs to enable more effective commercialization of their services.

By the end of 1991, 74 689 economic subjects had been registered in Slovenia (SURS 2004, p. 54). The majority of them were crafts units. The number of incorporated businesses was 21 527, but estimates suggest that only 60 per cent to 65 per cent of all registered companies actually operated (Glas 1993). In subsequent years, the number of registered and actually operating businesses increased rapidly, and for the year 2002, the Slovenian Business Register showed 140 982 registered units. However, this number is misleading as not all of them were operating and not all were companies.

Table 8.1 shows the number of companies actually operating, the number of employed people, and average added value per employee for the period 2002–07. During the same period, steady growth is evident, reflecting the positive momentum of the development of entrepreneurship in Slovenia. According to data collected by the Agency of the Republic of Slovenia for Public Legal Records and Related Services (AJPES), 111 201 active enterprises existed in Slovenia in 2007; of these, the majority had 1 to 9 employees and only 271 had 250 or more employees. Most enterprises fell within the industries of K – namely, real estate, renting and business services (22.3 per cent) – followed by the industries of G (trade, repair of motor vehicles, and household goods; 21.2 per cent), D (manufacturing; 15.8 per cent), F (construction; 15.5 per cent), and I (transport, storage, and communications; 8.2 per cent). All remaining industries combined accounted for 17 per cent of all enterprises.

Table 8.1   Companies according to class size in the period 2002–07

	Year	Companies according to class size (in number of employees)					TOTAL
		0	1 to 9	10 to 49	50 to 249	250 and more	
Number of enterprises	2002	9912	75346	4522	1162	308	91250
	2003	11081	76062	4641	1149	300	93233
	2004	12274	78301	5089	1186	284	97134
	2005	12794	82119	5328	1186	281	101708
	2006	13454	85721	5587	1249	262	106273
	2007	14059	89611	5966	1294	271	111201
Number of employees	2002		137732	90171	123360	210580	561843
	2003		137445	93737	121057	204241	556480
	2004		156927	98409	122927	199462	577725
	2005		161859	102668	123276	199163	586967
	2006		165918	106997	129555	196094	598564
	2007		173278	114926	131701	202493	622399
Average added value per employee (in EUR)	2002		17115	22927	22167	26812	22916
	2003		17669	24071	23652	28619	24068
	2004		16004	26076	25813	29801	24787
	2005		16121	27301	27480	32079	26061
	2006		17205	28549	28105	33879	27205
	2007		18330	31956	30332	36864	29513

Source: Rus and Rebernik (2009), according to data provided by AJPES – the Agency of the Republic of Slovenia for Public Legal Records and Related Services.

The bad news is that most Slovenian companies – a little more than one third (33.7 per cent) – are located in the Osrednje-slovenska region, including the capital city and nearby surroundings (37483), while the fewest are in the Zasavska region (1546), which also has the smallest number of enterprises per 1000 inhabitants (34.2). The Obalno-kraška region ranks far above the national average (55.1), with 74.6 enterprises per 1000 inhabitants; Osrednje-slovenska ranks second, with 74 enterprises per 1000 inhabitants. The fact that enterprises in Slovenia are very unevenly distributed throughout its territory is cause for concern. Undoubtedly, the economic prosperity of the region and the number of enterprises are interdependent: less developed regions have fewer enterprises, which makes them less developed. The number of enterprises is important not only for recruitment purposes, but also for the establishment of various entrepreneurship support systems, attainment of economies of scale, creation of support services, development of banking networks, attractiveness for the venture capital industry, a critical mass of social capital, the synergy of competences, and so on. Regions with a low density of companies not only suffer from higher unemployment and a lower level of development, but they also lack the possibilities of spillover effects that companies bring along (Rus and Rebernik 2009).

Currently, SMEs are important drivers of economic development and employment, representing 99.8 per cent of all enterprises in Slovenia and employing 419 906 people (two thirds of all employment). Although the number of employees in large enterprises has diminished over the past five years, the number of employees in SMEs has steadily increased. Although such growth in the number of companies and the importance of SMEs is satisfactory, comparisons to EU companies are not as favourable. The most recent available structural business data of the non-financial business economy for EU-27 and Slovenia show that the EU-27 created 5 650 billion € of added value, to which Slovenia contributed a modest 16 billion €. The average person employed in the non-financial business economy in the EU-27 created 42 300 € in gross value added, but only 29 640 € in Slovenia. The most productive employees were those from large enterprises, who tended to generate 24 per cent higher-than-average productivity. The least productive employees were from micro enterprises, who achieved only 64 per cent of average Slovenian productivity in 2007 in the non-financial business economy – less than in the EU-27 in this class size. The most productive people in the EU-27 and Slovenia worked for electricity, gas, and water supply, creating 120 000 € gross added value in the EU-27 and 53 600 € in Slovenia. Average productivity in the EU-27 was 1.7 times higher than Slovenian productivity (Močnik 2009).

Entrepreneurial Activity and Attitudes of Adult Population in Slovenia According to Global Entrepreneurship Monitor (GEM) Data

As previous research has confirmed (for example, Audretsch et al. 2006; Thurik 2008; Wennekers et al. 2005), a strong relationship exists between entrepreneurship and economic development. According to data from the 2008 Global Competitiveness Report, 43 GEM participating countries were clustered in factor-driven, efficiency-driven, and innovation-driven countries. Based on GDP per capita, Slovenia belongs to the group of innovation-driven countries, along with Belgium, Denmark, Finland, France, Germany, Greece, Iceland, Ireland, Israel, Italy, Japan, the Republic of Korea, the Netherlands, Norway, Spain, the United Kingdom, and the United States.

Several comparisons have been made between Slovenian entrepreneurship characteristics and clusters of innovation-driven countries from

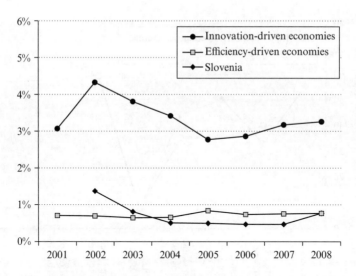

Source: Rebernik et al. (2009).

Figure 8.1 Total early stage entrepreneurial activity out of necessity

2002 to 2008. Within GEM, early stage entrepreneurial activity is evident among the adult population – namely, the share of those individuals who have already established a business that is between three and 42 months old (new businesses) or are in the process of establishing a business or having one younger than three months (nascent entrepreneurs). Early stage entrepreneurial activity is expressed in the TEA index, comprising nascent and new entrepreneurs. The GEM does not count registered businesses, but measures the entrepreneurial activity and attitudes of individuals. Slovenia joined the GEM in 2002, registering 4.6 per cent of the adult population being engaged in some way in early stage entrepreneurial activity in that year. By 2008, the engagement of adult population had increased to 6.4 per cent.

The majority of entrepreneurs in Slovenia started their careers not out of necessity, but because they wanted to exploit a promising opportunity, which is also a characteristic of entrepreneurship in more developed countries (see Figure 8.1). In 2008, the share of necessity-driven entrepreneurs among early stage entrepreneurs was less than 10 per cent.

From a policy point of view, it is important to realize that most people who establish a company make such a career move while they are employed. According to GEM 2008 data, less than 5 per cent of all entrepreneurs in Slovenia established their companies while they were unemployed. Encouraging unemployed people to establish their own company

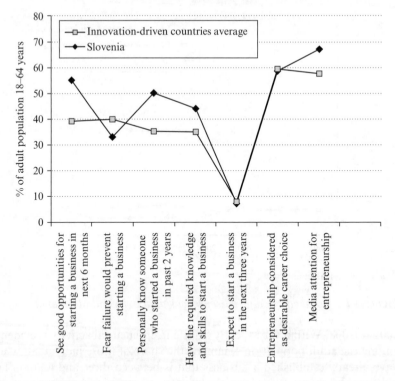

Source: Rebernik et al. (2009).

Figure 8.2   Entrepreneurial attitudes and perceptions in Slovenia and 18 GEM 2008 innovation-driven countries

and self-employ is obviously not appropriate for solving unemployment problems. The problem is clearly not in the number of entrepreneurs and companies, but in their quality. This is also where important differences between SME policy and entrepreneurship policy lie – the former focuses on the number of entrepreneurs with no regard to the type of business they create; as long as the unemployment rate decreases, while the latter looks to the type of businesses created (Lundström and Stevenson 2001).

Companies are created by individuals who see opportunity, have the required knowledge and skills to start a business, and regard entrepreneurship as a desirable career. Entrepreneurial attitudes and perceptions of the adult population in Slovenia compared to the average of 18 innovation-driven countries are displayed in Figure 8.2. The strong potential for further development of Slovenian entrepreneurship is clearly evident. The attitudes and perceptions of the adult population all favour starting a business: high opportunity recognition, low fear of failure, presence of role models, and confidence in having the necessary knowledge and skills. A similar pattern can be observed for the entire period of 2002 to 2008. Obviously, policy makers do not need to take any special efforts to encourage those capabilities; they are already here. They should start from here and build on it.

According to the GEM conceptual model, entrepreneurial activity varies within each country according to entrepreneurial framework conditions, which include the availability of financing, governmental policies and programmes, education and training, research and development (R&D) transfer, commercial and services infrastructure, market openness, physical Infrastructure, cultural and social norms, knowledge and skills, IPR protection, women's support during start-ups, and available resources for high growth (Reynolds et al. 2005). National experts in each GEM country answer a long list of questions every year and give their assessment of the situation with regard to entrepreneurial framework conditions on a scale from 1 to 5. Comparing the assessments in 2002 and 2008, some entrepreneurial framework conditions in Slovenia have improved significantly over the past seven years; at the general level, not much difference exists anymore between Slovenia and GEM 31 countries when we look at framework conditions as an average. Comparing the best-evaluated frameworks in particular countries to those in Slovenia indicates that significant differences still exist, expressed especially in the fields of government policies (support and regulations), market openness and velocity of changes, cultural and social norms, intellectual property rights, and focus on high growth (Rebernik et al. 2009). These are areas in which entrepreneurship policy should pay appropriate attention in the near future.

DEVELOPMENT OF ENTREPRENEURSHIP POLICY IN SLOVENIA

Slovenia had to develop its own entrepreneurship and SME policies when it became an independent country. After researching these two policy concepts, it can be concluded that Slovenia's history includes elements of both. Theory indicates that SME policy focuses on existing companies while entrepreneurship policy focuses more on entrepreneurs who are in the process of developing new businesses or have early stage companies. Therefore, the entrepreneurship policy is a broader concept, which – according to Lundström and Stevenson (2002, 2005) – includes measures to stimulate entrepreneurial culture, promote entrepreneurship, and support nascent and early stage entrepreneurs. For the purposes of this study, we used the framework proposed by Lundström and Stevenson (2002) in which an overlap between the two policies exists. The discussion herein focuses on showing a shift from SME policy toward entrepreneurship policy that was predominant in the first years after Slovenia's independence, thereby preparing the overview of covered entrepreneurship policy areas in a particular time period using the six areas proposed by Lundström and Stevenson (2005), as summarized in Tables 8.2 through 8.4:

- Entrepreneurship promotion;
- Entrepreneurship education;
- Environment for SMEs and start-ups;
- Start-ups and seed capital financing;
- Business support measures for SMEs and start-ups; and
- Target group strategies.

To better understand the development of entrepreneurship policy and supporting institutions in Slovenia, it is important to understand that not only entrepreneurship policies and institutions had to be built in Slovenia, but also the state itself. The timeline in Figure 8.3 depicts three periods, with some common characteristics highlighted.

The Making of the State (1991–96)

Starting in 1991, as an independent country, Slovenia's primary goals were to establish the state and replace the socialistic economy with a market economy. This was a twofold transition process in which the main tasks were to establish a capitalist state and form an environment that would enable economic growth. During this period, Slovenian national policy focused primarily on:

- Solving the unemployment problem and supporting self-employment;
- Forming a supportive environment for SMEs;
- Offering financial support to SMEs;
- Supporting crafts;
- Establishing institutions of innovative environment, such as technology parks;
- Supporting the technological development of SMEs; and
- Raising awareness among people about entrepreneurship.

The basic framework for new venture creation along with the rules of a market economy was established by the establishment of the Companies

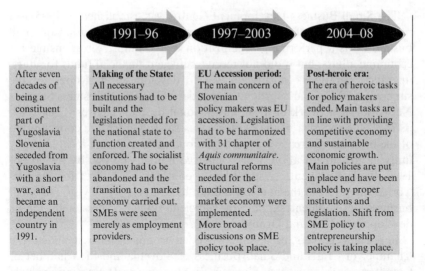

1991–96	1997–2003	2004–08
After seven decades of being a constituent part of Yugoslavia Slovenia seceded from Yugoslavia with a short war, and became an independent country in 1991.	**Making of the State:** All necessary institutions had to be built and the legislation needed for the national state to function created and enforced. The socialist economy had to be abandoned and the transition to a market economy carried out. SMEs were seen merely as employment providers.	**EU Accession period:** The main concern of Slovenian policy makers was EU accession. Legislation had to be harmonized with 31 chapter of *Aquis communitaire*. Structural reforms needed for the functioning of a market economy were implemented. More broad discussions on SME policy took place.	**Post-heroic era:** The era of heroic tasks for policy makers ended. Main tasks are in line with providing competitive economy and sustainable economic growth. Main policies are put in place and have been enabled by proper institutions and legislation. Shift from SME policy to entrepreneurship policy is taking place.

Source: Authors.

Figure 8.3   *Characteristic periods in the development of entrepreneurship policy in Slovenia*

Act as well as the Small Business Development Act. The latter was adopted in 1991 and created a framework for establishing support institutions for SMEs. Although this act created a legal framework for the Small Business Development Fund and the Small Business Development Centre, the entire system was developed step-by-step and is characterized by a lack of unified concept, modest financial resources, and quick changes in supportive concepts and programmes, leading to a gap between the needs and expectations of entrepreneurs and real possibilities. The Small Business Development Fund should enable easier access to SMEs' finance, providing guarantees and loans and subsidized interest rates; however, it had limited impact on SMEs' financing due to a lack of financial resources and its own financial troubles stemming from lengthy and bureaucratic procedures, an inappropriate legal basis, and limited professional knowledge (Glas 2004, pp. 7–8). Furthermore, it was undercapitalized, as its main source of revenues was realized through privatization purchases that limited its ability to provide sufficient financial support. Although the government rescued the fund from bankruptcy with an injection of additional capital, the negative publicity surrounding the management of the fund prompted a change in policy, which subsequently granted only subsidized bank loans to entrepreneurs (Glas and Drnovšek 1999).

The Small Business Development Centre was established in 1995 as a principal provider of entrepreneurship promotion and creation of small businesses as a performing organization of the ministry responsible for economic affairs, but it did not receive sufficient financial funds for start-ups and operations. Its mission was to develop soft measures for the support of SMEs and coordinate activities of the Small Business Support Network – a network of local and regional business centres (Glas 2004, p. 7). The basic idea of the network was to strengthen the coordination of the business centres' work at the national, regional, and local levels by unifying the organization; it has achieved limited success. By the end of 1996, the government re-established a considerable budget for the net-work's support, but the ministry did not have an elaborate vision of small business development support or sufficient skilled professionals for its development (Glas and Drnovšek 1999).

Important players in a supportive environment also included the Chamber of Crafts and Small Business of Slovenia and the Chamber of Commerce and Industry of Slovenia. In Slovenia, craft associations have a very long tradition, and the first Chamber of Trade, Craft and Industry was established as early as 1850. Organizational forms of the Chamber of Crafts changed over time. In 1990, it became an independent legal entity, and the state transferred some authority to it. Its legal status was changed with the Small Business Act of 1994. The Chamber's most important roles and activities have remained basically the same for two decades and include representing the interests of craftsmen and small entrepreneurs at the national level; providing consultancy, information, training, and education; organizing the annual International Trade Fair; and performing numerous public authorisations left by the state.

A similar organization is the Chamber of Commerce and Industry of Slovenia, which was established in 1962. With the introduction of the 1990 Chamber of Commerce Act, companies were legally obliged to become Chamber members. Over the years, more and more members became unsatisfied with the services and organization of the Chamber. In 2006 a new Chamber of Commerce and Industry Act was passed, bringing some significant changes into the chamber system in Slovenia, including voluntary membership, the establishment of new private chambers of commerce, and the transformation of the existing Chamber of Commerce.

As previously stated, unemployment was an extremely serious problem in the first years of independence. The number of employees decreased from 819000 in 1988 to 657000 in 1992. The average standard of living declined while social differences between people increased. Workers organized a number of strikes primarily due to poor and outstanding wages (Krašovec 2001). In addition, massive early retirement (the number of pensioners doubled), social relief, and other social benefits imposed a strong burden of debt on public finance. To solve the problem the government passed the Employment and Insurance against Unemployment Act in 1991 and established the Employment Service of Slovenia at the national level, with regional employment offices (Employment Service of Slovenia 2008), to offer different measures on an annual basis to support unemployed people and help them search for new jobs as well as gain new qualifications. Another of the government's goals was to raise awareness among people about entrepreneurship. In 1992, it had already started some programmes to promote entrepreneurial and creative thinking among young people, which were offered by private providers primarily by adapting similar programs from abroad (for example, the programme for entrepreneurship training of young people from elementary school to students launched in 1994).

To support innovative businesses, the ministry responsible for economic affairs sponsored the establishment of two business parks in 1992: Technology Park Ljubljana and Technology Park Maribor (Drnovšek and Glas 2006). However, the main problems were that financing was not stable and local networks were not developed. In addition, a conflict of interest became apparent as technological development was the responsibility of the Ministry of Science and Technology, whose funding was shifted from technology to science over the years. The proportion of funds for technology fell from 20 per cent in 1991 to 8 per cent in 1999 (Bartlett and Bukvič 2001). Moreover, the Slovenian Technological Development Fund was established by the government in 1994 as a first direct mechanism for stimulating and financing technological development, mainly through the assurance of loans for SMEs when introducing new, technologically improved products or new technology (Bučar and Stare 1998).

In 1995, the first strategic document at the national level, the Strategy of Economic Development of Slovenia, was adopted. The strategy was aimed at catching up to the developmental stage of Europe's most developed countries; it entailed the idea of sustainable development. Its developmental orientation included internationalization, polycentric development, market economy, the maintenance of relatively high social standards, and integral planning. However, implementation of the strategy was not well performed.

Summarizing the first period, it was mainly characterized by the formation of organizations and institutions, the passing of different laws, and the formulation of general conditions and a framework for SMEs' environment. During that time, national entrepreneurship policy was focused primarily on the area of business support measures for SMEs, while national policies focusing on the environment for SMEs and financing SMEs and start-ups were only partially covered.

EU Accession (1997–2003)

With the primary goal of becoming an EU member, Slovenia adopted the 'Strategy for the inclusion of the Republic of Slovenia into the European Union: Economic and Social Part' in 1998. During that time, Slovenia was not sufficiently developed to fulfil the EU admission criteria. To be successfully integrated into the economic and social field, the following reforms had to be successfully introduced:

- Economic stabilization;
- Economic transition, the regulation of property rights, and the implementation of structural reforms needed for the functioning of a market economy; and
- The adoption of rules and regulations to achieve the required degree of compatibility with the EU.

The most important among these requirements was economic stabilization, as no market economy can operate successfully if it has not resolved its main macroeconomic issues. The formal process of ownership transformation had already been completed, most companies had been restructured, and the rehabilitation of the banks was completed. Thus, the basic conditions for the creation of a market economy had been fulfilled. However, to support the entrepreneurial sector further, reforms were needed in the financial sector to enable higher competitiveness.

Table 8.2   Entrepreneurship policies in the first period

Policies	Not covered	Partially covered	Fully covered
Entrepreneurship promotion	x		
Entrepreneurship education	x		
The environment for SMEs and start-ups		x	
Start-ups and seed capital financing		x	
Business support measures for SMEs and start-ups		x	
Target group strategies	x		

Source: Authors.

The Slovenian national policy during this period focused on the following objectives:

- Restructuring the economy and increasing competitiveness;
- Supporting the transfer of technology from universities and other research and development organizations to the industry;
- Increasing companies' innovativeness;
- Internationalizing companies;
- Establishing appropriate entrepreneurship topics in the formal education system;
- Increasing entrepreneurial culture;
- Changing employment policies;
- Lessening administrative burdens;
- Developing sustainable regional development;
- Promoting entrepreneurship at the local level;
- Simplifying the procedures for establishing a company;
- Stimulating rural entrepreneurship;
- Supporting some entrepreneurship awareness-building events; and
- Fostering cooperation among companies.

One of the government's priorities during this period was also balanced regional development. For this reason, the Promotion of Balanced Regional Development Act was adopted in 1999 in an effort to reduce disparities in economic development among regions, with emphasis on an integrated approach to rural development. The act was very political and failed to contribute to more intensive development of entrepreneurship in less developed regions or build a more competitive regional economy.

Mainly after the year 2000, the number of measures, programmes, and projects in different areas for SMEs increased significantly. Although not integrated into one sustainable system, they provided some general development of the entrepreneurship field. In the area of promoting entrepreneurship and building entrepreneurial culture, several projects were implemented. The Ministry of the Economy's measures in the promotion of entrepreneurship and entrepreneurship education were carried out based on the 'Programme of Measures to Promote Entrepreneurship and Competitiveness for the Period 2002–2006'. The Ministry also introduced three programmes for promoting and supporting entrepreneurship among young people. First was the programme of development of entrepreneurship and creativity of young people between 2001 and 2004, implemented by the Small Business Development Centre, to boost the confidence of young people in their own abilities and knowledge, acquaint them with the basic values and principles of an entrepreneurial society, and develop the basic skills of entrepreneurship (it included approximately 4500 young people between the ages of 12 and 30 years annually). The second programme was Young Researchers for the Economy, which aimed to foster the inflow of R&D personnel into companies and strengthen their core businesses by co-financing part of the costs of young researchers recruited by the companies or technological and other development centres. The third programme was the system of dual education, which promoted different professional and vocational educations (implemented by the Chamber of Crafts and taken over by the Employment Service in 2005). In addition, the voucher advisory system for potential and existing entrepreneurs was launched in 2000 by the Small Business Development Centre as a pilot project in two regions and subsequently throughout Slovenia in 2002. Furthermore, the government has – through the Small Business Development Centre and the Ministry of the Economy – implemented a permanent promotion of entrepreneurship to improve entrepreneurial culture in Slovenia and self-employment for young people and women both in urban as well as in rural areas through counselling programmes, education, promotion, and financial support.

Because the procedures for establishing a new company were much too long, the Ministry of Labour, Family and Social Affairs and the Ministry of the Economy introduced the Anti-bureaucratic Programme in 2000. Its objectives were to (1) significantly reduce the cost of opening a new business; (2) reduce the time to start a new company; (3) abolish all administrative obstacles that prevent faster growth of small and medium enterprises; and (4) establish a system of employment and labour relations in the field of small business that will allow for sufficient flexibility for SMEs and ensure an adequate level of social security for employees. The ultimate goal of the Anti-bureaucratic Programme was to ensure that new businesses could be established in one place and that procedures would not take more than 14 days. In this sense the Small Business Development Centre began to establish the system of one-stop shops in 2001. In 2006, a network of one-stop shops with their e-mode was finally formally established – not only to register a company, but also to provide all necessary information to entrepreneurs by trained counsellors. During this period, the government also supported Euro Info Centres with the aim to help SMEs in their internationalization (the first was established in 1993 in Ljubljana, followed by Koper and Maribor in 2000).

At the national level, interest increased for supporting the cooperation of SMEs. The government offered strong support to the establishment of clusters starting to define a systematic approach to developing clusters through the mapping study steered by the Ministry of the Economy started in 1999 (Dermastia and Križnič 2000). Given the lack of practical experience, knowledge, and available instruments in starting up cluster development, the Ministry decided to launch pilot cluster development projects in the fields of automotive industry, tooling industry, and transport logistics in 2000. The results of clustering support have been encouraging; consequently, awareness of clustering has significantly increased. The Ministry launched the Programme of Fostering Cluster Development in Slovenia in 2001 and supported more than 20 initiatives before finishing it in 2004. The purpose of the programme was to enhance networking and cooperation among companies and knowledge institutions in Slovenia that could significantly accelerate investments in the development of new knowledge and technologies, specialization and increased competences of firms, development of knowledge and skills on the labour market for the needs of particular members, and improved marketing activities of individual members and/or groups of companies in international markets. Several of the clusters remain very successful (for example, the automotive and tooling industry).

In the framework of the supportive environment for SMEs, some additional activities were carried out. A renewed interest in business incubators was supported by different initiatives, such as PHARE and cross-border projects. Unfortunately, after 1996, the government lessened its interest in business incubators; consequently, only a few incubators have survived (Drnovšek and Glas 2006).

Summarizing the second period, national strategies were spread across all entrepreneurship policies. However, not all were covered consistently. One of the drawbacks was that the supportive environment for venture capital was still not developed. In addition, entrepreneurship support through sponsorship and the education system was not well developed. However, during this period, Slovenia addressed all the EU's harmonization requirements and fulfilled all the accession criteria.

Table 8.3   Entrepreneurship policies in the second period

Policies	Not covered	Partially covered	Fully covered
Entrepreneurship promotion		x	
Entrepreneurship education		x	
The environment for SMEs and start-ups			x
Start-ups and seed capital financing		x	
Business support measures for SMEs and start-ups			x
Target group strategies		x	

Source: Authors.

The End of an Heroic Era (2004–)

In 2004, after the establishment of the national state and the introduction of a relatively successful market economy, Slovenia became a regular member state of the EU. The era of heroic tasks for policy makers ended, and Slovenia's main goals became tightly connected to the question of how to compete with the most developed countries in the EU in order to provide sustainable economic growth. Slovenia's national policy became focused on:

- Faster economic growth,
- Sustainable development,
- Fostering of innovativeness and technological development,
- Education for entrepreneurship,
- Support of entrepreneurship among particular groups of people, and
- Venture capital support.

For the first time at the national level, all policies were focused on being constructed into one coherent system. In the first two years after joining the EU, programmes and strategies that started in 2000 to 2002 were implemented. In 2005, the main national document, 'Slovenia's Development Strategy', was adopted, setting five key developmental priorities:

- A competitive economy and faster economic growth;
- Effective generation, two-way flow, and application of the knowledge needed for economic development and quality jobs;
- An efficient and less costly state;
- A modern social state and higher employment; and
- Integration of measures to achieve sustainable development.

The main weaknesses of previous development strategies were their unsatisfactory implementation and the fact that they were not amended and upgraded on a regular basis. If Slovenia wants to improve its position and range among the most developed EU countries, it needs to improve its global competitiveness substantially. This, however, will require more radical structural reforms in order to resolve fundamental development problems and overcome resistance to faster social change.

In 2007, based on the 'Slovenia's Development Strategy', the 'National Research and Development Programme 2006–2010', the 'Framework of Economic and Social Reforms for Increasing Welfare in Slovenia', and the 'National Action Plan for the Lisbon Strategy', the government adopted the Programme of Measures for Promoting Entrepreneurship and Competitiveness 2007–2013, which should – during this period – form the basis for directing activities and the use of budgetary funds of the Ministry of the Economy. This programme is based on four fundamental interconnected pillars: (1) promoting entrepreneurship and an entrepreneur-friendly environment; (2) ensuring knowledge for business; (3) enhancing R&D and innovations in companies; and (4) promoting small and medium-sized enterprises with equity and debt instruments. The policies and corresponding measures are aimed at catching up with the most developed countries in the EU by 2013. As this is a very ambitious goal, the operation of all institutions at the national, regional, and local levels must be well coordinated, which is not yet the case, although some institutional changes have been made recently.

During the past four years, some other changes have also appeared in supportive environment legislation and, consequently, in organizations of the supportive environment. When the Small Business Development Act of 1991 became obsolete, it was replaced by the Supportive Environment for Entrepreneurship Act in 2004. In accordance with this act, the Small Business Development Fund was transformed into the Slovenian Enterprise Fund, which was allocated new tasks. The fund has been instrumental in directing European structural resources for development investments into the entrepreneurial sector since 2004. In 2004, the Public Agency for Technology of the Republic of Slovenia (TIA) was established as an independent public agency responsible for the enhancement of technology development and innovation with an aim to promote technological development and innovation. According to the Resolution on the National Research and Development Programme 2006–2010, the Agency implements programmes and measures to promote competitiveness and technological development mainly as grant programmes aimed at technology development and fostering the cooperation of R&D institutions and universities with industry.

In 2006, the Small Business Development Centre was reorganized into the Public Agency of the Republic of Slovenia for Entrepreneurship and Foreign Investments. Its main task is to look after the implementation of development policy designed to cater for the development of entrepreneurship and competitiveness in Slovenia, and to run programmes aimed at attracting foreign direct investments and company internationalization (JAPTI 2008). The Agency launched several programmes to foster entrepreneurship among particular groups of people (for example, Programme of Vocational Development of Women in 2002 and Entrepreneurship in the Countryside in 2002). In 2008, other institutional changes occurred

Table 8.4   Entrepreneurship policies in the third period

Policies	Not covered	Partially covered	Fully covered
Entrepreneurship promotion			x
Entrepreneurship education			x
The environment for SMEs and start-ups			x
Start-ups and seed capital financing			x
Business support measures for SMEs and start-ups			x
Target group strategies			x

Source: Authors.

as the Enterprise Europe Network was established, incorporating the activities of two organizations – namely, Euro Info Centres and the Innovation Relay Centre Slovenia. Finally, in 2007, Slovenia supported venture capital investment at the national level with the Venture Capital Companies Act, which should enable capital financing of fast-growing companies. Venture capital companies will be given tax concessions from capital investment, which is supposed to increase the share of venture capital in Slovenian companies.

The third period of the development of entrepreneurship policy and its adoption by institutions in Slovenia has been characterized by greater coherence in the integration of entrepreneurship policy. Although this integration is not yet complete, at least the established policies are in place and have been enabled by a corresponding legal background and implementation by institutions.

CONCLUSIONS

In evaluating the development of entrepreneurship policy in Slovenia and the country's relevant entrepreneurial institutions, it is clear that significant progress has been made. Not only has entrepreneurship developed significantly, but major institutions have been built and entrepreneurship policies have been implemented. The overview of policies in this chapter has shown that, from the early days characterized by the formation of organizations and institutions, passing of different laws, and formulation of general conditions and a framework for SMEs' environment, Slovenia has developed to a stage where partial policies, programmes, and measures have started to converge into more coherent entrepreneurship policy.

The entrepreneurship policy development in Slovenia can be systemized in three phases according to common characteristics of the particular time period. In the first period (1991 to 1996), Slovenia searched for an appropriate concept of SME development, established different organizations, and implemented instruments at the national level, but without a clear understanding of the concept of entrepreneurship. After gaining independence in 1991, Slovenia started to build its own legislation and institutions with the lack of governance know-how. As a result, the infrastructure for SME support was built ad hoc and partially following the short-time needs and identified shortages in particular areas. In addition, employees in institutions of supportive environments for SMEs and entrepreneurship were not suitably educated. Furthermore, the financing of those institutions at the national level was not addressed, and the financial support was defined on a yearly basis without long-term plans. Moreover, only at the end of the first period was the first strategy of economic development adopted at the national level.

A few achievements in the first period served as a basis for further development in phases to follow, including (1) development of key institutions that are still key players in supportive environment for SMEs (for example, Small Business Development Centre), (2) establishment of some instruments to support SMEs development (for example, technology parks), and (3) successful implementation of programmes for unemployed persons. This period can mainly be characterized as the period of SMEs policy, focusing on existing companies and on support measures for SMEs, and partially on developing environment for SMEs with strong support for unemployed persons and financial measures.

The second period (1997 to 2003) was mainly characterized by implementing all necessary legislation and instruments needed to access the EU. Within this period, certain elements of entrepreneurship policy can be identified. Generally speaking, the policy was extended from national to regional and local levels, particularly with the support of the Small Business Support Network. Meanwhile, entrepreneurship policy measures offered soft measures such as information and advisory, introduction of diverse financial support, R&D and technology development support, and entrepreneurship promotion.

Nevertheless, not all programmes, measures, and instruments were successful. The Anti-bureaucratic Programme achieved only limited success; declining interest in technology parks shifted to increased support of cluster development. In addition, at the national level, different measures and programmes were implemented to increase awareness, education, and information about entrepreneurship among people. The main weakness of such efforts was that they were not arranged in a coherent system, but were implemented separately by different institutions and at different levels, making them difficult to recognize in society. However, at the national level, development shifted to entrepreneurship policy, as demonstrated in the support and development of entrepreneurship promotion, technology and innovation, and nascent entrepreneurs as well as the focus on particular groups of people (for example, young people, women). At the end of this period, all entrepreneurship policy areas were at least partially covered.

The third period started after Slovenia's accession to the European Union in 2004. During this period, national strategies were for the first time organized into a coherent interconnected system. However, the assessment of implementation has not yet been completed as it can only be done after a certain period of time and the country is lacking analytical instrumentation.

The main challenge facing policy makers in Slovenia in regard to designing and implementing entrepreneurship policy in the years ahead is how to contribute to building an entrepreneurial society in which entrepreneurship is not only a socially desired activity, but also a career sought after by talented and highly educated individuals. To achieve this task, a careful selection of programmes and measures is needed as well as policy performance based on the permanent evaluation of the efficiency of current policies and measures. During society's transition from a managerial to an entrepreneurial one (Audretsch and Thurik 2007), the policies also have to transform. A thorough analysis of entrepreneurship policies – and of their successes and failures – is needed not only to formulate appropriate responses, but also to prevent the possibility that the abundance of instruments, measures, organizations, institutions, and policies will create confusion among entrepreneurs and policy makers. Evidence-based policy making is an important method for preventing such a situation, and researchers can contribute to this significantly.

REFERENCES

Audretsch, D.B., I. Grilo and R. Thurik (2007), 'Explaining entrepreneurship and the role of policy: a framework', in D.B. Audretsch, I. Grilo and R. Thurik (eds), *The Handbook of Research on Entrepreneurship Policy*, Cheltenham, UK and Northampton, MA, USA, pp. 1–17.

Audretsch, D., M. Keilbach and E. Lehmann (2006), *Entrepreneurship and Economic Growth*, Oxford: Oxford University Press.

Audretsch, D. and R. Thurik (2007), 'The models of the managed and entrepreneurial economies', in H. Hanusch and A. Pyka (eds), *Elgar Companion to Neo-Schumpeterian Economics*, Cheltenham, UK and Northampton, US: Edward Elgar, pp. 211–31.

Bartlett, W. and V. Bukvič (2001), 'Barriers to SME growth in Slovenia', *MOCT-MOST: Economic Policy in Transitional Economies*, **11** (2), 177–95.

Bučar, M. and M. Stare (1998), 'Prenos inovacij in tehnologij: Slovenske izkušnje', *Raziskovalec*, **27** (5), available at http://www.mszs.si/slo/ministrstvo/publikacije/znanost/mzt/raziskovalec/1998-1/ (accessed 10 December 2008).

Chamber of Crafts and Small Business of Slovenia (2008), 'About the Chamber', available at http://www.ozs.si (accessed 15 December 2008).

Dermastia, M. and A. Križnič (2000), *Spodbujanje povezovanja podjetij, specializacije v proizvodnih verigah in skupnega razvoja mednarodnih trgov po sistemu grozda: zaključno poročilo o raziskavi*, Ljubljana: Iteo.

Drnovšek, M. (2004), 'Job creation process in a transition economy', *Small Business Economics*, **23** (3), 179–88.

Drnovšek, M. and M. Glas (2000), 'Job creation by company size: main findings and recommendation for public policy in Slovenia', *Proceedings of the 30th European Small Business Seminar*, pp. 829–48.

Drnovšek, M. and M. Glas (2006), 'Women entrepreneurs in Slovenia: by fits and starts', in F. Welter, D. Smallbone and N. Isakova (eds), *Enterprising Women in Transition Economies*, Aldershot: Ashgate, pp. 143–70.

Employment Service of Slovenia (2008), 'History of the Employment Service', available at http://www.ess.gov.si/slo/Predstavitev/Zgodovina/Osamosvajanje.htm (accessed 10 December 2008).

Enterprise Europe Network (2008), 'About the Enterprise Europe Network', available at http://www.een.si/ (accessed 10 December 2008).

Glas, M. (1993), 'Slovensko malo gospodarstvo: stanje, problemi in možnosti' (Slovenian Small Business: condition, problems and opportunities), *Slovene Economic Review*, **44** (6), 551–58.

Glas, M. (2004), 'The Slovenian model of SME development', *Economic Commission for Europe, Expert Meeting on Good Governance for SMEs*, Paper No. 10, available at http://www.businessgrowthinitiative.org/ResourceCenter/Studies%20Enterprise%20Development/Slovenian%20Model%20of%20SME%20Development_.pdf (accessed 7 January 2009).

Glas, M. and M. Drnovšek (1999), 'Small business in Slovenia: expectations and accomplishments', paper presented at RENT XIII Workshop, London, available at http://miha.ef.uni-lj.si/_dokumenti/wp/glas6.doc (accessed 7 January 2009).

Glas, M. and M. Drnovšek (2003), 'Small business in Slovenia: expectations and accomplishments', in A. Watson and D.A. Kirby (eds), *Small Firms and Economic Development in Developed and Transition Economies: A Reader (Transition and Development)*, Aldershot: Ashgate, pp. 131–51.

Jaklič, M., A. Cotič Svetina and H. Zagoršek (2004), *Zaključno Poročilo: Evalvacija ukrepov za spodbujanje razvoja grozdov v Sloveniji v obdobju 2001–2003* (Final Report: evaluation of measures to foster cluster development in Slovenia in 2001–2003), Ljubljana: Ministry of the Economy, available at http://www.mg.gov.si/fileadmin/mg.gov.si/pageuploads/razpisi/analize_razpisov/evalvacija_ukrepov_spodbujanja_grozdenja_261104.pdf (accessed 10 December 2008).

JAPTI (2008), 'About JAPTI', http://www.japti.si/about-us, 10 December 2008.

Krašovec, T. (2001), 'Deset let gospodarskega razvoja v samostojni Sloveniji', available at http://www.zdruzenje-manager.si/si/publikacije-dokumenti/strokovni-clanki/deset-let/ (accessed 5 January 2009).

Lundström, A. and L. Stevenson (2001), *Patterns and Trends in Entrepreneurship/SME*

Policy and Practice in Ten Economies, Entrepreneurship Policy for the Future Series, vol. 3, Örebro: The Swedish Foundation for Small Business Research.

Lundström, A. and L. Stevenson (2002), *On the Road to Entrepreneurship Policy*, Örebro: Swedish Foundation for Small Business Research.

Lundström, A. and L. Stevenson (2005), *Entrepreneurship Policy – Theory and Practice*, New York: Springer.

Ministry of the Economy (2002), 'Program of measures to promote entrepreneurship and competitiveness for the period 2002–2006', available at http://www.rra-mura.si/jes/download/Programme%20of%20Measures%20to%20Promote%20Entrepreneurship%20and%20Compmpetitiveness%202002-2006.pdf (accessed 10 December 2008).

Ministry of the Economy (2007), 'Programme of Measures for Promoting Entrepreneurship and Competitiveness 2007–2013', available at http://www.mg.gov.si/fileadmin/mg.gov.si/pageuploads/DPK/Program_ukrepov_angl_071009.pdf (accessed 10 December 2008).

Močnik, D. (2009), 'Structural business statistics of nonfinancial business economy for the EU-27 and Slovenia', in K. Širec and M. Rebernik (eds), *Dynamics of Slovenian entrepreneurship: Slovenian entrepreneurship observatory 2008* (Slovenian entrepreneurship observatory), Maribor: Faculty of Economics and Business, pp. 27–46.

Petrin, T., R. Vitez and M. Mešl (2002), 'Sustainable regional development: experiences from Slovenia', in J.L. Pyle and R. Forrant (eds), *Globalization, Universities and Issues of Sustainable Human Development*, Cheltenham, UK and Northampton, US: Edward Elgar, pp. 48–69.

Rebernik, M., P. Tominc and K. Pušnik (2009), *Rast podjetniške aktivnosti v Sloveniji*, Maribor: Faculty of Economics and Business.

Reynolds, P.D., N. Bosma, E. Autio, S. Hunt, N. De Bono, I. Servais, P. Lopez-Garcia and N. Chin (2005), 'Global Entrepreneurship Monitor: Data collection design and implementation 1998–2003', *Small Business Economics*, **24** (3), 205–31.

Rus, M. and M. Rebernik (2009), 'Slovenian enterprises in 2007', in K. Širec and M. Rebernik (eds), *Dynamics of Slovenian Entrepreneurship: Slovenian Entrepreneurship Observatory 2008* (Slovenian entrepreneurship observatory), Maribor: Faculty of Economics and Business, pp. 11–25.

Slovene Enterprise Fund (2008), 'About the Slovene Enterprise Fund', available at http://www.podjetniskisklad.si/index.php?id=128 (accessed 6 January 2009).

Slovenian Technology Agency (2009), 'About the agency', available at http://www.tia.si/o_agenciji,261,0.html (accessed 6 January 2009).

Small Business Development Centre (2002), 'Projects', available at http://www2.pcmg.si/Pcmg/sprojekti05_down.htm (accessed 6 January 2009).

SURS (2004), *Stastistični letopis Republike Slovenije 2004: Poslovni subjekti* (*Statistical Yearbook of the Republic of Slovenia 2004: Business Subjects*), Ljubljana: Statistični urad Republike Slovenije.

Šušteršič, J., M. Rojec and K. Korenika (eds) (2005), *Slovenia's Development Strategy*, Ljubljana: Institute of Macroeconomic Analysis and Development.

Thurik, R. (2008), 'Entrepreneurship, economic growth and policy in emerging economies', *ERIM Report Series Reference No. ERS-2008-060-ORG*, available at http://ssrn.com/abstract=1276618 (accessed 6 January 2009).

Thurik, R. and S. Wennekers (2004), 'Entrepreneurship, small business, and economic growth', *Journal of Small Business and Enterprise Development*, **11** (1), 140–49.

Vahčič, A., R. Hisrich, M. Glas and B. Bučar (1998), 'Why Slovene public policy should focus on high growth SMEs', *Frontiers for Entrepreneurship Research 1998: Proceedings of the annual Babson College Entrepreneurship Research Conference*, pp. 487–89.

Vahčič, A. and T. Petrin (1990), 'Restructuring the Yugoslav economy through the development of entrepreneurship, and the role of the financial system', *Slovene Studies: Journal of the Society for Slovene Studies*, **12** (1), 67–73.

Wennekers, S., A. Wennekers, R. Thurik and P. Reynolds (2005), 'Nascent entrepreneurship and the level of economic development', *Small Business Economics*, **24** (3), 293–309.

Legislation

Chamber of Commerce Act, Official Gazette of the Republic of Slovenia, no. 14/1990.
Chambers of Commerce and Industry Act, Official Gazette of the Republic of Slovenia, no 60/2006.
Companies Act, Official Gazette of the Republic of Slovenia, no. 30/1993.
Employment and Insurance against Unemployment Act, Official Gazette of the Republic of Slovenia, no. 5/1991.
Promotion of Balanced Regional Development Act, Official Gazette of the Republic of Slovenia, no. 60/1999.
Resolution on the National Research and Development Programme 2006–2010, Official Gazette of the Republic of Slovenia, no. 3/2006.
Small Business Act, Official Gazette of the Republic of Slovenia, no. 50/1994.
Small Business Development Act, Official Gazette of the Republic of Slovenia, no. 18/1991.
Supportive Environment for Entrepreneurship Act, Official Gazette of Republic Slovenia, no. 40/2004.
Venture Capital Companies Act, Official Gazette of the Republic of Slovenia, no. 92/2007.

PART II

ENTREPRENEURSHIP POLICIES BEYOND THE EUROPEAN UNION

9 Entrepreneurship policy transfer: the case of the SME policy framework in Albania
Mirela Xheneti

INTRODUCTION

Policy transfer, convergence or transnational communication are amongst the terms that have been used to describe that part of the policy process which draws on knowledge accumulated in other countries or contexts. Globalization pressures have also contributed to this by improving the communication of ideas and knowledge. There is consensus in the literature that policy makers choose policy transfer for internal reasons related to the economical, political and social characteristics in their country or for external reasons related to pressures that might come from international organizations and their powerful discourses or their conditionalities (Dolowitz and Marsh 2000; Hoberg 2001; Stone 1999).

Entrepreneurship and small business policy has also been shaped by processes of knowledge transfer. The exchange of ideas and knowledge in this field has been influenced by the widely established assumptions that the small business sector is one of the driving factors for economic development. Dominating governmental discourses about entrepreneurship prescribe it as the answer to more jobs and more competitive economies, which many countries, whether developed or developing, are aiming to achieve. Academic research has also acknowledged the contribution of entrepreneurship and the conditions under which it can flourish in different contexts. This has led to a large number of policies and initiatives being developed and the transfer of those defined as 'best practice' from one context to another.

Entrepreneurship and small business development all over the world is promoted by the same functionalist arguments of economic development and job generation. Perren and Jennings (2005) identified three main discourses in guiding entrepreneurship policy throughout the world: the discourse of power, the discourse of subjugation and the discourse of legitimacy. According to them, many government programmes make explicit the expectations on the small business sector, and also the power of the governments to successfully intervene in facilitating their role. Along similar lines, Parkinson et al. (2009) argue that the enterprise discourse

Table 9.1   List of interviews conducted in Albania

Face to face interviews	Total
Public officials	
• Department of Business Promotion (Ministry of Economy)	
• Small and Medium Enterprise Development Agency (SMEDA)	3
Business Agencies/Associations	
• Regional Development Agencies	
• Agro-Business Council	
• Albanian Industrialists and Investors Association	3
Donor programmes	
• Southeast Europe Enterprise Development (SEED, World Bank)	
• Small Business Credit and Assistance (SBCA USAID)	
• German Agency for Technical Cooperation (GTZ)	3
Financial institutions	
• National Commercial Bank of Albania	1

Source: Author.

has become hegemonic and the entrepreneur is being seen as the cure to the economic and social ills of every society. These studies establish the successful transfer of the entrepreneurship discourse in many countries. However, their attempt does not indicate whether policy transfer has occurred only in the form of discourse adoption or in the broader sense of policy embeddedness. They also do not show whether different institutional settings, in terms of the political, economical and social contexts, give an account of the way the content of these policies is understood and used to create action programmes.

In this chapter, drawing on entrepreneurship (policy) discourses and on the policy transfer literature, analysis will consider how a genuine policy transfer process such as the endorsement of the SME Charter of the European Union (EU) in the post communist context of Albania is accompanied by a mismatch of policies and programmes, rather than by embedding the EU SME Charter into the Albanian context. This will be done through an analysis of (i) policy documents produced by the Government of Albania (GoA); and (ii) interviews with policy makers and organizations that have an impact on the development of entrepreneurship policy in Albania. Ten interviews were conducted in the period March–April 2004, with the original intention of understanding the entrepreneurship policy development process in Albania. Two interviews were conducted at the Department of Business Promotion and one for each of the other organizations presented in Table 9.1.

In 2005, there was a change of government, which was accompanied by some changes in the structure of the government as well as in some policies in the years up to 2008. Although the chapter is mainly based on data collected in 2004, the way policies have been affected by these changes will also be presented. Special emphasis is given to understanding how policy discourses have been developed, interpreted and integrated into the domestic policy making context as an attempt towards contributing to the policy transfer literature and entrepreneurship policy development in transition.

The first section provides an account of entrepreneurship discourses in general and their characteristics in a post communist setting, emphasizing the rationale for the transfer of the EU SME Charter. Section 2 will assess the policy transfer concept, its uses and limitations and its applications to post communist contexts. These two sections will provide the framework for the discussion of the entrepreneurship policy in Albania in section 3. In section 4, the features of the SME policy framework in Albania will be discussed and conclusions made.

ENTREPRENEURSHIP DISCOURSE(S), THE EU AND POST COMMUNIST ECONOMIES

The literature on entrepreneurship and small businesses has emphasized that academic research has been subject to a long standing influence of functionalist arguments on the economic and societal roles that small businesses and entrepreneurship play (Jennings et al. 2005). Accordingly, the field has been strongly linked to economic development, represented by increased employment levels, competitiveness and by a reduction of regional disparities (Audretsch and Keilbach 2004; Fritsch and Mueller 2004). Whilst academics have explored, although to a limited extent, different paradigms and different understandings of entrepreneurship, the functional or the economic discourse still seems to be predominant. The economic discourse and the creation of entrepreneurial societies have been given significant attention by various governments and international organizations all over the world, which in one way or another, attempt to push forward different policies on entrepreneurship and small businesses, all having as their cornerstone an individualistic ideology and minimal state intervention.

As early as 1991, Fairclough (1991, p. 40) warned towards the ambivalent use of the word 'enterprise' and the possibilities of manipulating it by varying the verbal context. He linked the strategic exploitation of the word enterprise in political speeches in Britain with achieving higher purposes such as the revaluation of a discredited private business sector at the time, which could benefit by an association with the culturally valued qualities of 'enterprisingness'. Other scholars have constructed and deconstructed our view of entrepreneurs (Nicholson and Anderson 2005; Ogbor 2000), have made links of entrepreneurship discourses and power (Perren and Jennings 2005) and have questioned the role that has been given to entrepreneurship as a cure for economic problems (Parkinson et al. 2009). It is claimed that policy aims and objectives very often bear little, or no resemblance at all, to what the entrepreneurs themselves want to achieve and that the drive for support policies in most cases is not articulated as a need by the entrepreneurs, whom governments are aiming to support (Dannreuther 2007; Perren and Jennings 2005).

Post communist economies also embraced the view that entrepreneurship had system transformation capacities (Xheneti 2006). Entrepreneurs have been perceived for a long time as carrying the values of hard work, self-reliance and determination that support the capitalist order, and upon which the prosperity of this system is based. Thus, the emergence of the private sector as an agent of change in 'achieving the norms, values and rules of conduct' was considered to be crucial to the performance of the market economy and therefore, in promoting the freedom of individuals through their free choices in post communist economies (Brezinski and Fritsch 1996; Scase 1997). Another important reason for the encouragement of entrepreneurship and SMEs was the unbalanced structure of entrepreneurial organizations with a focus on big firms as functional to the central planning, but abnormal to a market economy (Chilosi 2001; Smallbone and Welter 2001a). The shift towards a more balanced economic structure was accompanied by large dismissals, which the private small business sector was expected to absorb. Moreover, SMEs could introduce more flexible production processes and a wider range of products to consumers considering the inflexibility of production processes inherited from central planning (Smallbone and Welter 2001b).

However, the 'privatisation from below' (Boettke and Leeson 2002; Winiecki 2001) or 'bottom up transformation' (Brezinski and Fritsch 1996), which refers to the creation of enabling conditions for entrepreneurship, thus fostering the *de novo* private sector, did not receive proper attention. The 'bottom up transformation' that occurred in some of the countries in transition, like Poland or Hungary, initially was spontaneous. Only in later stages of transition has there been a more organized approach towards entrepreneurship and SMEs, with almost all post communist governments developing strategies and stating objectives for the development of the small business sector.

It does not require an extensive analysis of documents to understand that the stake placed by national governments and international organizations such as the EU or OECD on entrepreneurship is very high. The versatility of the concept (its different definitions) and also the different manifestations of entrepreneurship (in very different types of enterprises, that is, ranging from a one-person retail shop to a high-tech small company) have facilitated its use as an idealized economic subject in policy documents and government agendas according to the priorities of national governments or international organizations such as the EU (Dannreuther 2007).

In the community of discourses about entrepreneurship development, the EU has contributed increasingly by making explicit the stake it places on the SME sector and entrepreneurship, as a key to the creation of an internationally competitive Europe.

> more than 99 per cent of all European businesses are, in fact, SMEs. They provide two out of three of the private sector jobs and contribute to more than half of the total value-added created by businesses in the EU. Moreover, SMEs are the true back-bone of the European economy, being primarily responsible for wealth and economic growth, next to their key role in innovation and R&D.[1]

Moreover, the EU agenda places a very important role on the encouragement of entrepreneurial attitudes in the society, especially through entrepreneurship education.

> Europe needs to stimulate the entrepreneurial mindsets of young people, encourage innovative business start-ups, and foster a culture that is friendlier to entrepreneurship and to the growth of small and medium-sized businesses. The important role of education in promoting more entrepreneurial attitudes and behaviours, starting even at primary school, is now widely recognised (CEC 2008a, p. 10).

EU entrepreneurship and SME policy, as embodied in the EU SME Charter, is comprehensive and addresses issues related to both the external and internal[2] environment where small businesses operate. The Charter was approved in 2000 and consists of a package of policy instruments that will support the SME sector in ten different areas, with the aim of harmonizing the support to SMEs in all the EU and non EU countries that have endorsed the charter. These ten areas are:[3] education and training for entrepreneurship, cheaper and faster start-ups, better legislation and regulation, availability of skills, improving online access, more out of the Single Market, taxation and financial matters, strengthening the technological capacity of small enterprises, successful e-models and top-class small business support and develop stronger, more effective representation of small enterprises' interests at Union and national level.

One of the objectives of the EU SME Charter is to encourage public authorities to share their experiences and learn from each other. Each year, the Commission collects examples of good practice in the field of SME policy from across Europe. In 2004, the Member States reported on some 20 cases where they had based their own policy improvements on experience from other Charter countries. Over the years, the number of these cases has increased and the current exercise provides more than 40 of such cases (CEC 2008b[4]). In addition, the EU SME Charter has been given praise for helping candidate countries to structure their SME Policy in preparation for EU membership.

By 2003, the Charter had already established itself as an influential tool in supporting the SME sector and thereby was endorsed by the Western Balkan countries and Moldova. Although a voluntary decision, it could be argued that this also had a political dimension since the Balkan countries aspire future membership of the EU. Moreover, this was a move to increase the legitimacy of reforms in these countries. On the other hand, post communist countries have been very eager to learn from the EU and to build democracies and market economies according to the EU model.

As a result, policy transfer literature might assist in highlighting the development of SME policy in the post-communist context of Albania and the influences surrounding its development. The policy process is embedded in the institutional context and it also reflects the political context under which it is performed. Moreover, it defines who will be involved in the process and also how each of the participants in the policy process approach or use the Charter dimensions.

POLICY TRANSFER: FORMS, ACTORS, SUCCESS FACTORS

Dolowitz and Marsh (2000, p. 5) define policy transfer as 'the process by which the knowledge about policies, administrative arrangements, institutions and ideas in one political system (past or present) is used in the development of policies, administrative arrangements, institutions and ideas in another political system'. They are praised for drawing together a general framework of quite heterogeneous concepts such as policy convergence (Bennet and Michael 1992), policy diffusion (Walker 1969) or lesson drawing (Rose 2003) under the umbrella term of the policy transfer (Evans and Davies 1999). The range of objects to be transferred can be very broad and include policy goals, structure and content, policy instruments and administrative techniques, institutions, ideology, ideas, attitudes and concepts and negative lessons (Dolowitz and Marsh 1996, pp. 349–50).

A distinction has also been made between soft transfers that lead to substantial similarities of central ideas, concepts or attitudes between two policies, and hard transfers that involve substantial elements of specific programmes and implementation (Evans 2004; Evans and Davies 1999).

The literature distinguishes between entirely voluntary choices of policy transfer to impositions of the policy transfer, as the two ends of the continuum of the policy transfer process. The form that the transfer (voluntary or coercive) takes is very much dependent on: (i) the actors involved in the transfer (the borrower and the lender) and their motivations; (ii) the objectives of the transfer; and (iii) the circumstances under which the transfer takes place. In many cases, the voluntary involvement is for the policy actors to restore or establish legitimacy, or to respond to internal pressures in the political, economic and social environment where they operate. This can be argued to be the case in many East European Countries after the collapse of communism. However, almost every policy transfer is a mixture of voluntary and coercive factors. Whilst it can be argued that international organizations such as World Bank or International Monetary Fund (IMF) impose their policies through conditional loans, other organizations, such as the European Union or the OECD, although they sometimes place conditionalities, *drag* countries into a policy transfer process through their powerful discourses on certain issues as discussed in later sections with regard to entrepreneurship and small business policy in Albania. In addition, policy transfer can involve not only policy makers but also non-governmental actors (Stone 2000) or stakeholders of the policy (Radaelli 2005).

In addition, different criteria have been used to judge whether policy transfer has occurred or not and, if it has been successful or has failed. For example, Holzinger and Knill (2005, p. 776) distinguish between 'policy outputs (the policies adopted by a government) and policy outcomes (the actual effects of a policy in terms of goal achievement)'. For them policy outputs are what counts since implementation and outcomes are subject to influences from other intervening variables and actors. However, in analysing a transition country one cannot set aside implementation and outcomes of a policy, since they are an indicator of the progress made with transition.

The reasons for policy failure, though difficult to identify in practice, have been conceptually attributed to three conditions: *uninformed* transfer when the policy transfer is based on inaccurate or insufficient information about the original policy, *incomplete* transfer when crucial features of what made the policy successful in the original country are not transferred and *inappropriate* transfer when there are essential contextual differences between the policy originating country and the policy transferring one (Dolowitz and Marsh 2000; Dolowitz and Medearis 2009).

Thus, the literature provides us with a well defined and comprehensive conceptual framework to understand how far policy makers in a transition context are in the process. However, it would be interesting to understand: (i) how far entrepreneurship policy is transferred in practice; (ii) what is the role of influential discourses; and (iii) how particular institutional settings affect the transition from discourse as a soft aspect of transfer to actions, tools and implementation.

SME DEVELOPMENT STRATEGY IN ALBANIA: CONTENT AND IMPLEMENTATION

In this section, the third dimension of the EU Charter in the Albanian context will be analysed. One of its sub dimensions, the 'institutional framework', will be the focus of the analysis. It is concerned with, firstly, the design of an SME development strategy accompanied by evidence that all the components of the strategy have been implemented as demonstrated by time bound targets achieved and the number of assignments completed; secondly, the establishment of and full support for an SME policy implementation unit and, thirdly, effective coordination of different governmental actors in the policy process.

The analysis will focus on the two issues introduced in the conceptual sections. One aspect is policy transfer at the level of discourse which will be dealt with by analysing a number of policy documents on entrepreneurship and SMEs in Albania and the narratives of interviewees. This sub-section is inspired by Perren and Jennings (2005) who have provided an account of entrepreneurship and small business discourses all over the world.

The second aspect of the analysis will focus on actions and outcomes of the policy transfer process of endorsing the EU SME Charter. The aim of this section is to demonstrate whether the policy transfer process has moved beyond the soft transfer of adopting the discourse to actions and tools relevant to the Albanian institutional context.

Policy Transfer at the Level of Discourse: The Role of the EU

In this section, the soft aspect of entrepreneurship and small business policy transfer is explored, by highlighting *first*, the influence of entrepreneurship and small business assumptions and *second*, the role of domestic and international actors in transferring the entrepreneurship and small business discourse. GoA policy documents provide strong evidence of the transfer of entrepreneurship and small business policy discourse.

As discussed earlier, one of the most influential discourses of small

Table 9.2 Policy documents analysed in the empirical section

No	Title of the document	Author
1	National Strategy for Socio-Economic Development, Medium Term Programme of the Albanian Government Growth and Poverty Reduction Strategy (2002–04)	Government of Albania
2	Medium term strategy for the development of small and medium size enterprises (2001)	Government of Albania
3	SME Development Strategic Programme (2007–09)	Government of Albania
4	SME in Albania, Annual Report 2004	SMEDA
5	2004 Enterprise policy performance assessment (EPPA) – Republic of Albania	OECD
6	European Charter for small enterprises in Western Balkans and Moldova–Albania 2004	SMEDA

Source: Author.

business development is the *functionalist discourse* that has been promoted by both academic research and EU or other international organizations. Since 2000, the Albanian government has produced a number of documents that indicate the great importance it attaches to SME development. Although much spoken attention has been directed to this sector since transition started, few written policy instruments have been available until the year 2000, to complement what has been called a spontaneous development of the SME sector. In this respect, the National Strategy for Socio-Economic Development (NSSED), one of the main documents on socio-economic development in Albania published in November 2001, considers:

> (the) development of the private sector as the driving force behind growth and poverty reduction. The objective of the government is to stimulate the development of a dynamic private sector, increase the level of the competitiveness of the economy and create an attractive environment for private foreign investments through improvements of the legal and institutional framework that is directly related to the business sector (GoA 2001a, p. 63).

As importantly, the Ministry of Economy, Trade and Energy (MoETE) and, more specifically, the Department of Business Promotion in this ministry, which has the main responsibility for designing policies on SME development in Albania formulated for the first time in 2001 a Medium Term Strategy for the development of the SME sector (GoA 2001b). Albeit much delayed as a formalized step towards supporting SMEs, this strategy put forward a number of objectives and indicated the means to achieve them. In this respect, the following objectives in terms of SME development were identified (GoA 2001b, p. 18):

1. Encourage/support the expansion of existing enterprises.
2. Promote the creation of new businesses.
3. Transform traders into investors in production units.
4. Support production for export.
5. Promote joint-ventures at an SME level.

At first glance, the objectives that the government has articulated in this strategy do not differ much from similar strategies that have been adopted in other countries, reflecting some broadly accepted assumptions about SME development. These assumptions are based on economic approaches to entrepreneurship which are focused on the broader role of the entrepreneur in society and the particular societal interests (s)he may fulfil.

The legitimization of government policy and actions in relation to SMEs is carried out through functional discourses about job generation, the number of businesses, the contribution of the SME sector to GDP, and so on, all of which drive many government agendas on SMEs. To take just one example, one of the latest (and few) reports on the state of the SME sector in Albania states that:

> SMEs play a vital role in the economy . . . micro and small size enterprises comprise 99 per cent of firms' enterprise stock . . . SMEs provide about 75 per cent of employment in non-agricultural sectors (SMEDA 2005, p. 1).

The GoA spells out in its SME strategy that the main aim of SME policy in Albania is social and economic development with a focus on job creation and on a balanced sectoral development. It seems clear that the government would like to encourage a dynamic economy by not only fostering the expansion of already established businesses, but also by increasing the number of start-ups.

Moreover, a *discourse of subjugation or dependency* (Perren and Jennings 2005) is also evident in GoA documents. Accordingly, entrepreneurs are considered as very dependent on the government because otherwise they would not be able to utilize their full potential. A document on the general state of the SME sector, produced by the Small and Medium Enterprise Development Agency (SMEDA) in 2005, that makes reference to the steps undertaken after the formulation of the SME strategy states that 'these actions enabled the private sector to become the driving force for economic growth' (SMEDA 2005, p. 1). This is a very declarative statement that overestimates these steps and considers the business community as being dependent on government agendas. Going further in the strategy document, the same discourse of dependency is evidenced in the intention of the Albanian government to encourage manufacturing as an entrepreneurial activity:

> Start-ups and already existing enterprises, that intend to diversify, should be guided into more productive activities – away from trade and common services – namely into manufacturing, agro-industry, production of construction materials, tourism activities and the like. Some of them might also be encouraged to consider investing in high-tech ventures and to go into export activities (GoA 2001a, p. 25).

The encouragement of entrepreneurial attitudes in society, especially through entrepreneurship education, is a prominent feature of EU policy discourse. Before Albania joined the EU SME Charter, thus having to report annually on the different elements of the Charter, there was no reference in the GoA's documents of an entrepreneurship policy implying entrepreneurship and business policy were interchangeable or, otherwise, that this is a neglected policy area. This is an indication of the influence of the EU as a main 'policy pusher'.

The lack of entrepreneurship policy in many countries has been associated with the main belief that altering the characteristics of a society takes a long time. Therefore, the public policies' role in changing human orientations and preferences about business is insignificant in the short term (Baumol 1990). However, in the Albanian context, old prejudices about a lack of entrepreneurship activity during communism are still present and reflected in the attitudes of many state officials toward small businesses. This prejudice should have been a reason for the government to consider a policy on entrepreneurship. Yet, it is known in policy making that sometimes governments are more concerned about the time frame than about the task performance, which results in short-term oriented political agendas (Zahariadis 1999). In this regard, the EU Charter for SMEs that the Albanian government adopted in September 2003 can be considered a turning point. As a result, for the first time, the Business and Investment Development Strategy (GoA 2007) placed some emphasis on entrepreneurship culture and more specifically on its introduction into formal and vocational education and in training sessions with entrepreneurs, although nothing specific has been achieved, as yet, with regard to this objective. This lack of expression for a very long time puts some doubt onto the government's commitment to entrepreneurship policies, suggesting that its decisions are taken mainly to fulfil EU conditionality, in other words, to respond to the discursive emphasis of the EU.

Not surprisingly, this section highlighted two main points. First, the discourse of entrepreneurship and small business development as drivers of economic development has been successfully transferred to Albania. As in many other governments' policy documents, GoA's policy documents contain the same enterprise rhetoric of function and dependency (Perren and Jennings 2005). Second, the section illustrated the particular influence of the EU SME Charter in adopting the European entrepreneurial society discourse which shows that influential actors like EU and the incentives they offer (that is, membership prospects) are drivers of policy transfer in a variety of contexts.

Actions and Outcomes: Implementing the SME Strategy

The soft aspect of policy transfer was discussed in previous sections. In this section, the emphasis is on the link between discourse and actions. The experience of mature market economies has shown that entrepreneurship and SME policy framework is complex; comprised by a large set of loosely connected and uncoordinated initiatives; changeable over short period of times; and with responsibility for its delivery spread between various government departments (Curran and Storey 2002; Storey 2003). In transition economies, the 'hard' aspect of policy transfer is even more problematic, especially considering the poor record of transition economies with implementation due to a lack of capacities (for example Smallbone and Welter 2010), financial resources and developed institutional structures. In this respect, this section will highlight some of the issues with policy making in Albania from policy analysis to policy evaluation and lesson learning.

The interviews revealed a tendency for policy makers to initiate policy without doing any policy analysis, which was mainly due to lack of research institutes and lack of funding. It was mentioned earlier that the SME strategy places special emphasis on manufacturing and exporting activity, and balanced regional development. However, in the contents of the medium term plan, there is no reference to specific studies undertaken to identify any particular manufacturing activities in which the country has comparative advantages, or regional studies identifying the prospects of different regions in order to narrow the development gap between the centre and other areas of the country. The government made its commitment to implement the strategy by issuing a SME law dated October 2002 that would regulate the definition of SMEs, the legal framework for SME government support, and the creation of a development agency for SMEs. However, the evidence shows that it is dragging its feet when it comes to implementation.

The SME strategy (GoA 2001b) has been subject to various criticisms. Several interviewees observed that the strategy needs serious revision, in order to reflect more explicitly the national priorities for SME development. The South East Enterprise Development (SEED) interviewee mentioned that:

> The strategy lacks some focus and does not reflect a clear vision of where the country will be in 5–10 years . . . In this context it is necessary to make studies on the resources that are available whether natural, human or geographical that will give a competitive advantage in the future. The strategy was drafted in a period in which not too many things were evident. It is also necessary to consider some changes in the framework of the negotiations for the Association and Stabilisation Agreement. My point is that the development of the private sector should be oriented toward EU standards, if we want to integrate. I have in mind here the SME charter adopted by the government. It is necessary to set targets and who is going to do what and when.

A SME Agency started its operation in 2003 in line with the EU SME Charter that emphasizes the need for an SME implementation unit. In 2005, after the national elections, it was restructured and changed its name to the Department of Competitiveness and Enterprise Growth as part of a bigger governmental organization, Albinvest that deals with issues such as export and foreign direct investment.[5] These units were given the main responsibility for the administration of various government and donor SME funds, and for monitoring and coordinating the different programmes of SME support. The SME strategy states that:

> (the agency) must be adequately funded and well equipped, as well as have a limited but highly specialized staff and functional structure to fulfil its conceptual and coordinating mission adequately (GoA 2001a, p. 19).

However, interviewees were sceptical not so much about the agency itself in its conceptual design, but about its limited operational capabilities in terms of financial and human resources. One interviewee from a donor programme was very pessimistic about the role of SMEDA:

> I am not an optimist. It does not have the budget necessary. The people working there are not the brightest and at the same time there is no database of enterprises to start with.

In this respect, no budget was assigned for the implementation of the strategy until 2007, six years after its design. The director of SMEDA mentioned that the 'strategy is not an operational programme where the activities are expressed in financial terms'. That means that SMEDA, which has a very small budget and not enough staff, needs first, to design action plans on what its director calls 'reading between the lines of the strategy' and second, make them known to the donor community. Four years after the strategy was formulated, there were still no regional plans, and the ad hoc measures being used instead, lacked any informed knowledge of specific local areas and their needs for support. In 2007, an action plan was designed by MoETE for the development of SMEs with clearer objectives, an indication of the necessary budget for achieving these objectives and also the potential financing body for each of them. Unsurprisingly, the donor community has been given quite an extended role in financing the activities under this action plan. Although these activities can be considered as a step forward in the implementation of the strategy, they do not exclude the imposition of political agendas and donors' agendas on SME development in Albania (Xheneti 2005), which shows that countries like Albania are dependent on the international organizations not only about knowledge and expertise but also the funding to transfer this knowledge.

Moreover, the policy process does not go through the whole cycle from the design of policies to the monitoring of specific targets to evaluating how they have been fulfilled. The design of policies is a very government-centred process with very little inclusion of other policy actors or business themselves. Whilst an aspect of the EU SME Charter is related to businesses' inclusion in the policy making process, in order to ensure that the policy is responsive to their needs and problems, the interviews conducted in 2004 revealed that this is in practice mere political rhetoric on entrepreneurship and business development. To take just one example, the Prime Minister created a Business Advisory Council (BAC) in February 2002. The rationale for its creation was to facilitate the dialogue between business and government. However, this structure is yet another in the range of buzz initiatives of giving voice to businesses or making them heard. 'Voice of small businesses' has been considered as a catchy and memorable phrase (Perren and Jennings 2005), that has built into an influential discourse of representation by governments and international organizations such as the EU.

One of the main criticisms of this structure related to the composition of its members, which included mainly ministerial staff and representatives of structures that did not really represent the business community. In this respect, one interviewee reported that:

> the government drafts the laws and the council just comments on them. I think this is a deficient process . . . the voice of the businesses is not really heard in the form this is operating right now. This initiative was one of the many formalities.

No doubt initiatives of this kind not only give no credibility to government actions which are crucial for the implementation of reforms, but they increase the general distrust of the business community of institutions, including support structures or business associations that represent businesses in the council. In 2006, the Business Advisory Council's actions were institutionalized by law and the Council is now composed of 20 members, 13 of which are representatives of the business community.[6]

Other problems of the policy process relate to evaluation and lack of measurable or quantifiable targets until the year 2007, or certain negligence on this very important step of the policy process. A respondent from the Department of Business Promotion in the MoETE mentioned that no monitoring is done by government structures. According to the interviewee, official monitoring only takes place in donor-funded programmes, since donors typically are required to ensure the proper use of their funds.

The level of awareness the business community has about initiatives undertaken by the government and the available facilities for businesses is also of interest. It is striking what interviews revealed in this regard, namely that four years after the SME strategy was formulated and the SME law was passed in parliament, the majority of businesses were still not properly informed about the law and what the strategy offered to specific groups of businesses. The same concerns were presented in an OECD report of 2004 (OECD 2005). Interviews with public officials made it clear that the government sees its only role as initiator and designer of strategies and policies and not as 'awareness engineer'. This position makes the government a mere producer of nicely written documents with little interest in implementation and even less in the fulfilment of the stated objectives and targets. As one interviewee from public administration observed:

> Businesses that are interested find ways to get to know about the strategy. If not they are not going to learn about it.

Or with reference to the manufacturing sector as one of the priorities of the government, another public official mentioned that 'They should know themselves that they are being protected by the law.'

The evidence provided above shows that the government is more concerned with designing policies and action plans in line with the official EU or donor discourse than with their enforcement or with the real impact they will have on SMEs, and is not at all concerned about feeding back the results or outcomes of policies into the policy process.

FEATURES OF ENTREPRENEURSHIP AND SME POLICY IN ALBANIA

Evidence of the Albanian institutional framework for SMEs, with a special emphasis on the EU SME Charter and its application was discussed earlier. The sections above highlighted two main issues: (i) the influence of entrepreneurial discourses in adopting entrepreneurship and small business policy as evidenced by the language of policy documents; and (ii) the way structural and institutional factors influence the transition from discourse as a soft aspect of the transfer to actions and outcomes of the policy transfer process in a post communist context such as Albania.

The analysis of the GoA's policy documents showed that entrepreneurial discourses have also been embraced in Albania. Governmental discourses emphasize the functionality of the role of entrepreneurship and SMEs, consistent with Perren and Jennings (2005) and Parkinson et al. (2009). It is hard to explicate whether the zeal in embracing these discourses is strictly political, as a way to show the EU that the government has firm intentions towards EU membership, or whether it is genuine and there is a real belief (supported and influenced by discourses elsewhere) that entrepreneurship is the answer to economic and social problems of a transformation society, despite the evident ambiguity and lack of clarity in the objectives of the GoA with regard to entrepreneurship policy.

One of the reasons why countries engage in policy transfer is to learn from the experience of others. EU acts as a very influential platform in this respect in 'dragging' countries towards learning and convergence through tools such as the EU SME Charter. However, the lack of clarity about objectives and policies makes the process of learning in the Albanian policy-making community difficult.

These learning difficulties signal that little will be done to correct inconsistencies or revise various objectives or targets that the government has designed. Thus, the policy transfer process may turn into a mere exercise of using the words of (translating) policies elsewhere without being able to translate/adapt them into successful actions and outcomes for the Albanian context.

From the institutional framework perspective of the EU SME Charter, the Albanian government has an SME policy in place and an agency that plays the role of an implementation unit. The SME Implementation Unit and the Business Advisory Council created might not differ from those one finds in more developed economies in respect to their conceptual design, which comprises another soft aspect of the transfer. However, the analysis showed that the way they translate discourses into actions and tools is subject to various pressures and influences in the policy environment. As randomly happens in any policy environment, the proclivities of individual officials employed within these organizations influence the implementation process. Hodgson (2004), whilst criticizing the concept of organizations as social actors used by North (1990), states that individual members of these organizations might have conflicting objectives. Moreover, while specific individuals might know what their responsibilities are under a particular organizational framework, they might not be able or willing to place themselves in the broader picture of that organization.

In transition economies, such as in Albania, there is another issue that renders the job of the public administration more difficult. Lack of motivation, short-term horizons and a lack of capabilities are among the general reasons that have been cited (Eriksen 2007; SIGMA 2009) to explain the weak implementation of policies (failure of hard transfers) in a transition context. At the same time, the majority of the laws that are introduced in the country is not followed by implementation regulations and operational guidelines that would outline the responsibilities of the administration, restrict the space for discretionary use of power and compensate for lack of transparency and accountability (for similar examples from Belarus and Estonia see Smallbone and Welter 2010).

At a general level, policy is not regarded as a process that entails analysis of a problem and the different options for tackling it but rather as a mere technical exercise of drafting legislation, which implies that policy transfer will be uninformed and hence, their likelihood of failure will be higher. At a more practical level, there is a gap between the strategic orientation of national SME policies towards the EU SME Charter and the funding of programmes, which means that policy will fail because of incomplete transfer.

CONCLUSIONS

EU membership aspirations have been a major factor influencing enterprise policy in Albania. These policy changes that take the form of 'voluntary transfers', were evidenced in an emphasis on SMEs as main drivers of economic development, entrepreneurship education as essential in developing the entrepreneurial attitudes of the population, business inclusion in policy making and the orientation/adjustment of the SME policy towards the areas of the charter. Although the available data enabled me to discuss only a few aspects of the EU SME Charter, it can be concluded that the Charter's diffusion has happened mainly at the level of discourse and spoken commitment to it rather than a genuine commitment towards its proper implementation. The diffusion at the level of discourse is independent of the respective national context as entrepreneurship and small business are portrayed in the same way in the discursive practices of many other countries.

Albeit some convergence is noted in terms of the instruments and the agencies involved in SME policy making and implementation, the same does not apply to their functioning. The EU SME Charter is a multidimensional policy tool that has been adopted by countries, including Albania, and the transfer is voluntary since the EU does not set priorities for how governments should implement the Charters' dimensions. However, the case of Albania shows that policy transfer might be deficient (in spite of good intentions) in contexts where the policy process is characterized by (i) a reformulation of problems by different political actors; (ii) frequent changes in solutions; (iii) frequent reshuffling and unclear competences of different departments; and (iv) by a set of attitudes that have not yet positively embraced the underpinnings of these policies and most importantly the meaning of, and the cultural predisposition towards entrepreneurship.

This chapter attempted to show that the policy transfer concept is a useful concept in understanding the road towards EU integration in South East Europe. In addition, the policy transfer concept has value in understanding, what policies are adopted, why and under what influences they are adopted and the actions and outcomes they produce. Implementation and outcomes of the transfer process are very important aspects to look at in a transition economy because that is where a distinction is made between political rhetoric and transformational change.

The major point of the discussion is that policy transfer is a very necessary process in contexts like Albania, where entrepreneurship and consequently entrepreneurship policy did not exist during communism. However, the policy transfer will never be a genuine policy transfer process if it is not accompanied by policy learning that is necessary to adapt a policy to contextual conditions. As Hirschman (1973, pp. 239–40) states: 'Genuine learning about the problem will sometimes be prevented not only by the local policy makers' eagerness to jump to readymade solutions but also by the insistent offer of help and advice on the part of powerful outsiders . . . such practices will tend to cut short that "long confrontation between man and a situation" (Camus) so fruitful for the achievement of genuine progress in problem-solving.' This has implications for future research on the links between policy transfer and learning.

NOTES

1. http://ec.europa.eu/enterprise/policies/sme/facts-figures-analysis/index_en.htm.
2. The internal environment refers to all those internal forces operating within the organization itself, such as the company's objectives and goals, nature of the organization's products and/or services, communication processes and networks within the organization, and the educational background of employees (Duncan 1972).
3. http://ec.europa.eu/enterprise/enterprise_policy/charter/index_en.htm#charta.

4. http://ec.europa.eu/enterprise/entrepreneurship/charter_en.htm.
5. http://www.albinvest.gov.al/.
6. http://www.kkb.gov.al/.

REFERENCES

Audretsch, D. and M. Keilbach (2004), 'Entrepreneurship capital and economic perform-ance', *Regional Studies*, **38** (8), 949–59.
Baumol, W.J. (1990), 'Entrepreneurship: productive, unproductive and destructive', *The Journal of Political Economy*, **98** (5), 893–921.
Bennet, C. and H. Michael (1992), 'The lessons of learning: reconciling theories of policy learning and policy change', *Policy Sciences*, **25** (3), 275–94.
Boettke, P.J. and P. Leeson (2002), 'An "Austrian" perspective on public choice', George Mason University, Global Prosperity Initiative Working Paper 11, Washington, D.C., available at http://www.gmu.edu/departments/economics/working/WPE_02/02_15.pdf (accessed 5 August 2009).
Brezinski, H.D. and M. Fritsch (eds) (1996), *The Economic Impact of New Firms in Post-socialist Countries: Bottom-up Transformation in Eastern Europe*, Cheltenham, UK and Brookfield, VT, USA: Edward Elgar.
CEC (2008a), *Entrepreneurship in Higher Education Especially in Non Business Studies*, Final Report of the expert group, Brussels: Enterprise and Industry Directorate General, EC.
CEC (2008b), *European Charter for Small Enterprises – 2008 Good Practice Selection*, Brussels: Enterprise and Industry Directorate General, EC.
Chilosi, A. (2001), 'Entrepreneurship and transition', *Moct-Most*, 11, 327–57.
Curran, J. and D.J. Storey (2002), 'Small business policy in the United Kingdom: the inheritance of the Small Business Service and implications for its future effectiveness', *Environment and Planning C: Government and Policy*, **20** (2), 163–77.
Dannreuther, C. (2007), 'A zeal for a zeal? SME policy and the political economy of the EU', *Comparative European Politics*, **5**, 377–99.
Dolowitz, D.P. and D. Marsh (1996) 'Who learns what from whom: a review of the policy transfer literature', *Political Studies*, **XLIV**, 343–57.
Dolowitz, D.P. and D. Marsh (2000), 'Learning from abroad: the role of policy transfer in contemporary policy making', *Governance: An International Journal of Policy and Administration*, **13** (1), 5–24.
Dolowitz, D.P. and D. Medearis (2009), 'Considerations of the obstacles and opportuni-ties to formalising cross-national policy transfer to the United States: a case study of the transfer of urban environmental and planning policies from Germany, *Environment and Planning C: Government and Policy*, **27** (4), 684–97.
Duncan, R.B. (1972), 'Characteristics of organizational environments and perceived envi-ronmental uncertainty', *Administrative Science Quarterly*, 17, 313–27.
Eriksen, S. (2007), 'Institution building in Central and Eastern Europe: foreign influences and domestic responses', *Review of Central and Eastern European Law*, 32, 333–69.
Evans, M. (2004), *Policy Transfer in Global Perspective*, Aldershot: Ashgate.
Evans, M. and J. Davies (1999), 'Understanding policy transfer: a multi-level, multi-disciplinary perspective', *Public Administration*, **77** (2), 361–86.
Fairclough, N. (1991), 'What might we mean by "enterprise discourse"?', in R. Keat and N. Abercrombie (eds), *Enterprise Culture*, London: Routledge, pp. 38–57.
Fritsch, M. and P. Mueller (2004), 'Effects of new business formation on regional develop-ment over time', *Regional Studies*, **38** (8), 961–75.
GoA (2001a), *National Strategy for Socio-Economic Development, Medium Term Programme of the Albanian Government Growth and Poverty Reduction Strategy (2002–2004)*, Tirana: Government of Albania.

GoA (2001b), *Medium Term Strategy for the Development of Small and Medium Size Enterprises*, Tirana: Government of Albania.

GoA (2007), *Business and Investment Development Strategy 2007–2013*, Tirana: Government of Albania.

Hirschman, A.O. (1973), *Journeys Toward Progress: Studies of Economic Policy-making in Latin America*, New York: Norton.

Hoberg, G. (2001), 'Globalization and policy convergence: symposium overview', *Journal of Comparative Policy Analysis: Research and Practice*, **3**, 127–32.

Hodgson, G.M. (2004), *The Evolution of Institutional Economics*, Routledge: London.

Holzinger, K. and C. Knill (2005), 'Cause and conditions of cross-national convergence', *Journal of European Public Policy*, **12** (5), 775–96.

Jennings, P.L., L. Perren and S. Carter (2005), 'Guest editors' introduction: alternative perspectives on entrepreneurship research', *Entrepreneurship Theory and Practice*, **29** (2), 145–52.

Nicholson, L. and A.R. Anderson (2005), 'News and nuances of the entrepreneurial myth and metaphor: linguistic games in entrepreneurial sense making and sense giving', *Entrepreneurship, Theory and Practice*, **29** (2), 153–72.

North, D.C. (1990), *Institutions, Institutional Change and Economic Performance*, Cambridge University Press: Cambridge.

OECD (2005), *2004 Enterprise Policy Performance Assessment – Republic of Albania*, Paris: Organisation for Economic Cooperation and Development, European Bank for Reconstruction and Development, available at http://www.oecd.org/dataoecd/12/52/35443365.pdf (accessed 5 August 2009).

Ogbor, B.M. (2000), 'Mythicizing and reification in entrepreneurial discourse: ideology-critique of entrepreneurial studies', *Journal of Management Studies*, **37** (5), 605–35.

Parkinson, C.R., C.A. Howorth and A. Southern (2009), 'Does enterprise discourse have the power to enable or disable deprived communities?', in D. Smallbone, H. Landström and D. Jones-Evans (eds), *Entrepreneurship And Growth In Local, Regional And National Economies Frontiers in European Entrepreneurship Research*, Cheltenham, UK and Northampton, MA: Edward Elgar, pp. 281–311.

Perren, L. and P.L. Jennings (2005), 'Government discourses on entrepreneurship: issues of legitimisation, subjugation, and power', *Entrepreneurship Theory and Practice*, **29** (2), 173–84.

Radaelli, C.M. (2005), 'Diffusion without convergence: how political context shapes the adoption of regulatory impact assessment', *Journal of European Public Policy*, **12** (5), 924–43.

Rose, R. (2003), 'When all other conditions are not equal: the context for drawing lessons', in C. Jones Finer (ed.), *Social Policy Reform in Socialist Market China: Lessons for and from Abroad*, Aldershot: Ashgate, pp. 5–22.

Scase, R. (1997), 'The role of small businesses in the economic transformation of Eastern Europe: real but relatively unimportant?', *International Small Business Journal*, **16** (1), 13–21.

SIGMA (2009), *Albania-Policy Making and Coordination Assessment*, Brussels: European Commission.

Smallbone, D. and F. Welter (2001a), 'The distinctiveness of entrepreneurship in transition economies', *Small Business Economics*, **16** (4), 249–62.

Smallbone, D. and F. Welter (2001b), 'The role of government in SME development in transition economies', *International Small Business Journal*, **19** (76), 63–77.

Smallbone, D. and F. Welter (2010), 'Entrepreneurship and government policy in former Soviet Republics: Belarus and Estonia compared', *Environment and Planning C: Government and Policy*, **28** (2), 195–210.

SMEDA (2005), *SME in Albania, Annual Report 2004*, Tirana: Small and Medium Enterprise Development Agency.

Stone, D. (1999), 'Learning lessons and transferring policies across time, space and disciplines', *Politics*, **19** (1), 51–9.

Stone, D. (2000), 'Non governmental policy transfer: the strategies of independent policy institutions', *Governance: An International Journal of Policy and Administration*, **13** (1), 45–62.

Storey, D.J. (2003), 'Entrepreneurship, small and medium sized enterprises and public policies, in Z.J. Acs and D.B. Audretsch (eds), *Handbook of Entrepreneurship Research*, Dordrecht: Kluwer, pp. 473–511.

Walker, J.L. (1969), 'The diffusion of innovations among the American states', *American Political Science Review*, **63**, 880–99.

Winiecki, J. (2001), 'The role of the new, entrepreneurial private sector in transition and economic performance in light of the successes in Poland, the Czech Republic and Hungary', BOFIT Discussion Papers No. 12, Bank of Finland Institute for Economies in Transition.

Xheneti, M. (2005), 'Exploring the role of the business support infrastructure in Albania: the need for a rethink?', *Environment and Planning C: Government and Policy*, **23**, 815–32.

Xheneti, M. (2006), 'Barriers to SME growth in transition economies – the case of Albania', Bristol University PhD thesis.

Zahariadis, N. (1999), 'Ambiguity, time and multiple streams', in P.A. Sabatier (ed.), *Theories of the Policy Process*, Oxford: Westview Press, pp. 73–96.

Webpages

http://ec.europa.eu/enterprise/enterprise_policy/charter/index_en.htm#charta.
http://ec.europa.eu/enterprise/entrepreneurship/charter_en.htm.
http://www.albinvest.gov.al/.
http://www.kkb.gov.al/.

10 Entrepreneurship and SME policies in fragile environments: the example of Russia

Alexander Chepurenko

INTRODUCTION

Crises mark watersheds in two decades of entrepreneurship development in post-Soviet Russia. These include the systemic crisis of 1990–92, the financial crisis of 1998 and, finally, the economic crisis that has been in progress since autumn 2008. The latter one will presumably be a starting point for new trends in the development of private sector in Russia and for re-conceptualizing government policy concerning entrepreneurship and SME. State authorities in Russia never clearly distinguished between entrepreneurship policy and SME policy, not surprisingly, because even researchers and experts lack understanding of these two approaches. Audretsch (2002) emphasized that SME policies focus on existing enterprises, while entrepreneurship policy also includes potential entrepreneurs, therefore fostering change processes, and paying attention to the overall framework for businesses and aspiring entrepreneurs, whereas SME policy is focused exclusively on the enterprise level.

In a rapidly changing environment, like in Russia during the transition process, government policies to support SMEs and entrepreneurship cannot be explained and understood without a general understanding of the main trends and developments within the SME sector. Therefore, the next section outlines SME development and the main characteristics of small businesses in Russia during the last decade, before the chapter turns to discuss the evolution of SME and entrepreneurship policies since the beginning of transition. In a huge country like Russia the role of regional disparities in SME development and policy approaches of regional authorities becomes crucial and is discussed in the next section. The chapter continues to shortly summarize the role which international programmes and donor organizations played in implementing core principles and institutions of a SME policy in Russia. Finally, conclusions are formulated on possibilities of a new entrepreneurship policy in Russia after the current crisis.

SME DEVELOPMENT IN RUSSIA AFTER THE 1998 CRISIS

The main aspects of entrepreneurship and SME development in Russia in the early-mid 1990s have been discussed in a number of studies (for example, Black et al. 2000; Centre for Co-operation with the Economies in Transition 1998; Earle and Sakova 2000; Frye 2004; Gaddy and Ickes 1998; Iwasaki 2003; Moers 2000; Murrell 2005; Welter and Smallbone 2003; Yakovlev 2001). Therefore, we will concentrate on a more detailed explanation of the last period in the evolution of small businesses in Russia (1999–2008), because this period has not yet been explored sufficiently in international publications. However, what is more important, without such an observation the shift in the State policy from 'classical' SME support schemes towards a more entrepreneurship policy oriented approach would not become clear.

In 1998 the crisis opened new opportunities for the development of 'free entrepreneurship', that is, entrepreneurship based on the recognition and use of opportunities rather than on ways to secure rent income after the departure of bigger players from the market. This is particularly true of those small and medium-sized enterprises whose business relied on local resources and was covering demand by the middle class, gradually recovering and growing in numbers. Many of the current Russian *gazelles*, which represent the second or third tier of Russian business (mostly in food processing, clothes and footwear manufacture, business services, IT, consulting) emerged at that time. In the mid 2000s, the percentage of gazelles was estimated at 12 to 15 per cent of the total number of acting ventures, compared to 4 to 8 per cent in developed countries (Yudanov 2008).

In the early 2000s, new developments and trends in the evolution of entrepreneurship in Russia occurred. The increasing wages (+10–20 per cent per year) provided fuel for a fast growth of consumer demand, resulting in a boom in retailing, services and public catering and in a new format, too – there is a multiplication of trade chains, which became the core customers of national manufacturers of basic goods. Additionally, the federal government made a conscious choice in favour of the authoritarian modernization model very similar to the South Korean version of the 1960s and 1970s. A 'business capture' by the State led to the growing role of state-owned corporations and their strategic advantages.

In this context there is an increasing tendency towards 'business capture' by the State (Yakovlev 2006b). The weakness of civil society and the absence of real political competition and formal regulations for the recruitment of civil servants lead to government agencies and civil

Table 10.1   SME development in Russia from 2002–07, in per cent

	2002	2003	2004	2005	2006	2007
Average number of full time employees (without freelancers and external contractors)	14.3	15.0	15.9	16.7	17.8	18.9
Average number of freelancers	34.4	36.6	38.7	39.6	40.5	39.5
Average number of external contractors	21.4	22.6	22.0	22.8	19.8	22.4
GDP share[1]	–	9.8	12.5	12.0	11.6	–
Turnover	–	–	–	26.0	26.3	26.6
Investment	2.9	2.4	3.5	3.3	3.6	3.9

Note: 1.   Share of small firms' added value at GDP in market prices.

Source: Rosstat (2008), Table 1.1.

servants becoming ever more noticeable in their drive to use their office of regulators and overseers to secure rent incomes. This results in corruption acquiring a new dimension: isolated bribes and gifts develop into a system of contractual relationships between business and bureaucrats. The problem has become so urgent that it is targeted by a special plan orchestrated by the new president Dmitry Medvedev himself.

But the dynamics of small business growth in Russia is on the whole positive. For example, the number of incorporated small businesses increased from 1999 to 2008 from 900 000 to 1.34 million, and the number of employees from 6.2 to 11.4 million. (Nabiullina 2009).[1] According to official SME statistics for 2007–08, however, no significant upward trend in small business development appeared in the pre-crisis period (Table 10.1). Alternative data, for example, the early entrepreneurship index (TEA), as measured by the Global Entrepreneurship Monitor (http://www.gemconsortium.org), shows the same tendency for nascent entrepreneurship: whereas in 2006 Russia was ranked tenth from the bottom in terms of this indicator, in 2007–08 it was already the last but one out of the 42 countries surveyed. In other words, the share of owners of small business start-ups in Russia in the employable adult population was not only very low, with the 2006–08 indicator at 4.9, 2.7 and 3.3 per cent, respectively, but it dropped even lower in the last two pre-crisis years.

It is obvious that, given the faster growth of wages in the non-market sector and the ever higher economic and administrative barriers (especially the corruption of several inspections monitoring small firms), private enterprise was no longer an attractive alternative for potential entrepreneurs. This fact can only be interpreted as evidence of the business development in Russia being unfavourable for start-ups and even for already established small firms. According to the 'Doing Business 2010' survey of the World Bank, Russia takes the 120th place among 183 participating countries (http://www.doingbusiness.org/EconomyRankings/).

SME POLICY AND ITS ENVIRONMENT

Macroeconomic Stabilization Instead of SME Policy at the Beginning of Transition

The dominating group of the nation's political elite in early 1990s – first of all, the liberal wing of Russia's experts and government officials under Yegor Gaidar subscribed to the World Bank's concept of the 'Washington consensus', that is structural assistance through macroeconomic policies and deregulation measures (Earle and Estrin 2003). However, the advocates of targeted small business support, represented by lobbyists and staff of numerous governmental and non-governmental organizations that are part of the small businesses support infrastructure, disagreed with them. In 1991, this was a result of limited resources and a lack of tools for supporting small businesses, as well as of the fact that in the absence of an established macroeconomic environment any fine-tuning intervention by the state would inevitably misfire. It was decided that formulating effective antitrust policies, backed by privatization, would make it possible to put in place the preconditions *necessary* for establishment of small business at the grassroots level. The conditions sufficient for sustainable growth would be addressed at a later stage.

Privatization was an important institutional precondition for small business emergence, but its implementation and outcomes in the post-Soviet environment were not what had been expected. In the absence of institutions of market infrastructure or legally accumulated private capital, in an environment of high political risks, non-transparent prices for assets to be privatized, and, above all, with no concerted support available from major groups of the civil society, the initial radical concept of privatization, which provided for stricter restrictions on the bidding by so-called 'red directors', could not have been kept without undergoing major changes. Major concessions had to be made to populist interests and allowances for the actual alignment of forces within the society, including the clout of the former economic elite (Black et al. 2000, Radygin 1995). Once the privatization was completed, private businesses created from scratch did not, in fact, receive any access to the property and other assets of former state-owned enterprises, and the commercial space (offices, workshops and so on) lease mechanism made it to all intents and purposes dependent on the administration of post-privatized enterprises.

The Emergence of 'Traditional' SME Policy since the Mid-1990s

From 1994 to 1995 onwards, after a complete change of the government team, a concept for small business support started to be developed. At that time, small businesses seemed to be a fast growing sector, and its protection should be used to solve problems of the labour market and of some specific groups of population such as former officers of the declining Army.

In May 1995 the Federal Law 'On State Support of Small Business in the Russian Federation' was adopted. The Law identified small enterprises and the basics of government policies towards small business. The Federal Foundation for Small Business Support (FFSES) was appointed to coordinate financial measures for governmental support of small business. At the same time, according to the above mentioned law, the State Committee for Small Business Support and Promotion (SCSESP of Russia) was set up. It was charged with the implementation of government policies in the area of small business, the formation of comprehensive infrastructure for small business support, including consulting, information and financial support, as well as the coordination of the Federal Fund's activities.

It was during that period that a system of organizations and institutions for the support of small firms was started to be put together both at the federal and territorial levels, including territorial foundations and centres for the support of private enterprise. Until 1998, 73 regional funds and centres of entrepreneurship support were set up, in 44 Russian regions agencies for small business support were established (consulting, audit and so on), 36 business training and information centres, some science parks across the country, as well as legal and accounting/auditing firms, which catered to small business (http://www.xserver.ru/user/ffpmp/).

Local tax exemptions were introduced and funds were allocated from local treasuries for the development of a small business support infrastructure. Also, financial support for small businesses was provided at both federal and territorial levels, drawing on the funds of dedicated foundations. However, even the envisaged small-scale funding of the programmes (for example, in the last adopted Federal Programme for 2000–01 it was foreseen to use sources of different federal authorities in order to fund

RUR 120 billion in 2000 and RUR 210 billion in 2001, that is less than EUR 10 billion in total), both on federal as well as on regional level, never was provided in full ('Realisaciya', without year).

Government policies and institutional arrangements for small business support saw continuous changes; and reorganizations and reshuffles took place on a regular basis. For example, the FFSES saw seven CEOs come and go between 1993 and 2002. In 1998, just before the crisis, SCSESP was dismantled, and the functions of small business support were reassigned to the Ministry of Antitrust Policy. The situation being what it was, one could hardly expect consistency in the implementation of practical measures. According to the Law 'On State Support of Small Business' (1995), Russia was to provide support for small businesses through the development and implementation of relevant programmes at federal, territorial and municipal level.

Until 2002 four special federal programmes, as well as over a hundred territorial programmes, had been adopted and implemented. The implementation of federal programmes in the 1990s helped establish an infrastructure for the support of small businesses at the federal and territorial levels, gain experience, review the support practices abroad, and identify best practices.

There was no appreciable effect, however, made by the said programmes to improve conditions for the growth of small businesses as such. Macroeconomic and political risks (like high inflation) undermined the special support measures. Moreover, serious faults manifested themselves in the established system of state-sponsored support for small businesses. They included its orientation towards allocating solely budgetary resources, inadequate recognition of the needs of the entrepreneurs themselves when choosing support measures and tools, low transparency of activities of the organizations involved, and lack of competition for the governance of resources to be allocated. The major fault of federal (as well as of most territorial) programmes was the failure to monitor the results of the implementation of previous programmes; under such preconditions a waste of resources and corrupt practices were usual features of the state programmes and implementing activities.

New Agenda: Roots of Entrepreneurship Policy in the Early 2000s

The very limited results of the policies implemented in the second half of the 1990s caused the renewed government under Putin's presidency to dismantle the bulky, inadequately funded and poorly performing system of small business support organizations. The FFSES was scrapped as early as the beginning of the 2000s, and the functions of think tank for private enterprise support were transferred from the Ministry of Antitrust Policy to the Ministry for Economic Development and Trade (MEDT). The system of support organizations that emerged in the 1990s in most territories which was merely built on donations from the Federal centre collapsed in most regions as soon as the FFSES was shut down.

The government made a choice to change policies in favour of the World Bank-supported concept of indirect support of economic growth by way of structural reforms because in the conditions of a fragmented and weak state and highly opportunistic behaviour of public officials the effects of tax reliefs and exemptions, subsidies and the like were totally neutralized by rampant corruption (Yakovlev 2006a, pp. 248–50). Moreover, the policy of structural regulation did not target any specific groups in need of focused support, although it prioritized the problems of growing SME. The early 2000s saw the dominance of an indirect support strategy of small entrepreneurs by reducing red tape and lowering the costs of entry and administration of business. According to MEDT estimates, by 2001 red-tape overheads were as high as 5 to 7 per cent of the GDP.

The main idea of the programme developed in 2000–01 ('Long-term priorities of social and economic development of the Russian Federation') regarding small business support, was to diminish state intervention in the economy, abandon excessive bureaucratic regulation in order to ease bureaucratic pressures on businesses and to improve the performance of government agencies in areas where their involvement is absolutely necessary. Core measures included lowering market entry barriers for businesses; eliminating technical barriers for manufacturing enterprises (reform of the standardization and certification system); eliminating excessive and ineffective administrative regulation of business activities; coordinating the actions of federal and territorial government agencies, in particular developing a mechanism to represent the interests of citizens and organizations through self-regulating organizations, statutory separation of the functions of regulatory and oversight agencies.

The government planned to address these tasks based on a package of new federal laws, together with a complete overhaul of the legislation governing business activities. It proved, however, impossible to implement the plan: laws were put in place at long intervals (August 2001 – June 2003); at least two of them were dropped (Law 'On Self-Regulating Organisations' and amendments to the law 'On Consumer Rights Protection'). The 'cleaning-up' of former laws was not completed either. Moreover, the survey of administrative costs of business activities conducted by Russia's think tank CEFIR (2002–07) suggests that the deregulation policy also produced only limited results, if any, although the overall results for 2007 (2000 firms polled from 20 territories in seven federal districts of Russia) revealed a number of positive changes in some areas of state regulation. For example, the average term of licences has increased, approaching the statutory requirement; a majority of oversight agencies committed fewer breaches of legislation, in particular, they undertook unscheduled inspections on a less frequent basis; the total number of inspections decreased significantly; the incidence of pressure applied by civil servants with the aim to solicit a bribe in the course of registering ownership or lease of properties was much reduced and the transparency of the procedure increased.

However, CEFIR researchers also recorded deterioration in some areas. For example, the increased importance of personal connections for completing the registration procedure casts doubt on the effectiveness of the so-called one-stop; inspections in general and those by tax authorities in particular became more of a problem, compared to 2004; entrepreneurs feel that the situation with competition has worsened (presumably, they refer to the clout of big business used to unfair advantage at the negotiation table) and that corruption has increased (CEFIR 2007).

It is no coincidence that in her first public address on policies for the support of SME in 2008, the newly appointed Minister for Economic Development, Elvira Nabiullina, formulated a number of measures which to all intents and purposes usher in a 'second wave' of the drive to cut red tape for business (Nabiullina 2008). But even earlier, in the mid 2000s, as in the aftermath of dismantling the former system a vacuum in the area of support for private enterprise became more and more apparent, the government started to rethink its policies towards small business and entrepreneurship. In 2007, the efforts culminated in a new Federal Law 'On Small and Medium-sized Entrepreneurship in the Russian Federation', which was adopted after being in the pipeline for more than five years in different versions. Its main feature is that it identifies for the first time, in addition to small businesses, micro and medium-sized enterprises. It modifies and supplements the criteria for classification of private enterprise under these categories – these include, in addition to the structure of authorized capital and number of employees, limits on annual revenues. Moreover, the law identifies schemes and forms of governmental support for SME.

However, the law is seriously defective in that it fails to identify the sources of funding for the policies to support SME (the 'old' law allocated – at least on paper – some of the federal fiscal revenues from the privatization of state-owned assets), or the procedure for the selection of SMEs that would qualify for support. These drawbacks significantly impair the performance of this law as a regulatory framework for government policies.

Even before the new law postulated schemes and forms of support for small and medium-sized businesses, work began on a 'Target-oriented programme for the support of SME in 2005–08'. In spite of the legislation lacking many of the required preconditions (including the status of a 'target-oriented programme' as such and the concept of 'medium-sized enterprise'), the programme introduced principles and mechanisms stemming from the new understanding of both the role of small and medium-sized business and the capabilities and tasks of the state. What was new in the programme is that, first, it focused on crucial target groups in the SME sector. These included innovative firms (the programme provided for access to resources and to facilitate entry into new markets), start-ups (development of expertise and access to resources), and sustainable growing SME (access to new markets and to resources). Other groups of SME were to receive indirect support in the form of legalization (development of the necessary regulatory framework) and assistance in the development of management skills. For the first time ever, some of the measures implemented as part of the programme were aimed at supporting nascent entrepreneurs. In addition, the 'Target-oriented programme for the support of SME in 2005–08' outlined not only the targets, but also indicators which can be used to measure the degree of their attainment.

Finally, the Programme provided a rationale for its basic support principles, namely, decentralization of SME support mechanisms, co-funding (Federation and regions), a combination of entrepreneurship policy in the advanced territories and SME support in economically weaker territories, competition between state bodies and public organizations in the area of SME support, identification and dissemination of best practices, priority support for firms with high growth potential and lowering of exit barriers for less successful SME and incentives for cooperation between small, medium and large businesses.

Of special note is the need for open and transparent implementation of the Programme based on monitoring its progress and a regular evaluation of its performance, including the mechanism of third-party assessment as a means of minimizing the conflict of interest for the parties involved in the development and implementation of the Programme. The programme's initiators insisted on an annual update of the set of measures and funding objectives which was based on the evaluation of its performance in the previous year. In this sense, the concept of the programme was very close to what is meant under a 'six steps' assessment procedure (Storey 2005).

In the course of in-house coordination and subsequent implementation, however, many of the principles formulated for the renewal of the state programme got lost or were seriously distorted. For example, support was withheld for the idea of competition-based selection of an independent company to coordinate the programme's implementation, and the functions were left with the Ministry itself – thus, a conflict of interests

*Table 10.2   Structure of federal budget expenditures and results of the
Programme for SME Support in Russia, 2005–07*

Measures	Expenditures (RUR, mln)	Results
Support of business incubators formation	2730	Co-funding of 111 local, municipal and universities-based business incubators
Formation of venture funds	2151	21 funds, market capitalization – RUR 8 400 mln
Co-funding of regional SME support programmes	1593	SME support programmes in 56 RF oblasts and krays co-funded
Formation of guarantee funds	1556	23 funds, market capitalization – RUR 3 300 mln
Export support	170	380+ companies

Source: 'Maly bizness: ot inertsii k innovatsii' (2008).

was guaranteed. No public hearings were held on its interim stages and adjustments required, if any. There was no public platform organized (not even on the MEDT website) in order to reach out to and inform possible beneficiaries and civil society. Government also failed to arrange a balanced approach to implement the programme as several of the priorities identified received much more funding than other thrusts without any sound substantiation (Table 10.2).

Moreover, setting priorities and defining the next steps in the implementation of the programme for each following year took place behind closed doors of the MEDT. This makes it difficult to ascertain the success of the programme. In any case, the impact of the programme on the dynamics of the SME sector was relatively low, if assessed by official statistics which show that the input of SME in main economic indicators remained more or less stable and very modest (Table 10.1). Meanwhile, the slowest progress was made in supporting new ventures, exporting SMEs and increasing the involvement of SME in public procurement. GEM data for 2006–08 show that Russia still belongs to the group of countries with lowest share of nascent entrepreneurs in the adult population. Moreover, statistical data also illustrate that no significant change was achieved in the modest state of innovative small firms (Rosstat 2009). The share of small firms' participation in state procurement remains, according to expert estimations, at 1–5 per cent, far under the estimated target indicator of 15 per cent of public procurement turnover.

The outbreak of the economic crisis in autumn 2008 put on hold the implementation of further mid- and long-term plans. In late December 2008, support of SME was put on the 'List of Priority Measures of the Government of the Russian Federation' as part of its action against the effects of the global financial crisis. In April 2009 a comprehensive and complex anti-crisis programme of the Russian government was adopted, including a list of measures addressed to support SME and entrepreneurship policy. Measures aimed at increasing the lending programme of the federal main agent in the area of financial support for SMEs, Vneshekonombank, to RUR 60 billion and to provide RUR 10.5 billion from the federal treasury to fund the formation of small business start-ups. The latter includes measures such as lending, interest rate subsidies, provision of government guarantees, development of infrastructure such as science parks and business incubators, allocation of grants and implementation of training programmes. Moreover, the government was to provide a law for preferential treatment of small businesses in state and municipal procurement with a minimum quota of SME's goods and services in public purchases of 20 per cent. This measure provides SMEs with extra 800 billion roubles public purchases. Other measures referred to a resolution to lower the charge for power grid connection of low-consumption facilities and real estate funds for SMEs which provide SME with discount and long-term rental rates. Moreover, territories and municipalities are obliged to involve SME in the fulfilment of government and municipal orders and to remove administration barriers to entrepreneurial activities, including restrictions on access to local markets. Additionally, measures have been implemented to reduce the tax burden on SME. Russian regional governments are in their own right to reduce the so-called single tax on imputed income from 15 per cent to 5 per cent. Deregulation measures minimize administrative burdens for start-ups in order to decrease start-up capital. For example, from July 2009 the registration of a small business has become simplified. An entrepreneur only has to inform the government that he or she is starting a new business. Administrative inspections of SME activity in Russia are restricted to once in three years; and any additional inspections have to be permitted by a state prosecutor.

How efficient may the measures proposed be? As for facilitating access to credit facilities, the problem is not so much the level of credit as credit terms and guarantees, on which federal budget allocations have little direct effect, if any. It will naturally benefit SMEs if their power grid connection charge is lowered and they are granted the right of first refusal to buy state and municipal assets which they have been renting for years and which have already been significantly improved. Measures to reduce tax burden – by way of lowering the profit tax – can be important for the few sustainable growing companies, which are still in the black despite the crisis in progress. However, the share of such successful SME diminished very significantly, whilst the main goal of an anti-crisis protection should be to support those SMEs who are suffering from finance shortage. However, as for the right granted to territories to lower at their discretion the rate of single tax on imputed income, in the context of the territories' rising budget deficit this measure can be regarded as passing the buck to them rather than a real step in bringing relief to small businesses.

Having been portrayed by and large as priorities, the measures can hardly make a significant impact because they have too little focus on different target groups and fail to factor in the pending changes in the structure of the sector of small and medium-sized business (fewer profit-making and fast-growing firms and more 'weak' firms, inevitably rising number of necessity entrepreneurs, and so on).

Regional Differences in Entrepreneurship Development and Support Policies

A major roadblock to the development of SME and entrepreneurship in Russia has been, and remains, its uneven spread across the country, as well as the widely differing degree of territorial authorities' readiness to facilitate the conditions for the development of effective private enterprise. Small businesses are spread across Russia in a very uneven pattern, with several groups of territories identifiable in terms of its development, as suggested by a survey on the development of private enterprise in Russian territories, which was conducted in 2005 by the National Institute of Systemic Research of Entrepreneurship (Migin 2006). The survey identified eight territorial clusters with significant differences in terms of small business development (Table 10.3).

Small business development differs widely between individual territories in Russia as does the gross territorial product. There can be no doubt that these widely different territories need different ways and means regarding small business support policies, based on objectives that differ in terms of complexity, different levels of fiscal capacity, as well as differences in the level of relevant infrastructure development.

Regional differentiation of support policies, however, is hindered by external circumstances. The fundamental changes that took place in the 2000s limited budgetary powers and burdens, thus significantly decreasing the budgetary base of most regions of Russia. The federal and budgetary reform of the early 2000s led to a situation where the territories still had to honour most of their financial commitments, but with their funding sources significantly reduced. The importance of federal co-funding is highlighted by the fact that in only seven Russian territories federal

Table 10.3 Small business development in the regions of the Russian Federation

Cluster / Indicator	1	2	3	4	5	6	7	8
Number of SE per thousand workforce	37.56	12.72	10.41	14.41	8.54	6.07	5.52	6.14
Average SE staff on payroll per thou. workforce	268.62	99.66	99.63	107.79	79.93	55.69	45.16	42.92
Labour productivity per SE (per employee)*, RUR000's	201.27	372.32	329.21	271.48	251.10	228.64	258.86	648.74
Average number of investments into equity per SE*, RUR000's	28.13	141.70	255.28	70.62	97.42	267.42	45.27	96.52
Receipts of STSTS [single tax under simplified taxation scheme] and STII [single tax on imputed income]*, RUR000000's	2771.42	2644.11	1060.91	783.44	478.42	284.46	277.31	272.03

Note: * With the consumer basket cost factored in for inter-territorial comparison of purchasing power.

Source: Migin (2006).

transfers amount to less than 5 per cent of the revenues in the consolidated budget, whilst the rest of the 80 territories are subsidized from the Centre to a much greater extent.

Given the current crisis, one cannot expect the governments of a vast majority of Russian territories to be in a position to implement any support measures whatsoever other than cutting red tape. The biggest problem of entrepreneurship and SME policies in times of the crisis is the contradiction between a need in locally targeted and operated policies and the lack of funding abilities (and often adequate concepts) on the regional level.

Summing Up: Progress with Government Policies

Government policies towards SME and entrepreneurship in Russia have passed through a number of periods. In the early 1990s the government followed the concept of the macroeconomic policy to establish main institutions required for a market-driven economy which were at that time considered more important than SME focused policies. In this context, the policy of financial stabilization and privatization aimed at supporting preconditions for any kind of private entrepreneurship in general rather than targeting specific groups of entrepreneurs and firms such as start-ups and high growing SME. From the mid 1990s preference was given to the concept of supporting small firms by measures of a 'traditional' SME policy. Those are efficient under conditions of a balanced macro-, meso- and microeconomic policy in established market economies with a transparent system of efficient state regulating authorities. However, in the absence of any well functioning and recognized institutions, especially at the micro level, and a lack of financial resources, this policy did not have any impact on SME development. During the crisis of 1998, this system of state support for small business began to collapse. Circles close to the government were convinced not only of its inefficiency, 'radicals' complained about the total irrelevance of the small business support concept. As a consequence the pendulum swung back to the idea of entrepreneurship policy instead of SME policy.

By the mid 2000s, government started to realize the need to implement, alongside improving general conditions for business development, a targeted entrepreneurship policy, to provide specific assistance to key groups of SMEs. With the crisis in progress, starting in late 2008 any large-scale support for nascent entrepreneurs is again all but abandoned in favour of fast-response measures.

There are several and recurring mistakes made in the development and implementation of government policies towards SME and entrepreneurship. This includes, amongst others, a limited involvement of civil society stakeholders in the process of policy development and implementation; absence of comprehensive analysis of policy background, progress and results; the failure to grasp not only the common features, but also the differences between policies to support small businesses (that is, firms) and those to boost the entrepreneurial potential of the society (that is, of persons), the latter being obviously underrated and finally, the absence of policy coordination at the federal and territorial levels.

THE ROLE OF FOREIGN TECHNICAL ASSISTANCE IN SME AND ENTREPRENEURSHIP SUPPORT IN RUSSIA

The development of government policies for supporting entrepreneurship in Russia, especially in the period of early reforms, was undertaken with support from major Western partners. That included first of all the EU and the USA, international organizations such as the EBRD, the World Bank, the IMF and the IFC, as well as so-called bilateral programmes, which involved bilateral cooperations with most developed countries. Of the 21 foreign donor organizations involved, the most prominent were USAID, the German Ministry for Economic Co-operation, the European Commission and EBRD (FEED).

As of the beginning of the 2000s, Russia has received technical assistance worth more than $3 billion from a variety of donor organizations, 20 per cent of which (or 2000 projects) was dedicated to supporting and developing small businesses. That included mainly professional training and exchanges, while policy support, consultations and equipment for small businesses accounted for about 10–15 per cent of the total technical assistance. Moreover, technical assistance is unevenly distributed across the Russian territory, with 'the major portion being gained by the Central and North-Western regions and the Urals region' (FEED, no date p. 34).

SME support programmes and projects of technical assistance had different thrusts. Some focused on analytical and advisory support for reforms, monitoring business growth and business climate, while others concentrated on institution building such as microfinance organizations and credit institutions, business associations and business networks, business education centres, or offered management and business-related training. For example, the European Commission provided technical assistance, equipment and initial funding for the Moscow Agency of

Entrepreneurship Development and 23 other regional Development Agencies for SME Support. USAID focused on institution building at regional level. It created 19 business incubators, approximately 140 locations of technical aid and its credit lines totalled more than $600 million (FEED, no date).

Western technical assistance made it possible to quickly gain command of the legal and regulatory framework of developed market economies regarding the development and implementation of relevant policies, institution building, first of all lending and financial establishments, and the formation of a business education system. However, the eclipse of the authority of international financial institutions in the wake of the Asian crisis of 1997 and Russia's default of 1998, as well as the growing political antagonism between Russia and the West caused SME support activities of Western organizations in Russia to be rolled back, starting in the first half of the 2000s.

Moreover, the overall situation had changed: Russia was experiencing sustainable growth in the 2000s, which rendered the model of technical assistance, put in place in the 1990s in an environment where institutions and governmental experiences in implementing and developing market institutions were lacking, superfluous. It was time to move to a dialogue on a peer-to-peer basis which however, proved increasingly difficult to realize because of the mutual disappointment in the aftermath of the turbulent 1990s. Many Western projects, which provided for the implementation of 'best practices' in an environment of 'bad' institutions failed to prevent the emergence of 'crony capitalism' in Russia. The Russian elite, on the other hand, seemed disappointed with the 'unwillingness' of Western organizations to take into consideration the rules (path dependency) and norms (rather informal than written) of a transition economy and with their belief in 'universal' schemes and notions of international financial institutions.

CONCLUSIONS

Based on the description of SME development, as well as of the small business and entrepreneurship policy in Russia from the late 1990s onwards, we argue that shortcuts of the state policy towards SME and entrepreneurship were unavoidable. The reasons include a lack of adequate institutions (among them, a lack of experience in developing and implementing adequate policy) and strategic failures in selecting policy priorities. During the period of systemic transition, Russia would have been in dire need of an entrepreneurship policy which promoted an environment for new ventures and thus could have helped to establish a broader stratum of 'productive small businesses'. Instead, the government tried to establish SME policies similar to that in developed market economies during the 1950s–70s. As a result, other – rent seeking oriented – forms of entrepreneurship ('unproductive' or even 'destructive', Baumol 1990) became dominant. Under such circumstances, the 'old fashioned' SME policy was obsolete. It could merely conserve established enterprise structures, namely micro business with little added value creation, predominantly in retail trade and so on, but had no influence on shaping conditions for high growth new ventures. A new agenda from the early 2000s onwards combined traditional SME policies and some important entrepreneurship policy measures. However, the agenda was still implemented in the old bureaucratic manner with no transparency, no feedback from the SME sector, no monitoring according to clearly defined criteria. Therefore, it did not lead to a fundamental policy change. Moreover, in 2008, after the last SME promotion programme was completed, the crisis occurred, resulting in reactive instead of proactive approaches to designing policies and support.

The chapter shows that in Russia, the strategic objective of government policies must be to support productive entrepreneurship and limit the options for rent-oriented or even parasitic growth of unproductive or destructive entrepreneurship. But this task must be recognized by governmental authorities. Moreover, it involves fundamental changes in the system of ownership rights and the entire structure of social relations, because the domination of unproductive and 'destructive' entrepreneurship is inseparable from the system of ownership power, which disguises itself as the system of private ownership and resists eradication. While mostly entrenched in the segment of the so-called super large and large business, unproductive and 'destructive' entrepreneurship is actually rooted in close personal ties of business owners and managers with the ruling political elite. An alternative is 'productive entrepreneurship', which is mostly based in the segment of SME. However, it is forced to put up with the government's veiled attempts to gain control and is not free itself from opportunistic behaviour patterns. Nevertheless, the sources of its income are still based in a different area – in the area of realignment of market resources for the production of new benefits. Under such circumstances, traditional SME policies providing support for any kind of private enterprise do not undermine the positions of unproductive and 'destructive' entrepreneurship. On the other hand, entrepreneurship policy, focused on providing advice and help for starting 'productive' businesses can foster the consolidation of the latter.

Overall, SME policies in Russia have never been consistent, penetrating or comprehensive in their nature as this would contradict the interests of principal beneficiaries of abortive reforms in Russia. Hence, to outline and conduct a balanced entrepreneurship policy, a sufficiently strong coalition to support such policies is needed. The groundwork for such a coalition to be put together needs the involvement of 'productive entrepreneurship', new professionals (since the value of knowledge will inevitably depreciate if dominated by unproductive and destructive entrepreneurship), new regional leaders (because they have no potential allies or sources, other than SME, for fuelling the social and economic development of the territories under their jurisdiction), and the – at least – tacit consent of the nation's leadership (because the ambitious goals set by it for the innovation-oriented economy under development cannot be achieved as long as Russia is dominated by unproductive entrepreneurship).

The current crisis seems to be a long one, and the measures announced by the federal government to promote SME and entrepreneurship appear to have little impact on SME and entrepreneurship development and especially on the motivation to establish new ventures. Changing the currently dominating inconsistent agenda for entrepreneurship policy is obviously required to create better preconditions for public supported policy which would be in favour of productive entrepreneurship.

NOTE

1. Note that in Russia up to the 2008 statistics have been gathered for *small* and *incorporated* firms only; the number of sole traders, according to the census of 2007, amounts to 2.5 million.

REFERENCES

Audretsch, D. (2002), 'Entrepreneurship: a survey of the literature', available at http://www.ec.europa.eu/enterprise/entrepreneurship/green_paper/literature_survey_2002.pdf.
Baumol, W.J. (1990), 'Entrepreneurship: productive, unproductive, and destructive', *Journal of Political Economy*, **98** (5), 893–921.
Black, B., R. Kraakman and A. Tarasova (2000), 'Russian privatization and corporate governance: what went wrong?', *Stanford Law Review*, **52** (6), 1731–1808.
CEFIR (2007), *Monitoring administrativnykh barierov na puti razvitiya malogo biznesa v Rossii. Raund 6 (Monitoring of Administrative Barriers for Small Business in Russia. Round 6)*, available at http://www.cefir.ru/index.php?l=rus&id=34&yf=2007.
Centre for Co-operation with the Economies in Transition (ed.) (1998), *Entrepreneurship and Small Business in the Russian Federation*, Paris: OECD.
Earle, J.S. and S. Estrin (2003), 'Privatization, competition, and budget constraints: disciplining enterprises in Russia', *Economics of Planning*, **36** (1), 1–22.

Earle, J.S. and Z. Sakova (2000), 'Business start-ups or disguised unemployment? Evidence on the character of self-employment from transition economies', *Labour Economics*, **7** (5), 575–601.
Forum for Entrepreneurship and Enterprise Development (FEED) for the Russian Federation, *Policy Guidelines and Recommendations*, not dated.
Frye, T. (2004), 'Credible commitments and property rights: evidence from Russia', *American Political Science Review*, **3** (98), 453–66.
Gaddy, C. and B. Ickes (1998), 'To restructure or not to restructure: informal activities and enterprise behavior in transition', *William Davidson Institute Working Paper Series*, WP 134, mimeo.
Iwasaki, I. (2003), 'The governance mechanism of Russian firms: its self-enforcing nature and limitations', *Post-Communist Economies*, **15** (4), 503–31.
'Maly bizness: ot inertsii k innovatsii' ('Small business: from inertia to innovation'), available at http://www.economy.gov.ru (accessed 13 May 2008).
Migin, S. (2006), *Klassifikatsiya subyektov Rossiiskoi Federatsii po urovnyu razvitiya malogo predprinimatelstva* (*Classification of Russian Federation Members in Terms of Small Business Development*), available at http://www.nisse.ru/analitics.html?id=ks_RF.
Moers, L. (2000), 'Determinants of enterprise restructuring in transition: description of a survey in Russian industry', *Post-Communist Economies*, **12** (3), 307–32.
Murrell, P. (2005), 'Institutions and firms in transition economies', in C. Menard and M.M. Shirley (eds), *Handbook of New Institutional Economics*, Dordrecht: Kluwer Academic Press, pp. 667–700.
Nabiullina, E. (2008), 'Maly i sredny biznes – osnova sotsialno-ekonomicheskogo razvitiya Rossii v XXI veke' ('Small and medium-sized businesses: the backbone of Russia's social and economic development in the 21st century'), summary of the contribution by the Minister for Economic Development of the Russian Federation to All-Russia Forum, available at http://www.economy.gov.ru (accessed 26 May 2009).
Nabiullina, E. (2009), 'O proekte "Razvitie malogo i srednego predprinimaelstva" perechnya proektov po realizacii Osnovnykh napravleniy deyatelnosti Pravitelstva Rossiyskoj Federacii na period do 2012 goda' ('On the project "Development of small and medium sized business" of the list of projects on the main tasks of the Government of the Russian Federation until 2012'). Theses of the contribution by the Minister for Economic Development of the Russian Federation to the Government of Russian Federation, available at http://www.economy.gov.ru, 18 May.
Radygin, A. (1995), *Privatization in Russia: Hard Choice, First Results, New Targets*, L.: CRCE – The Jarvis Print Group.
'Realisaciya meropriyatij gosudarstvennoy poddershki malogo predprinimatelstva' ('Realisation of measures of State support of small entrepreneurship'), available at http://http://www.mbm.ru/content/document_r_45DD8847-42E5-4297-B7F7-6D5AD538C675.html.
Rosstat (2008), 'Maloe predprinimatelstvo v Rossii 2008. Rosstat' ('Small entrepreneurship in Russia in 2008, Federal Statistical Agency'), Moscow.
Rosstat (2009), 'Maloe i srednee predprinimatelstvo v Rossii 2009. Rosstat' ('Small and medium sized business in Russia 2009, Federal Statistical Agency'), Moscow.
Storey, D. (2005), 'Entrepreneurship, small and medium sized enterprises and public policies', in Z.J. Acs and D.B. Audretsch (eds), *Handbook of Entrepreneurship Research*, New York: Springer, pp. 473–511.
Welter, F. and D. Smallbone (2003), 'Entrepreneurship and enterprise strategies in transition economies: an institutional perspective', in D.A. Kirby and A. Watson (eds), *Small Firms and Economic Development in Developed and Transition Economies: A Reader*, Hampshire: Ashgate, pp. 95–114.
Yakovlev, A. (2001), '"Black cash" tax evasion in Russia: its forms, incentives and consequences at firm level', *Europe-Asia Studies*, **53** (1), 33–55.
Yakovlev, A. (2006a), *Agenty modernizatsii* (*Modernization agents*), Moscow: HSE.

Yakovlev, A. (2006b), 'Evolution of business-state interaction in Russia: from state capture to business capture?', *Europe-Asia Studies*, **58** (7), 1033–56.

Yudanov, A. (2008), *Opyt konkurentsii v Rossii: prichiny uspekhov i neudach* (*Competition in Russia: the Causes of Success and Failure*), Moscow: KnoRus.

Webpages

http://www.gemconsortium.org.

http://www.doingbusiness.org/EconomyRankings/.

http://www.innovbusiness.ru/pravo/DocumShow_DocumID_120.html.

http://www.xserver.ru/user/ffpmp/.

11 Fostering women's entrepreneurship in Ukraine

Nina Isakova

INTRODUCTION

The International Labour Office (ILO) stated in its annual report 'Global Employment Trends for Women' that the economic crisis was expected to increase the number of unemployed women by as much as 22 million, and that the global job crisis was expected to worsen sharply with the deepening of the recession in 2009 (ILO 2009). However, the entrepreneurial potential of women could be used as a source of economic growth and therefore as a solution to social problems such as unemployment. Women do business in a wide variety of countries and increasingly contribute to economic growth – in particular in low- and middle-income economies, but a systematic and significant gender gap, which is more characteristic of opportunity-driven rather than necessity-driven entrepreneurs, has been identified, as we know from the Global Entrepreneurship Monitor research project performed in 41 countries (Allen et al. 2008). Encouraging entrepreneurship among women seems to be a challenge worldwide, and this is equally true for countries which are still in transition from a planned to market economy. In Ukraine the participation of female entrepreneurs remains low in relation to that of male entrepreneurs, it is also low compared to the ratio of women in the population. More progress could probably be made if an appropriate policy was in place.

Fostering women's entrepreneurship, it is argued, depends on formal and informal institutions related to gender and entrepreneurship. The main topic of this chapter will be discussed from these two points of view: a gender perspective and an entrepreneurship perspective.

Most research on gender and entrepreneurship in the context of transition economies has studied differences between the sexes in areas such as features of sector and business, motivation, education and previous experience, psychological characteristics of entrepreneurs, finance, barriers to development and growth, and networking (Aidis 2006; Ashwin 2000; Bruno 1997; Drnovsek and Glas 2006; Fajth 2000; Kiblitskaya 2000; Koncz 2000; Lokar 2000; Mrcozkowski 1997; Wells et al. 2003; Zhurzhenko 1999). To date, few studies have focused on the importance of gender norms and values and their influence on the nature and extent of female entrepreneurship in a transition context (for example, Aidis et al. 2007; Welter and Smallbone 2008; Welter et al. 2006).

The theme of entrepreneurship policy has been widely addressed in the recent academic and practical literature and remains at the top of the research agendas of scholars in many countries (Hart 2003). Modern entrepreneurship is a multi-faceted phenomenon, which requires that an inter-disciplinary approach be used in research and policy making (Audretsch et al. 2007). Given the important role of entrepreneurship in transition economies, several studies have investigated this phenomenon, evaluated institutional characteristics to promote entrepreneurship, analysed government policies and the business environment fostering (female) entrepreneurship, and compared countries in different stages of transition (Aidis et al. 2007; Manolova and Yan 2002; Manolova et al. 2008; McIntyre and Dallago 2003; Smallbone and Welter 2001a, 2001b; Welter et al. 2006; Williams and Round 2007).

In this regard, Welter and Smallbone (2008, p. 506) argue that 'an institutionalist perspective is a particularly appropriate guiding frame of reference in a post-socialist context, where formal market institutions have yet to be installed and informal codes of conduct and path dependency are a major influence on entrepreneurial behaviour'. By discussing some of the transition-specific features of female entrepreneurship policy in terms of formal and informal institutions in Ukraine, this chapter aims to contribute to the international knowledge base regarding female entrepreneurship policy. First, the chapter describes the Ukrainian economic and national policy context, then progress achieved with entrepreneurship and small business development since the early 1990s and the entrepreneurial potential of men and women. This is followed by a section analyzing those policies and institutions which have an impact on women's entrepreneurship in Ukraine. The chapter ends with some conclusions.

UKRAINIAN ECONOMIC AND NATIONAL POLICY CONTEXT: AN OVERVIEW

Since 1991 Ukraine has been known as one of the transition countries attempting to move from socialism to democracy and from a planned to a market economy. At present Ukraine is a republic under a mixed parliamentary/presidential system, with separate legislative, executive, and judicial branches (Constitution of Ukraine 1996). Initially the country was viewed as a republic with favourable economic conditions in comparison to other regions of the ex-Soviet Union. However, it experienced a deeper economic slowdown than some of the other republics. From 1991 to 1999, Ukraine lost 60 per cent of its GDP, and suffered five-digit annual inflation rates. The first years of independence were characterized by large deficits in the state budget, hyperinflation, loss of personal savings and former markets in other ex-Soviet republics, suspended manufacturing, and a population growing increasingly disappointed with the inability of the government to deliver basic services. After 17 years of independence and market reforms Ukraine has failed to be promoted to the category of advanced transition countries (EBRD 2008). By 2008, the systemic transformation in the country had largely been completed, but reforms had been taking place at a pace which was insufficient to allow Ukraine to advance at the same pace as other economies with whom it competes for investment and markets (World Bank 2009).

After several years of relatively stable growth, in 2008 the economic situation in Ukraine started to worsen. The gross domestic product decreased by 2.1 per cent in October and 14.4 per cent in November 2008. This was caused by the world financial crisis, lack of trust in the Ukrainian banking system, lowering world commodity prices and a tightening domestic policy (Pogarska and Segura 2009).

Sustainable development in the economy and society is slow because many of the institutions indispensable for establishing a Western societal model are still either missing or underdeveloped in Ukraine (Romanchuk 2008). In 2006 it was recommended by the US–Ukraine Policy Dialogue Project that the Cabinet of Ministers set up a new system for formulating and implementing economic policy, introduce effective measures to combat corruption, bring order to the regulatory and tax systems and promote the development of institutions to build a civil society (ICPS 2007). The Ukrainian government has clearly failed to build strong democratic institutions and to ensure the economic freedom needed to achieve improved social results. According to the 2009 assessment by the Heritage Foundation, Ukraine's economy is 48.8 per cent free, ranking 152 out of 183 economies (Heritage Foundation 2009).

After the 'Orange Revolution',[1] which initially gave rise to hope for a better society, no major change has taken place in economic policy. The Ukrainian economic and national policy context, which is now aggravated by the world economic crisis, has had a negative impact on all spheres of human activity – including small business and entrepreneurship – by adding to the turbulence of the national business climate and fragility of institutions. Moreover, gender analysts argue that the process of market transition has tightened gender discrimination in the economy, reduced economic opportunities for the female workforce and contributed to the overall deterioration of conditions for their careers (Kisselyova 2008).

DEVELOPMENT OF (FEMALE) ENTREPRENEURSHIP SINCE THE EARLY 1990S

The important role of small businesses and entrepreneurship in the nation's economy has been repeatedly acknowledged at the highest political level, but significant change to support them has, to date, been modest. In the early 1990s the following three groups of businesses were identified in the country: former Soviet nomenclature-owned businesses, shadow businesses and legal businesses (Smallbone and Welter 2001a). A subgroup of enterprises, those registered but not operating, was also a characteristic of the Ukrainian entrepreneurship landscape. Over the years, enterprises in the first and second group have evolved into legal businesses. The processes which have occurred in the 'legal enterprises' group are those typical for businesses all over the world: some businesses were more successful than others and started to grow, some were just able to survive, and some companies closed down. However, in the light of unfavourable macroeconomic conditions, underdeveloped formal institutions and the still strong influence of Soviet societal norms, small enterprises have not received the necessary momentum for rapid growth, as can be seen in Table 11.1. As in many less successful transition countries, enterprises remain small and lack growth and innovation potential, furthermore there is almost no vertical integration with large enterprises (Dallago 2003).

Table 11.1   *Characteristics of small enterprises development in Ukraine*

Year	No. of small enterprises	No. of small enterprises per 10 000 inhabitants	No. of small enterprises hired employees, 1000	Share of small enterprises' hired employees in total employment	Share of small enterprises in total volume of products (services)
2000	217930	44	1709.8	15.1	8.1
2001	233607	48	1807.6	17.1	7.1
2002	253791	53	1918.5	18.9	6.7
2003	272741	57	2034.2	20.9	6.6
2004	283398	60	1928.0	20.2	5.3
2005	295109	63	1834.2	19.6	5.5
2006	307398	66	1746.0	19.0	4.8
2007	324000	70	1674.2	18.4	4.4

Source: Osaulenko (2008).

A large number of Ukrainian entrepreneurs are (or started as) small traders, and among these women form a significant proportion. The economic crisis and growing unemployment pushed the majority of (potential) small entrepreneurs to start businesses, which helped to avoid social unrest in the early 1990s. While in the first years of reforms small business played a role in fighting shortages of food and consumer goods by exploiting the opportunities of informal import from China, Poland, Turkey and other countries, in more recent years entrepreneurs have started to respond to growing demand by setting up small construction firms, consumer- and business-oriented services and manufacturing businesses.

Data on female entrepreneurship is difficult to obtain. Much to the disappointment of researchers on female entrepreneurship, the Ukrainian State Statistics Committee does not collect data on woman-owned businesses. In the absence of independent statistics agencies it is impossible to find data on such information as the percentage of women entrepreneurs in the female population or among the total number of entrepreneurs.[2] Woman-owned enterprises in the Ukraine, similar to their counterparts all over the world, are reported to be on average smaller, be concentrated in particular sectors, have fewer internal (capital) resources and demonstrate lower performance and growth levels compared to men (Aidis et al. 2007; Isakova et al. 2006). The most recent in-depth report on women in Ukrainian business is a survey commissioned in 1999 by the US Agency for International Development (Kiev International Institute of Sociology 2000). According to this report, in Ukraine there were about 1.5 million woman-owned or controlled businesses. The vast majority of these were small firms with fewer than 50 employees; 69.6 per cent of woman-owned businesses were in wholesale or retail trading. Different types of services made up 23.2 per cent, while manufacturing (and mining) and construction were less common, amounting to just 3 per cent of such enterprises. Many female-run businesses have never been registered or partly operate in the informal economy and do not intend to legalize themselves.

A recent study of Ukrainian society (Vorona and Shulga 2008), which was carried out in April 2008 by the Institute of Sociology in the National Academy of Sciences of Ukraine, contains newer data on the entrepreneurial potential of Ukrainian women. The sample consisted of 1800 respondents and was representative of the adult population of the country (those over 18 years of age) in terms of geographical location, gender, occupation, age and education. The percentage of female entrepreneurs in the total number of women of all occupations (professions) in the sample is low, comprising 0.6 per cent for large and medium enterprises (compared to 1.6 for men) and 2.8 per cent for small entrepreneurs and sole proprietors (6.2 per cent for men).

Table 11.2 Attitude to the development of private entrepreneurship in Ukraine by gender, in per cent

Attitude to the development of private entrepreneurship in Ukraine	Male	Female
Absolutely disapprove	7.8	7.3
Rather disapprove	11.2	13.7
Hard to say whether approve or disapprove	20.2	28.3
Rather approve	37.8	33.1
Absolutely approve	23.0	17.5
Total number of respondents	807	942

Source: Based on Vorona and Shulga (2008).

Table 11.3 Expressed wish of Ukrainians to start own business by gender, in per cent

Would you like to start your own business?	Male	Female
No	23.7	33.7
Rather no	11.2	12.0
Hard to say	11.6	14.9
Rather yes	16.4	17.2
Yes	37.1	22.2
Total number of respondents	830	969

Source: Based on Vorona and Shulga (2008).

When asked whether they approved or disapproved of private entrepreneurship, more men than women had a favourable attitude (Table 11.2). Likewise, Table 11.3 shows that more men than women (37.1 per cent compared to 22.2 per cent) would like to start their own business. The same tendency is observed in the attitudes of men and women towards the privatization of large, medium and small enterprises. Women were less in favour of privatization: 'rather positive' was the attitude of 11.5 per cent of women to the privatization of large enterprises (16.9 per cent for men) and the attitude of 40.8 per cent of women to privatization of small and medium enterprises (49.7 per cent for men). This may be a result of women not feeling themselves part of this process, and not having the attitude of potential shareholders, which reflects the still-dominant belief that business, especially large business, is a male domain.

The general tendency of female entrepreneurs to concentrate on particular sectors accords with trends in the development of female entrepreneurship worldwide, but it is also attributed to specifics of a transition environment. For instance, in Russia 'women who succeed in becoming entrepreneurs are usually limited to specific sectors, such as services or the production of cultural/educational activities or textile and fashion businesses where interference of organized crime and perceived risks are lower' (Bruno 1997, p. 57).

However, it is important to emphasize that female entrepreneurship is not limited to the trade and services sectors, since in practice they pursue a much wider range of entrepreneurial activities. Ukrainian business women are a heterogeneous group in terms of type of business, aims and ambitions, strategies and growth orientation (Welter et al. 2003). The young largely rely on enthusiasm, Western methods of education and training and work experience as employees in the non-state sector. Older generations use human capital accumulated under the Soviet regime (high levels of education, life-long work and management experience in state-owned companies) to successfully exploit the opportunity to do business in professional spheres of education, healthcare, finance, legal and audit services and the like. As a consequence, female success stories are to be found in different sectors, and very often it is their human capital that helps women to adapt to new market realities, more than special government policy initiatives to foster female entrepreneurship.

POLICIES AND INSTITUTIONS WHICH AFFECT WOMEN'S ENTREPRENEURSHIP

This section sets out to contribute to the understanding of why women's potential is under-used in Ukraine and why policy measures are not always effective. It is argued that the task of fostering female entrepreneurship is not limited to the sphere of entrepreneurship, but spreads to the wider issue of gender. Regarding female entrepreneurship, one might expect that it is determined by two groups of factors: those associated with the gender of entrepreneurs, and those related to the entrepreneurship environment. In terms of institutional theory, these factors include formal and informal institutions in both areas.

Taking into account the specific transition context it is necessary to note that, as mentioned above, Ukraine is on its way to developing and setting up a wide range of formal institutions conducive to political stability and economic growth. This process concerns also the specific areas of gender on the one hand, and entrepreneurship on the other, and these are discussed in more detail later in this chapter. The goal of establishing effective formal institutions is difficult to attain for a number of reasons (financial, political, organizational, educational) and existing informal institutions are one of the serious hindrances to this process. New laws and regulations affecting gender and entrepreneurship would remain ineffective unless the values, attitudes, perceptions and the behaviour of the public change. In this respect, informal institutions related to gender and economic activity and inherited from the previous regime represent additional obstacles to the task of fostering female entrepreneurship.

In light of this, the discussion of the issue of fostering female entrepreneurship will be approached by describing, first, gender-related formal and informal institutions and, second, entrepreneurship-related formal and informal institutions. As in many complex social systems, no clear-cut picture can be drawn. In real life the overlapping and interaction of institutions is inevitable and this is manifested at the level of the study of individual female entrepreneurs as well as at the more general level of female entrepreneurship in the state.

Gender Perspective

Gender-related formal institutions which are relevant to fostering women's entrepreneurship include first of all the Constitution, which ensures equal opportunities for women and men. More specific formal institutions include labour laws allowing equal access to employment, family policies such as specific tax regulations, and the overall infrastructure for childcare (Welter et al. 2002).

From a gender perspective, it is important to assess the policy environment for female entrepreneurship in terms of gender equality. This is reflected in, for example, the representation of women in the labour force, or their participation in political life. Forming 53.9 per cent of the population and playing a key role in economic life, women are not victims to obvious discrimination in Ukraine. However, there is still a significant discrepancy between the ideal of gender equality and the reality. Gender equality in Ukraine is guaranteed by laws: special provisions are placed under general law, primarily in the Constitution (Article 24), which prohibits privileges or restrictions on several grounds, including sex (Constitution of Ukraine 1996). The Equality Act of January 1, 2006 prohibits gender discrimination, including that in the labour market, and guarantees protection by the state. However, there have been no judicial precedents, which protect women against gender discrimination in the labour market: as of today, the courts in Ukraine have never examined such cases (Kisselyova 2008).

Under the Soviet regime women were fully integrated into the labour force and granted a number of rights that were legally enforced (Isakova et al. 2006). A fairly equal ratio of women to men in the labour force is a continuing feature of the modern situation in Ukraine: 63.5 per cent of the working age women are employed, compared to 69.8 per cent for men, 6.7 and 7.0 per cent of the female and male working population, respectively, are unemployed (Osaulenko 2008). However, these figures have no bearing on decision-making positions or the remuneration of men and women (Pavlychko 1997). From a gender perspective, the introduction of more women into institutions which wield state power is strongly needed in Ukraine, to make government policies in employment and entrepreneurship more gender-sensitive.

Equality within the family was never achieved by Soviet women and in the new socio-economic conditions they are still left with an unequal burden in raising children and performing household chores, alongside with their participation in economic activities. However, the end of socialism resulted in economic and political instability which entailed a change in gender order. Modern society does offer a range of gender role models, but the identity of housewife still tends to be emphasized (Zhurzhenko 2001). With the double burden of participation in economic activities and bearing household and family responsibilities, women have a much more insecure life situation than men and they face greater risks than men of experiencing poverty and social exclusion (lower pay, childcare obligations, career breaks and so on). Moreover, once transition started, many women were excluded from the gains derived from economic freedom and entrepreneurship. Ukrainian society became polarized, with a rich minority and poor majority. The transition process led to changes in values and perceptions, which for many women resulted in social exclusion and difficulties in adjusting to a market-based value system (Ruminska-Zimny 1997).

Interestingly, while gender inequalities exist, the level of gender awareness in Ukrainian society is still low. Gender issues are considered by many (men and women alike) as an imported notion that has no real significance for them. The majority of the population does not perceive any gender inequality, as Table 11.4 shows that 60.5 per cent of men and 55.2 per cent of women considered women and men to have equal rights at work and in the family.

Conflict between family needs, women's responsibilities and individual wishes (Ashwin 2000) is an example of when informal institutions can overrule the existing formal gender equality in legislation. Indeed, although family needs have been a push factor for many Ukrainian women to start businesses, and thus added to an increase in the female share among the total number of entrepreneurs, family responsibility and household duties,

Table 11.4   Opinion of Ukrainians on gender equal rights at work and in the family, in per cent

In your opinion, do women and men have equal rights at work and in the family?	Male	Female
Women have equal rights with men at work and in the family	60.5	55.2
Women have equal rights only at work, while in the family they are subordinate to men	12.2	10.4
Women have equal rights only in the family, while at work women are treated as second best workers mainly	9.9	10.2
Both at work and at home a woman is considered to be a second best person	7.3	12.8
Hard to answer	10.1	11.4
Total number of respondents	811	988

Source: Based on Vorona and Shulga (2007).

which are still considered the domain of women, often do not permit female entrepreneurs to further contribute to the development and growth of their businesses. This has a particular influence on the age profile of female entrepreneurs: for example, in an international project[3] on female entrepreneurship the most representative group in the Ukrainian sample were women of 40 to 49 years (36.7 per cent), that is women with grown-up children. The issue of harmonizing family and business responsibilities by female entrepreneurs was investigated in the above-mentioned project at the start of this decade. Results show that female entrepreneurs typically did not perceive business as interfering with family life. Nevertheless, 19 per cent of respondents considered that business was a hindrance to family life and they were lacking time for their children. Evidence from case studies demonstrated that women with young children would not be able to combine running a business and raising children without any external help from the family. In this regard the improvement of social policy, in particular childcare institutions, would help attract younger women into business.

The social capital of women within the existing gender order is obviously influenced by their networking activities, these, as a way of overcoming traditional role models, may well be more important for women than men. Networking can facilitate entry into markets, influence the choice of business field and assist in daily operations in transition (as well as other) environments. Ukrainian female entrepreneurs usually engage in networking with other women and (mostly) fail to cooperate with their male counterparts. The fact that there are more women than men among female entrepreneurs' external links serves to limit their opportunities to enlarge their external resources base, and keeps them within the bounds of the typical female business sectors described above (Welter et al. 2004).

As a compensatory interim measure to deal with this deficiency of contacts, women could take steps to set up or join associations, which would facilitate establishing relationships with a wider range of external contacts. Strengthening associations of business women could serve as a policy instrument to promote networking by female entrepreneurs and to develop a 'new' business culture, which would be more suited for a market economy. In Ukraine there are about 700 women's organizations of different types (Smolyar 1999), which differ in their missions, scope and membership. Women's organizations contribute to the adjustment of legislation to the requirements of gender equality, lobby policy-making affecting gender issues, raise public awareness of gender problems and simply help women in everyday life or, more importantly, in critical situations (for example, cases of domestic violence against women or trafficking). Business women's organizations, in particular, aim to improve the business climate – including regulation and overall entrepreneurship policy – which governs how women are able to start and continue doing business.

It could be argued that the efforts of NGOs in improving the existing gender policy and attitudes may be insufficient, and a public–private partnership is needed to bridge the gap in gender standards and formal institutions, which exists between Ukraine and developed countries. With this aim, a project supported by international organizations was launched by the government in 2009 to promote the inclusion of gender issues in policy-making. The project's main goal is to support the efforts of government and civil society in promoting gender equality between men and women in all spheres of life and to improve the status of women in Ukraine as an instrument towards achieving sustainable human development and Ukrainian 'Millennium Development Goals' (UNDP 2009).

Thus, the formation of a gender culture with new values, and persisting stereotypes concerning the role of women in society and the economy, are still a challenge for Ukraine. From a gender perspective it is highly necessary to increase public awareness of gender issues, to change the existing gender order towards genuine equality of rights, and promote self-employed and business women as successful social role models. Meanwhile persisting and traditional informal institutions are argued to have a negative influence on more active participation of women in the economy, as well as on the nature and extent of female entrepreneurship.

Entrepreneurship Perspective

The development and realization of female entrepreneurial potential depends on the general business environment. This section therefore reviews and analyses government policy and the formal institutional framework supporting (female) entrepreneurship. It is also intended to examine the influence of informal institutions with reference to codes of conduct, values and norms, that is, those attitudes and mental perceptions (Denzau and North 1994) which are embedded in a society. It is important to emphasize that in developing institutional environments, like the one which exists in Ukraine, formal and informal institutions are intertwined and interdependent and both have an impact on business development (Welter et al. 2002).

From an entrepreneurship perspective, formal institutions encompass government organizations in charge of enterprise development, national and regional programmes to support SME development, existing business legislation and regulations. Informal institutions which impact on entrepreneurship include the business culture, the attitudes and behaviour of entrepreneurs and informal means (for example, bribery) used by entrepreneurs to adjust to a largely unfavourable business environment.

The government bodies responsible for entrepreneurship development and support at the national level include the State Committee of Ukraine for Regulation Policy and Entrepreneurship, the Ministry of Economy, the Ministry of Labour and Social Policy, and the Ukrainian Fund for Entrepreneurship. At regional and local levels such bodies include regional representative offices of the State Committee, economic departments of regional state administrations, local self-governments, employment centres and small business support funds (Welter et al. 2002).

Government institutions are responsible for creation and realization of programmes for small business support, which have to a great extent failed to achieve their objectives because there were no effective means of implementing them. Factors which have led to this implementation gap include a lack of financial resources, insufficient interest in implementing the programmes on the part of authorities, subjectivity in selecting private companies for the implementation of particular measures, corruption and incompetence of local authorities. Some of these, like subjectivity and corruption, have roots in the dominant informal institutions of society.

Case-study interviews with entrepreneurs in Western Ukrainian regions in 2006 revealed that the weaknesses in delivery of the national and regional programmes are still felt by small (female) entrepreneurs, and that these problems are even stronger at the regional level (Isakova et al. 2008). Such important tasks as SME access to markets and promotion of entrepreneurship and skills are poorly (if at all) addressed by regional support programmes.

Legislation is a key component of the formal framework for entrepreneurship. Private entrepreneurship was legalized in Ukraine in the 1990s with the adoption of the laws 'On Property', 'On Enterprises in Ukraine' and 'On Entrepreneurship'. However, the process of further adjustment of Ukrainian legislation to the development of a market economy is ongoing. Recently, new laws were passed or amended which are aimed at further facilitating entrepreneurial activities.[4] These changes typically have an effect on individual businesses which is opposite to that intended. Frequent changes in and adjustments to the legal framework are one of the major obstacles for business, particularly for smaller companies. In a recent Ukrainian survey, most respondents assessed the performance of the central and local authorities in 2004 as poor, due to frequent changes in legislation (78 per cent of respondents), corruption within state authorities (about 30 per cent of respondents made unofficial payments to civil servants) and a lack of effective mechanisms for defending the rights of entrepreneurs (80 per cent of respondents) (IFC 2005).

Regarding female entrepreneurs, Ukrainian legislation as related to entrepreneurship is gender-neutral and female entrepreneurs enjoy equal rights to their male counterparts. Considering the fact that female-owned businesses mostly belong to the category of small enterprises,[5] which have problems in complying with the constantly changing laws and regulations, a conclusion can be drawn that this factor significantly hampers female-run business. Indeed, as results from our international project on female entrepreneurship (which ran between 2001 and 2003) demonstrate, the problem of 'regulation and law' was mentioned by 31.2 per cent of female respondents as being among the top constraints at start-up and by 33.2 per cent as among the main constraints at more advanced stages of business. The taxation and law issue was at the top of reasons given for 'shadow' operations, with 82.5 per cent of female respondents selecting this reason compared to 69.2 per cent of the male control group (RWI 2003). These evaluations by entrepreneurs provide an explanation of why the hidden enterprise culture in Ukraine is still flourishing (Williams and Round 2007).

Data from our project also demonstrate that female entrepreneurs do not perceive that they are discriminated against in any way when dealing with government at the local level, but considering the scale and sectors of female entrepreneurship, one might argue that insufficient attention to the needs of micro and small businesses is limiting the growth of new female-owned businesses in the small business sector. Moreover, the development of female entrepreneurship is restrained by government policy in the taxation and financial system. Female entrepreneurs perceived high taxes as a constraint on their businesses at start up (reported by 35.8 per cent of respondents) and at more advanced stages high taxes were identified as a barrier by 52.9 per cent of respondents. At the same time women tend not to relate these constraints to their gender. The financial system is another important formal institution which affects entrepreneurship. Limited access to (and use of) external financial resources is a problem for small entrepreneurs, in particular for female-owned enterprises (mainly due to their size and sector); and female entrepreneurs mainly use their own savings or informal loans to start or invest in businesses (Isakova et al. 2006). The burden of taxes and limited access to external finance are argued to prevent growth and the development of small firms, which should put measures to improve Ukrainian SME growth potential at the top of the government policy agenda.

In post-Soviet Ukraine, the inefficiency of (female) entrepreneurship policy is also affected by the impact of informal institutions inherited from the previous regime. Excessive government regulation and a lack of transparency were typical for Soviet society and economy. Soviet codes of conduct, values and norms are opposed to deregulation efforts, which have been pursued for about ten years with little effect on the business environment. Entrepreneurs continue to report the interference of the authorities as destructive, the permit system to be too complicated and the control over business activity by a large number of state agencies too intense – consuming time and money (IFC 2005; 2007). In this light, cutting red tape seems to be an urgent necessity for Ukrainian government policy. Under these circumstances, (female) entrepreneurs are forced to find illegal ways to comply with the constantly changing rules, thus contributing to the image of Ukraine as having a highly-corrupt economy. Bribery is a widely used mechanism to solve problems and it is typical for Ukrainian entrepreneurs to buy registration, permits and inspection services from either private consulting companies associated with government agencies or from local officials directly. On the other hand, some of the Soviet legacy, in terms of skills and habits has had a positive effect on female entrepreneurship. This includes a high average level of education and work experience, women's skills at managing scarce finance, informal networking and strong family relations (Ledeneva 1998).

In the absence of government gender-specific business policy, a significant contribution to fostering female entrepreneurship has been made by business women's associations with the technical assistance of donors, particularly at the beginning of the transition in the 1990s. With regard to female entrepreneurs, Western donors were the first to draw the attention of the government and business communities to gender issues. The

Winrock International (USAID-funded) projects and the Renaissance gender projects are well-known examples of assistance to women business associations, and they have been active since the beginning of market reforms in early 1990s (Welter et al. 2002).

As a result of Western assistance, the issue of support for female entrepreneurs has been included in many regional programmes (sometimes alongside aid for young entrepreneurs and disabled entrepreneurs). However, female support (sub-) programmes have been mere declarations, lacking focus and finance and with no real effect. There are examples of regional administrations and business communities organizing competitions for women in business, and awards (such as 'Business Lady of the Year'). Although such actions have no direct effect on female entrepreneurship they help to strengthen dialogue and consultation between the government and entrepreneurs and contribute to the formation of positive attitudes to women in business. They also increase public awareness of the issue thus helping to combat values, which suppress women's inclusion in business.

All in all, the Ukrainian case is an example of a business environment in which, although formal market institutions have been introduced, government policy is not conducive to entrepreneurship development and often hampers individual entrepreneurial initiative. The weaknesses of government policy with respect to (female) entrepreneurship are, the author of this chapter believes, aggravated by the dominant business culture, values, norms and modes of behaviour.

CONCLUSIONS

Woman-owned or controlled businesses constitute a significant section of small and medium enterprises in Ukraine, but female entrepreneurship has not yet become a major economic force. A variety of factors influence the nature and extent of female entrepreneurship, related to economic development, developmental stage and general conditions for entrepreneurship, but also gender-specific issues. Ukrainian female entrepreneurs have never perceived themselves as different from their male counterparts, in this context improvement of the general business climate in the country would inevitably have a positive effect on women's businesses. On the other hand, the experiences of Ukrainian female entrepreneurs are very similar to women in business in other countries, both developed and developing.

Global experience of fostering female entrepreneurship might help in the selection of effective policy formulation. The review of relevant literature undertaken in this chapter suggests that policies for fostering female entrepreneurs should focus on two main issues, namely a gender perspective and an entrepreneurship perspective. Similar to other complex socio-economic phenomena, policies in these two areas not only have their own weaknesses (especially in finance, methods of delivery of support programmes, evaluation and control), but they are also not convergent. The Ukrainian situation described in this chapter could be improved, provided policy-makers comprehend and be willing to implement the following recommendations.

From a *gender perspective*, it is required to include gender in mainstream policy-making, increase the public awareness of gender issues, include more women in institutions holding state power, contribute to change in the existing gender order towards genuine equality of rights, promote a positive image of female entrepreneurs in the mass media and improve social provisions, in particular childcare institutions.

From the *entrepreneurship perspective* Ukrainian policy-makers could make use of comprehensive EU policy to support SMEs, which includes areas such as promoting entrepreneurship and skills, improving SMEs' access to markets, cutting red tape, improving SMEs' growth potential and strengthening dialogue and consultation with SME stakeholders. It should be emphasized that, while drawing upon good practice examples from a range of other countries, Ukraine policy goals must reflect the national socio-economic context. Evaluating and measuring the economic impact of small business support programmes (not only in terms of number of small enterprises per thousand inhabitants, but reflecting qualitative characteristics) might be an effective policy instrument.

As was discussed in this chapter, policy and formal institutions may fail to achieve the goal (for example, increase the participation of women in business) because of the dominant informal institutions and their adverse impact. In this context, it could be argued that the creation of a vibrant entrepreneurship culture is a primary task in transition countries, which aim to make full use of the entrepreneurial potential of women. However, the experience of developed markets does not always work in transition states (Dallago 2003) because of differences in informal institutions, and hence should be drawn on with caution.

The final necessity for research and policy in Ukraine is to pay attention to gender-specific statistics on business development, because such statistics are crucial for the mainstream inclusion of gender into policy (UNDP/UNECE 2004). Meanwhile, there is no accurate data on the scale of female entrepreneurship except for evaluations based on small-scale research. In this respect, one of the recommendations provided by the Transition Economies Forum on Entrepreneurship and Enterprise Development – to monitor the structure, performance and needs of the small and medium-sized business sector through the collection of comprehensive statistics and research on the sector, and use this information to adapt policies and programmes – should be another priority for policy makers (OECD/UNIDO 1999).

NOTES

1. The Orange Revolution was a series of protests and political events that took place in Ukraine from late November 2004 to January 2005, in the immediate aftermath of the run-off vote of the 2004 Ukrainian presidential election – which was compromised by alleged massive corruption, voter intimidation and direct electoral fraud.
2. This absence of gender-specific data is a feature of many countries. The lack of sex-disaggregated data in most of the 27 transition countries was reported by UNDP/ UNECE (2004) in key gender areas, including entrepreneurship. These data gaps are broadly associated with the low capacity of such countries to devote adequate resources to gender statistics and, in particular, a low capacity to promote gender in their current data-collection activities.
3. Here and further in the text (if not otherwise indicated) Ukrainian results are from an international research project ('Female entrepreneurship in transition economies: the example of Ukraine, Moldova and Uzbekistan', Intas 00-0843). The methodology employed in the project involved a literature review, analysis of secondary data, a standardized survey of female entrepreneurs (297) and male control group (81) in selected sectors, and semi-structured case-study interviews with female and male entrepreneurs, as well as a policy evaluation. The survey was conducted in 2002, case studies were carried out in 2003. Results are published in Isakova et al. (2006); RWI (2003); Welter et al. (2003).
4. The laws of Ukraine: 'On State Support for Small Business', 'On the Fundamentals of Regulation Policy in Economic Activities Sphere', 'On State Registration of Legal Entities and Natural Persons – Entrepreneurs', 'On the National Programme for Small Business Support in Ukraine'. Decrees of the President of Ukraine: 'On a Simplified System of Taxation', 'Book-keeping and Accounting for Small Business Subjects', 'On Measures for Further Support of Entrepreneurship Development', 'On Liberalisation of Entrepreneurial Activity and State Support of Business', 'On Some Measures for State Regulatory Policy Implementation' (Gamzyan 2006).
5. In Ukraine small businesses include sole proprietors (physical persons in terms of the Ukrainian legislation) and small enterprises (legal entities), with fewer than 50 employees and an annual gross income under 70 million UAH (6.5 million EUR); fixed at 500 000 EUR per annum until 2009. Large enterprises are those with employment exceeding 250 people and gross income exceeding 100 million UAH (9.2 million EUR); other enterprises fall into the category of medium enterprises

REFERENCES

Aidis, R. (2006), 'From business ownership to informal market traders: the characteristics of female entrepreneurship in Lithuania', in F. Welter, D. Smallbone and N. Isakova (eds), *Enterprising Women in Transition Economies*, Aldershot: Ashgate, pp. 119–42.
Aidis, R., F. Welter, D. Smallbone and N. Isakova (2007), 'Female entrepreneurship in transition economies: the case of Lithuania and Ukraine', *Feminist Economics*, **13** (2), 157–83.

Allen, E., A. Elam, N. Langowitz and M. Dean (2008), *Global Entrepreneurship Monitor 2007. Report on Women and Entrepreneurship*, Babson: The Center for Women's Leadership.

Ashwin, S. (2000), 'Introduction: gender, state and society in Soviet and post-Soviet Russia', in S. Ashwin (ed.), *Gender, State and Society in Soviet and Post-Soviet Russia*, London: Routledge, pp. 1–29.

Audretsch, D.B., I. Grilo and A.R. Thurik (eds) (2007), *Handbook of Research on Entrepreneurship Policy*, Cheltenham, UK and Northampton, MA, USA: Edward Elgar.

Bruno, M. (1997), 'Women and the culture of entrepreneurship', in M. Buckley (ed.), *Post-Soviet Women: From Baltic to Central Asia*, Cambridge: Cambridge University Press, pp. 56–74.

Constitution of Ukraine (1996), available at http://www.rada.gov.ua/const/conengl.htm (accessed 10 September 2008).

Dallago, B. (2003), 'Small and medium enterprises in Central and Eastern Europe', available at http://src-h.slav.hokudai.ac.jp/pdf_seminar/031210smes_3.pdf (accessed January 2009).

Denzau, A.T. and D.C. North (1994), 'Shared mental models: ideologies and institutions', *Kyklos*, **47** (1), 3–31.

Drnovsek, M. and M. Glas (2006), 'Women entrepreneurs in Slovenia: by fits and starts', in F. Welter, D. Smallbone and N. Isakova (eds), *Enterprising Women in Transition Economies*, Aldershot: Ashgate, pp. 143–70.

EBRD (2008), *Transition Report 2008: Growth in Transition*, available at http://www/ebrd.com/pubs/econo/series/tr.htm (accessed 19 May 2009).

Fajth, G. (2000), 'Women in transition: themes of the UNICEF MONEE project', in M. Lazreg (ed.), *Making the Transition Work for Women in Europe and Central Asia*, World Bank Discussion Paper No. 411, Washington, DC: World Bank, pp. 89–101.

Gamzyan, A. (2006), 'Ukraine', *Proceedings of the Conference SMEs in the BSEC Region – Reality and Vision*, Istanbul, 16–18 March, available at http://www.konrad.org.tr/BSEC/21.arman.pdf (accessed 9 February 2008).

Hart, D.M. (ed.) (2003), *The Emergence of Entrepreneurship Policy. Governance, Start-ups, and Growth in the U.S. Knowledge Economy*, Cambridge, UK: Cambridge University Press.

Heritage Foundation (2009), available at http://www.heritage.org/research/features/index/country.cfm?id=Ukraine (accessed 10 May 2009).

ICPS (2007), 'What economic policy Ukraine needs: recommendations to the government', *International Centre for Policy Studies Newsletter*, **1** (348), Kiev, 1–2.

IFC (2005), *Business Environment in Ukraine*, Kiev: International Finance Corporation.

IFC (2007), *Business Environment in Ukraine*, Kiev: International Finance Corporation.

ILO (2009), *Global Employment Trends for Women report (GET)*, available at http://www.ilo.org/wcmsp5/groups/public/ (accessed 10 March 2009).

Isakova, N., O. Krasovska, L. Kavunenko and A. Lugovy (2006), 'Entrepreneurship in the Ukraine: a male female comparison', in F. Welter, D. Smallbone and N. Isakova (eds), *Enterprising Women in Transition Economies*, Aldershot: Ashgate, pp. 17–43.

Isakova, N., O. Krasovska, V. Gryga, F. Welter and D. Smallbone (2008), 'Perspectives of the development of entrepreneurship and cross-border cooperation: analysis of their inter-dependence on the example of Western Ukrainian oblasts', *Sociology: Theory, Methods and Marketing*, **2**, 151–64. (In Ukrainian and Russian.)

Kiblitskaya, M. (2000), 'Russia's female breadwinners: the changing subjective experience', in S. Ashwin (ed.), *Gender, State and Society in Soviet and Post-Soviet Russia*, London: Routledge, pp. 55–70.

Kiev International Institute of Sociology (2000), *Women and Entrepreneurship*, USAID Newbiznet project, unpublished report, Kiev.

Kisselyova, O. (2008), 'A gender analysis of the European Union developmental aid for Ukraine', *EU-CIS Gender Watch*. The Network of East-West Women – Poland, Gdansk.

Koncz, K. (2000), 'Transitional period and labor market characteristics in Hungary', in

M. Lazreg (ed.), *Making the Transition Work for Women in Europe and Central Asia*, World Bank Discussion Paper No. 411, Washington, DC: World Bank, pp. 26–41.

Ledeneva, A.V. (1998), *Russia's Economy of Favours: Blat, Networking and Informal Exchange*, Cambridge: Cambridge University Press.

Lokar, S. (2000), 'Gender aspects of employment and unemployment in Central and Eastern Europe', in M. Lazreg (ed.), *Making the Transition Work for Women in Europe and Central Asia*, World Bank Discussion Paper No. 411, Washington, DC: World Bank, pp. 12–25.

Manolova, T. and A. Yan (2002), 'Institutional constraints and entrepreneurial responses in a transforming economy: the case of Bulgaria', *International Small Business Journal*, **20** (2), 163–84.

Manolova, T., R. Eunni and B. Gyoshev (2008), 'Institutional environments for entrepreneurship: evidence from emerging economies in Eastern Europe', *Entrepreneurship Theory and Practice*, **32** (1), 203–18.

McIntyre, J. and B. Dallago (eds) (2003), *Small and Medium Enterprises in Transitional Economies*, Houndsmill, UK and New York: Macmillan.

Mrcozkowski, T. (1997), 'Women as employees and entrepreneurs in the Polish transformation', *Industrial Relations Journal*, **28** (2), 83–91.

OECD/UNIDO (1999), *Transition Economies Forum on Entrepreneurship and Enterprise Development. Policy Guidelines and Recommendations*, available at http://www.oecd.org/dataoecd/22/43/33959424.pdf (accessed 3 August 2008).

Osaulenko, O. (ed.) (2008), *Statistical Yearbook of Ukraine 2007*, Kiev: State Statistics Committee of Ukraine.

Pavlychko, S. (1997) 'Progress on hold: the conservative faces of women in Ukraine', in M. Buckley (ed.), *Women and the Culture of Entrepreneurship, Post-Soviet Women: from Baltic to Central Asia*, Cambridge: Cambridge University Press, pp. 219–34.

Pogarska, O. and E.L. Segura (2009), 'Ukraine macroeconomic situation, January 2009', SigmaBleyzer Private Equity Investment Group, available at http://www.unian.net/eng/news/news-250091.html (accessed 10 February 2008).

Romanchuk, J. (2008), 'The transition problem: the unhampered state as an obstacle to democratic and market reforms', available at http://www.cipe.org/publications/fs/pdf/091508.pdf (accessed 10 September 2008).

Ruminska-Zimny, E. (1997), 'Human poverty in transition economies: regional overview for HDR 1997', available at http://www.undp.org/en/reports/global/hdr1997/papers/ewa_ruminska.pdf (accessed 10 September 2008).

RWI (2003), *Female Entrepreneurship in the Ukraine, Moldova and Uzbekistan: National Report on Survey Data for the Ukraine*, Essen: RWI.

Smallbone, D. and F. Welter (2001a), 'The role of government in SME development in transition economies', *International Small Business Journal*, **19** (4), 63–76.

Smallbone, D. and F. Welter (2001b), 'The distinctiveness of entrepreneurship in transition economies', *Small Business Economics*, **16** (4), 249–62.

Smolyar, L. (1999), 'Women private organisations in the system of civil society', in L. Smolyar (ed.), *Gender Analysis of Ukrainian Society*, Kiev: UNDP, pp. 19–38. (In Ukrainian.)

UNDP (2009), 'Equal opportunities and women's rights in Ukraine programme', available at http://www.undp.org.ua/en/project-list-all (accessed 10 March 2009).

UNDP/UNECE (2004), *Report on the Status of Official Statistics Related to Gender Equality in Eastern Europe and the CIS Countries*, UNECE Statistical Division, UNDP Bratislava Regional Center, Geneva.

Vorona, V. and M. Shulga (eds) (2007), *Ukrainian Society 1992–2007. Dynamics of Social Change*, Kiev: Institute of Sociology of the National Academy of Ukraine. (In Ukrainian.)

Vorona, V. and M. Shulga (eds) (2008), *Ukrainian Society 1992–2008. Sociological Monitoring*, Kiev: Institute of Sociology of the National Academy of Ukraine. (In Ukrainian.)

Wells, B., T. Pfantz and J. Bryne (2003), 'Russian women business owners: evidence of entrepreneurship in a transition economy', *Journal of Developmental Entrepreneurship*, **8** (1), 59–71.

Welter, F. and D. Smallbone (2008), 'Women's entrepreneurship from an institutional perspective: the case of Uzbekistan', *International Entrepreneurship Management Journal*, **4**, 505–20.
Welter, F., D. Smallbone and N. Isakova (2006), *Enterprising Women in Transition Economies*, Aldershot: Ashgate.
Welter, F., D. Smallbone, E. Aculai, N. Isakova and N. Schakirova (2003), 'Female entrepreneurship in post soviet countries', in J. Butler (ed.), *New Perspectives on Women Entrepreneurs*, Greenwich, CT: Information Age, pp. 243–70.
Welter, F., D. Smallbone, N. Isakova, E. Aculai and N. Schakirova (2002), *Female Entrepreneurship: A Conceptual and Empirical View*, Schriften und Materialien zu Handwerk und Mittelstand, 15, Essen: RWI.
Welter, F., D. Smallbone, N. Isakova, E. Aculai and N. Schakirova (2004), 'Social capital and women entrepreneurship in fragile environments: does networking matter?', paper presented at Babson College-Kauffman Foundation Entrepreneurship Research Conference, University of Strathclyde, June.
Williams, C. and J. Round (2007), 'Entrepreneurship and the informal economy: a study of Ukraine's hidden enterprise culture', *Journal of Developmental Entrepreneurship*, **12** (1), 119–36.
World Bank (2009), 'Ukraine: country brief 2009', available at http://web.worldbank.org/ WBSITE/EXTERNAL/ COUNTRIES/ECAEXT/UKRAINE, (accessed 20 May 2009).
Zhurzhenko, T. (1999), 'Gender and identity formation in post-socialist Ukraine: the case of women in the shuttle business', in R. Bridgman, S. Cole and H. Howard-Bobiwash (eds), *Feminist Fields: Ethnographic Insights*, Ontario: Broadview Press, pp. 243–63.
Zhurzhenko, T. (2001), 'Free market ideology and new women's identities in post-socialist Ukraine', *The European Journal of Women Studies*, **8** (1), 29–49.

PART III

CHALLENGES FOR ENTREPRENEURSHIP POLICIES IN A WIDER EUROPE

12 Conclusions and outlook
David Smallbone and Friederike Welter

PUBLIC POLICY AND ENTREPRENEURSHIP IN THE WIDER EUROPE

The chapters selected for inclusion in this handbook demonstrate the variety of ways in which policy makers can influence the nature and extent of entrepreneurship development, both directly through direct interventions and indirectly through their influence on the environment for entrepreneurship, even if sometimes their influence is inadvertent. This is illustrated, for example, in Chapter 11 on Ukraine where Isakova argues that some regulations have a greater impact on women entrepreneurs because of their sectoral specializations.

To be effective, creating a facilitating environment for entrepreneurship also requires close cooperation between national and local policy makers, since it is at the local level that entrepreneurs typically come into contact with public policy, as well as being highly susceptible to the effects of the local economic context. Whilst this once again emphasizes the importance of the institutional dimension, it also draws attention to the need for policy to be sensitive to local conditions, which is a key theme in Chapter 2. As Hofer and Welter point out, where public policy involves the state working in partnership with other key players, this sometimes results in conflicts because of differences in the goals of public and private sector actors. The chapter demonstrates the challenges faced as the relationship between the state and business activity needs to be redefined and the mechanisms and institutions required implementing policies in a market environment to be established.

Whilst some chapters in the book show how the policy environment for entrepreneurship in some Central and East European countries is improving, in others the evidence suggests that without stronger commitments to entrepreneurship on the part of governments the potential contribution of entrepreneurs to economic and social development in the wider Europe will remain under-fulfilled. Chapter 3, for example, is mainly a call for policy action with respect to encouraging entrepreneurship in Europe's new member border regions, many of which suffer from being peripheral and a legacy from the 1960s which did not encourage cooperation with neighbours outside the Soviet bloc. EU membership provides an opportunity to address these issues through access to financial and technical resources, although this is unlikely to have much impact on the ground in the absence of political will.

A good example of political commitment to the promotion of entrepreneurship is reported in Chapter 6, which refers to the introduction of an introductory course 'Basics of Entrepreneurship' in Polish secondary schools, although its implementation has been hampered by a shortage of teachers with appropriate qualifications and attitudes. Interestingly one of the weaknesses identified in this chapter is that university-level entrepreneurship education still focuses on the traditional small business environment rather than stimulating entrepreneurial initiatives by students in the emerging sectors of the economy.

The inspiration to join the EU can result in a rather uncritical acceptance of policies as the case of Albania illustrates (Chapter 9). The appropriateness of crude policy transfer is a recurrent theme in the development literature. But, as Xheneti argues, there is a need for countries to take ownership of their development strategies, although achieving this requires a strong commitment to institutional capacity building by recipient countries as well as by those seeking to influence their development, which Chepurenko also emphasizes for the Russian Federation in Chapter 10.

ASSESSING PROGRESS WITH INSTITUTIONAL CHANGE AND CREATING A FACILITATING POLICY ENVIRONMENT FOR ENTREPRENEURSHIP

Approaching the end of the second decade after the collapse of socialism throughout Central and Eastern Europe, there is considerable variation between post-socialist countries in the extent to which a facilitating environment for the development of entrepreneurship has been created. The contrasting experience described in the chapters in this book reflects differences in the level of commitment to market reforms, as well as in the knowledge and resources available to the state to implement what is required. In Central, Eastern and South East European countries, the process of accession to the European Union has contributed significantly to policy development, interacting with ongoing processes of market reform to influence the path of private enterprise development. At the same time, the experiences of some of the new EU member countries, such as Bulgaria (Chapter 3) and Latvia (Chapter 5), illustrate the considerable challenges still faced in creating a facilitating policy environment for entrepreneurship development across the enlarged EU.

The case of Latvia demonstrates how formal institutional changes (as necessary as they are), which have been associated with EU accession (or the preparation for it) are only one element in the institutional changes required. Informal institutions, which are reflected in the attitudes to entrepreneurship demonstrated by some civil servants and public officials, as well as by attitudes to risk on the part of the population at large, may take a generation to change.

In contrast, in some of the former Soviet republics, as for example Ukraine (Chapter 11), the Russian Federation (Chapter 10) and other formerly centrally planned economies such as Albania (Chapter 9), the basic framework conditions required for private business development are not fully established and policy pronouncements typically suffer from an implementation gap. In many former Soviet Republics, the process of market reform has been delayed because of a lack of recognition and commitment on the part of the state to creating the conditions to enable entrepreneurs to make a full contribution to economic development. In such conditions, the extent of productive entrepreneurship is limited and the behaviour of entrepreneurs is necessarily shaped by institutional deficiencies, which often leads to entrepreneurs needing to allocate resources to activities which for them are not productive (Smallbone and Welter 2006). Informal institutions also have a negative effect, including for example a negative public perception of entrepreneurs. The role of the state in these countries frequently resembles the authoritarian control of Soviet times, which in some of the former Soviet republics (such as Belarus) includes the use of Presidential decrees and an absence of effective governance mechanisms. Poorly specified and frequently changing legislation leaves too much discretionary power in the hands of (underpaid) officials responsible for its implementation, thus fostering corruption. From a governance perspective, the behaviour of public institutions is far from open and the power of the state absolute. This is part of a wider absence of accountability, with poorly defined roles for public institutions involved in regulating and influencing private business activity; and a frequent lack of connection between policy pronouncements and actions by the state, particularly with respect to financial support measures. Under such conditions, improving the quality of laws and regulations are key policy challenges, in order to establish the framework conditions that are necessary for economic and democratic development, but so too are effective, efficient and consistent implementation mechanisms.

At the same time, institutional change, initiated by changes in the formal (legal) framework, has created opportunities for entrepreneurs in all transition countries. For example, the administrative reforms at the start of the transition process made it possible for private enterprises to legally exist. Entrepreneurs can also contribute to institutional change, when it becomes apparent that existing institutional arrangements are incompatible with a market based approach. However, whether or not this is translated into formal institutional change is likely to depend on the government's underlying commitment to market reforms, as well as on entrepreneurs having an effective voice to influence policy makers. One example is through their involvement in self governing organizations, such as Chambers of Commerce, although as in many mature market economies, entrepreneurs and small business owners can be slow to actively support such organizations. However, entrepreneurs can also foster informal institutional change by contributing to a growing acceptance of entrepreneurship within the population at large.

In those CEECs which have joined the European Union, institutional change has made a more positive contribution to entrepreneurship because EU membership led to the state becoming an important agent of formal and informal institutional change and an enabling factor as far as entrepreneurship is concerned, as the case of Slovenia demonstrates in Chapter 8. Certain framework conditions are particularly relevant to entrepreneurship development, such as simple and inexpensive procedures for licensing and regulation; a non-prohibitive and transparent tax system; stable legislation and regulations; and access to capital.

ONGOING POLICY CHALLENGES TO PROMOTE ENTREPRENEURSHIP DEVELOPMENT

The importance of institutional change, highlighted in Chapter 1, draws attention to one of the key challenges facing economies in transition, which is to redefine and adapt the role of the state in the economy (and society). The process of market reform requires a fundamental change in the role, type and behaviour of public institutions, as well as the establishment of new forms of governance. This in turn reflects a need for a more fundamental shift in the role of the state in the economy, as government replaces its roles as planner of resource allocation and price setter, owner and financier of enterprise activity through subsidies and transfers, with a role as regulator and facilitator of private enterprise activity, with all that involves. Not surprisingly, the experience in this regard has varied considerably between countries as the chapters in this book illustrate, despite the fact that these countries share a common socialist heritage.

Despite the progress made, institutional capacity building remains the most challenging aspect of the reform process and one that is central to the continued development of entrepreneurial capacity in a wider Europe. The effects of administrative and regulatory burdens on entrepreneurship can be used as litmus test for the effectiveness of the wider system of policy development and governance with respect to, entrepreneurship. Although one of the key roles of government policy during transition was to create an enabling environment for entrepreneurship, governments also needed to ensure that entrepreneurs operated within rules designed to balance a need to encourage and promote enterprise with wider social interests and the public good. This issue has been the subject of considerable debate in mature market economies, with some divergence of views (Bannock and Peacock 1989; Kitching 2004; Storey 1994). However, in a post-socialist context, establishing an appropriate balance is particularly challenging because of the lack of any tradition of the state as a regulator of private business activity.

In countries such as Albania, Ukraine or the Russian Federation, where the overall process of transformation is slow, the main difficulties facing entrepreneurs include frequent regulatory interferences as reflected in, for example, excessive regulations and procedures or numerous visits by various regulatory bodies, combined with an authoritarian role of the state. A highly imperfect regulatory environment also breeds corruption, thus constraining institutional change. In contrast, in those countries in Central and South East Europe which over the past decade have become members of the European Union, regulatory reform has been a priority issue, in line with EU priorities, although this has not been without difficulties, as these countries sought to simultaneously simplify legislation and adopt the *acquis communitaire*, as a condition of EU membership.

At the same time, there are still unresolved questions, such as the most effective consultation mechanisms to help governments to 'think small first', as small firms and entrepreneurs are typically a difficult to reach group for consultation purposes, as their limited involvement in social dialogue in Hungary and other new member states of the EU illustrates (Chapter 4). As emphasized in Chapter 2, effective institutionalization of entrepreneurship policy involves different forms of partnership between government at different levels and various private sector bodies. Organizations to represent the interests of entrepreneurs and businesses act as an interface between individual businesses and government, forming one of the mechanisms by which entrepreneurs can potentially influence institutional change (Kalantaridis 2007). However, in circumstances where there is no recent tradition of self governing organizations, the creation of effective organizations and business associations also can be a challenging task.

Developing effective institutional arrangements for the governance and support of entrepreneurship and small business development is a challenge faced in all countries, including mature market economies. In this regard, countries in Central and Eastern Europe which joined the European Union face many challenges shared by other EU countries. The process of EU accession has undoubtedly contributed to establishing an institutional framework for the longer term development of productive entrepreneurship. At the same time, institutional changes driven by the state on the supply side of the economy need to be matched by institutional change on the demand side, in which entrepreneurship education at different levels has an important potential role to play. This may be illustrated with reference to Poland (Chapter 6), where government has shown a willingness to take a lead in introducing entrepreneurship into the secondary school curriculum. Interestingly, in higher education, the introduction of entrepreneurship into public universities has been constrained by the conservatism of the academic establishment, keen to protect its disciplinary interests, demonstrating once again the role of institutional influences.

Whilst the promotion of entrepreneurship is likely to depend on the ability of the education system to generate interest in entrepreneurship as a career option and equip students with the skills to follow this up, investing in entrepreneurship education also will take some time to generate significant returns, thus rendering it an unattractive option for many politicians. Ultimately entrepreneurship is dependent on the drive and commitment of individuals. Government can facilitate the development of productive entrepreneurship through an appropriate and effective functioning institutional frame, although the state cannot substitute for individual entrepreneurial endeavour.

Another challenge facing former socialist economies concerns the development of market-oriented innovation systems, as illustrated in Chapter 7 for a Polish region. Many of the new EU member countries are currently attempting to build market-oriented innovation systems to support higher value added entrepreneurship and small business development. This is an institutional and policy priority, which more mature market economies must have more experience of but cannot claim to have always successfully completed. For example, developing effective links to promote innovation between higher education organizations and businesses is a policy priority throughout the EU. However, achieving this can be a slow process, constrained by the rewards system and career structure of university staff, as well as by other institutional factors which contribute to many higher education institutions not being fully committed to fulfilling their economic development role. This shows that policy priorities and challenges of new member countries have been converging with those of more mature economies in the EU, although in most of the former Soviet republics and other transition countries in Eastern Europe they remain at a more basic level.

OUTLOOK

As a result of divergent developments over the past two decades, the specific policy priorities for entrepreneurship and small business development vary between individual countries in the wider Europe, although there are commonalities. One of the key underlying themes is the importance of institutional development and capacity building, over which governments exert a key influence, coupled with a need to contextualize entrepreneurship policies. In countries such as Albania, Ukraine or the Russian Federation, the establishment of an appropriate and effective institutionalization of entrepreneurship policy is still one of the main preconditions that need to be fulfilled before productive entrepreneurship can become embedded. This includes strengthening the role of regional and local authorities in promoting and facilitating entrepreneurship, since it is at the local level that public policy and institutional influences touch entrepreneurs most directly.

Assessing the role of government in countries, such as those featured in this book, also underlines the importance of taking a broadly based view of what constitutes 'policy', as far as enterprise developments is concerned. 'Small business' or 'entrepreneurship' support policies either do not exist, or exist but are not implemented, or are implemented but affect so few businesses that they may be considered a marginal influence on the development of entrepreneurship. But policies related to taxation and the regulatory environment affect most businesses to some degree, which highlights the importance of a policy approach towards establishing the general framework conditions for entrepreneurship.

The evidence presented in this book also illustrates the complex relationship between institutional change and entrepreneurship, even in contexts which share a common heritage. In this regard, the book reinforces the importance of analysing entrepreneurship in its social context (Baker et al. 2005; Davidsson 2003). The nature of state-entrepreneurship relationships is an important part of that social context, indicating a need to also contextualise entrepreneurship policies.

REFERENCES

Baker, T., E. Gedajlovic and M. Lubatkin (2005), 'A framework for comparing entrepreneurship processes across nations', *Journal of International Business Studies*, **36** (5), 492–504.

Bannock, G. and A. Peacock (1989), *Governments and Small Business*, London: Paul Chapman for the David Hume Institute.

Davidsson, P. (2003), 'The domain of entrepreneurship research: some suggestions', in J.A. Katz and D.A. Shepherd (eds), *Cognitive Approaches to Entrepreneurship Research*, Amsterdam: JAI, pp. 265–314.

Kalantaridis, C. (2007), 'Institutional change in post-socialist regimes: public policy and beyond', *Journal of Economic Issues*, **XLI** (2), 435–42.

Kitching, J. (2004), 'Burden on business? Reviewing the evidence base on regulation and small business performance', *Environment and Planning C: Government and Policy*, **24**, 799–814.

Smallbone, D. and F. Welter (2006), 'Conceptualising entrepreneurship in a transition context', *International Journal of Entrepreneurship and Small Business*, **3** (2), 190–206.

Storey, D.J. (1994), *Understanding the Small Business Sector*, London: Routledge.

Index

abortive reforms in Russia
principal beneficiaries of 207
academic entrepreneurship, Poland
104–6
academic research in entrepreneurship
169, 177
Academy of Sciences of Latvia 97
accession prices in European Union 87
accountability of public institutions 8
accounting services in Petrich, Bulgaria
54
acquis communitaire as condition of
EU membership 237
administrative capacity of Bulgarian
local authorities
inadequacy of 59
administrative inspections of SME
activity, Russia 200
adult population attitudes, Slovenia
146–9
advantage, competitive and
constructive 133
ageing population, Kyustendil,
Bulgaria 55
age profile of female entrepreneurs
219
agricultural sector, decrease in share,
Bulgaria 50
agriculture in Petrich, Bulgaria,
development potential
tomatoes, peppers, spinach, tobacco,
fruits 54
agro-industry, Albania 179
Albania
change of government, 2005 171
policy transfer process, necessity of
13, 186
slow transformation process
regulatory interference 237
SME development strategy 176–83
transition economy
weak implementation of policies
185

Albinvest, government organization
on export and foreign direct
investment 181
appreciation for entrepreneurship 41
'artificial' differences, Bulgaria, Serbia,
Macedonia, for political reasons
58
Asian crisis of 1997 205
assimilation process for
entrepreneurship students 118
Association of Construction
Contractors 94
Association of Textile and Clothing
95
Austrian SME representation in EU
68
authoritarian control of Soviet times
235
automation and robotization 132
automotive and tooling industry 157
autonomous industrial relations, lack
of experience of 70
autonomy, orientation towards 69

Baltic States
all private business illegal 74
bankruptcies of large companies,
Slovenia 142–3
bankruptcy law 4, 85
'Basics of Entrepreneurship' course in
secondary schools, Poland 103
Berlin Wall, fall 1989
six new *Länder* in federal Republic
of Germany 23
bilateral agreements with other
countries, Bulgaria
hindrance of external events 57
bilateral dialogue, weakness of, in new
EU members 70
bilateral efforts for cross-border
cooperation 59
Bologna System, defining levels of
tertiary education 111